Writing Voyage

A PROCESS APPROACH TO BASIC WRITING

FIFTH EDITION

Thomas E. Tyner
Kings River College

 Wadsworth Publishing Company

I T P® **An International Thomson Publishing Company**
Belmont · Albany · Bonn · Boston · Cincinnati · Detroit · London
Madrid · Melbourne · Mexico City · New York · Paris
San Francisco · Singapore · Tokyo · Toronto · Washington

English Editor: *Angela Gantner Wrahtz*
Editorial Assistant: *Royden Tonomura*
Production: *Melanie Field*
Composition: *Thompson Type*
Print Buyer: *Barbara Britton*
Permissions Editor: *Robert Kauser*
Cover Photograph: *Onne van der Wal / Stock Newport*
Interior Design: *Christy Butterfield*
Cover Design: *Delgado Design, Inc.*
Printer: *Quebecor/Fairfield*

Printed in the United States of America

1 2 3 4 5 6 7 8 9 10

For more information, contact Wadsworth Publishing Company:

Wadsworth Publishing Company
10 Davis Drive
Belmont, California 94002, USA

International Thomson Publishing Europe
Berkshire House 168-173
High Holborn
London, WC1V7AA, England

Thomas Nelson Australia
102 Dodds Street
South Melbourne 3205
Victoria, Australia

Nelson Canada
1120 Birchmount Road
Scarborough, Ontario
Canada M1K 5G4

International Thomson Editores
Campos Eliseos 385, Piso 7
Col. Polanco
11560 México D.F. México

International Thomson Publishing GmbH
Königswinterer Strasse 418
53227 Bonn, Germany

International Thomson Publishing Asia
221 Henderson Road
#05-10 Henderson Building
Singapore 0315

International Thomson Publishing Japan
Hirakawacho Kyowa Building, 3F
2-2-1 Hirakawacho
Chiyoda-ku, Tokyo 102, Japan

Library of Congress Cataloging-in-Publication Data
Tyner, Thomas E., 1944–
    Writing voyage : a process approach to basic writing / Thomas E. Tyner. — 5th ed.
      p.   cm.
    Includes index.
    ISBN 0-534-51748-X
    1. English language—Rhetoric.   2. English language—Grammar.   I. Title.
PE1408.T96   1996
808'.042—dc20   96-15376

This book is printed on acid-free recycled paper.

Writing Voyage

Titles of Related Interest

College Writing Basics, Fourth Edition, Thomas E. Tyner (1996)

Composing Through Reading, Second Edition, Peter Elias Sotiriou (1994)

Critical Thinking: Reading and Writing in a Diverse World, Second Edition, Joan Rasool, Caroline Banks, and Mary-Jane McCarthy (1996)

Critical Thinking and Writing: A Developing Writer's Guide with Readings, Kristan Cavina (1995)

Developing Writers: A Dialogic Approach, Second Edition, Pamela Gay (1995)

Inside Writing: A Writer's Workbook, Form A, Third Edition, William Salomone, Stephen McDonald, and Mark Edlestein (1996)

Inside Writing: A Writer's Workbook, Form B, Third Edition, William Salomone, Stephen McDonald, and Mark Edlestein (1997)

Making Connections Through Reading and Writing, Maria Valeri-Gold and Mary P. Deming (1994)

Patterns and Themes: A Basic English Reader, Third Edition, Judy R. Rogers and Glenn C. Rogers (1993)

The Research Paper, Seventh Edition, Audrey Roth (1995)

Texts and Contexts: A Contemporary Approach to College Writing, Third Edition, William Robinson (1997)

Views and Values: Diverse Readings on Universal Themes, Kari Sayers (1996)

Writing as a Life-Long Skill, Sanford Kaye (1994)

Writing Paragraphs and Essays: Integrating Reading, Writing, and Grammar Skills, Second Edition, Joy Wingersky, Jan Boerner, and Diana Holguin-Balough (1995)

Writing with Writers, Thomas E. Tyner (1995)

Acknowledgments

Page 21: Paul Kaser, "Cross Country Skiing," is reprinted by permission of the author.

Page 23: Anne Tyler, "Still Just Writing," from *The Writer on Her Work, Volume I,* by Janet Sternburg. Copyright © 1980 by Janet Sternburg. Reprinted by permission of W. W. Norton & Company, Inc.

Page 27: Rob Hoerburger, "Gotta Dance!," from *The New York Times Magazine* July 18, 1993. Copyright © 1993 by The New York Times Company. Reprinted by permission.

Page 52: Donna Smith-Yackel, "My Mother Never Worked," first appeared in the *Women's Liberation Journal*.

Page 55: David R. C. Good, "Science," is reprinted by permission of the author.

Page 56: Maxine Hong Kingston, "The Woman Warrior," is from *The Woman Warrior* © 1975, 1976 by Maxine Hong Kingston. Reprinted by permission of Alfred A. Knopf, Inc.

Page 87: Susan Penny, "What's Your Best Time of Day?," is reprinted with the permission of Rawson Associates/Scribner, an imprint of Simon & Schuster from *The Secrets Our Body Clocks Reveal* by Susan Perry and Jim Dawson. Copyright © 1988 Susan Perry and Jim Dawson.

Page 89: Mary Mebane, "Black Wasn't Beautiful," is from *Mary* by Mary Mebane. Copyright © 1981 by Mary Elizabeth Mebane. Used by permission of Viking Penguin, a division of Penguin Books USA, Inc.

Page 92: Thomas French, "Long Live High School Rebels," is from *The St. Petersburg Times,* November 22, 1987. Reprinted by permission of the publisher.

Page 124: Richard Lynn, "Why Johnny Can't Read, but Yoshio Can," from *National Review,* October 28, 1988, pp. 40–43. © 1988 by National Review, Inc., 150 East 35th Street, New York, NY 10016. Reprinted by permission.

Page 129: Margaret Atwood, "Canada Through the One-Way Mirror," is from *The Nation.* © 1986 by The Nation Company, Inc. Reprinted by permission of the publisher.

Contents

Readings by Rhetorical Mode

Preface

*T*he purpose of this text is to provide an integrated writing experience for students. Textbooks often isolate basic elements of writing from the developmental process itself. Students are left with a fragmented approach to writing, in which connections between textbook work and real writing are difficult to see.

Writing Voyage, Fifth Edition, folds these writing elements into the process so that students write papers and work concurrently on specific writing skills to apply at different stages of the drafting process. Students learn what elements of writing are most important at each stage of the process, and they understand that a mastery of a variety of skills is crucial to the effective communication of the writer's ideas.

The following eight features help make *Writing Voyage* an effective writing text.

Focus on Process

In each unit, students are taken through the process of prewriting, drafting, revising, and proofreading their papers. The text emphasizes that writing is a process that develops in general stages that most writers go through. As students progress through the book, they tailor the process to their needs and preferences. By the book's end they are well versed in the basic elements of effective writing and in command of a process that works for them.

Content Orientation

Throughout the text, the primary emphasis is on writing content: what the writer wants to communicate to his or her readers. All other elements of effective writing—organization of ideas, paragraphing, wording, correctness —are addressed as a *means* to communicate a writer's ideas most effectively. Substance is always emphasized before structure, and structure is evaluated by how it contributes to the reader's appreciation of the substance.

Rotating Format

Writing texts frequently introduce a subject in one unit and then virtually abandon it. From my teaching experience, students who have been taught parallel construction in the first unit may have forgotten what they learned by the third or fourth unit unless the topic has been regularly reinforced. Therefore, this text is designed so the basic elements of writing—prewriting, audience/purpose consideration, paragraphing, sentence structure, organization—are covered in every unit. Many students in basic writing courses have problems that cannot be solved with the traditional block-coverage textbook approach. *Writing Voyage* provides reinforcement of basic writing skills throughout the book.

Emphasis on Writing

Assuming that students cannot learn to write well without writing often, the text provides constant writing opportunities: free writing, drafting essays, paragraph writing, copying exercises, sentence combining exercises, and a variety of sentence writing activities. In addition to the major assignments that students take through the writing process in each unit, there are numerous shorter writing assignments, each emphasizing a particular aspect of the process.

Student Writing Samples

Throughout the text, students will find student writing samples that relate to the kinds of writing they are doing. The writing samples are interesting to read, provide realistic models for students, and supply material to be analyzed from a number of angles: thesis development, purpose, audience consideration, organization, paragraphing, style, originality, and overall effectiveness. Each unit also contains first-draft writing samples through which students can sharpen their revising skills. Throughout the text, students will analyze and learn from the essays of other student writers.

Peer Editing

Often students share their writing with no one but their instructor. This text is designed for students to share their writing with classmates at each step in the process. They use their classmates as audience, and they develop their critiquing and revising skills by helping other writers. Students learn to view writing as a shared communication rather than a "please the teacher" effort, and they see the effects that their ideas have on readers.

Selected Readings

A selection of essays by professional writers, including a number of new readings, appears at the end of each unit. The readings and subsequent "Questions for Discussion" sections are tied in with the writing emphasis for that unit. These essays serve as models for structural and content analysis, provide a link between the related skills of writing and reading, and offer additional reading experiences that will benefit most students.

Final Editing

Grammar, punctuation, and spelling receive thorough treatment in each unit of the text. All of the major problem areas—run-ons and fragments, comma usage, subject-verb agreement, pronoun-antecedent agreement, irregular verbs—are covered in detail. Each section contains a number of exercises for students to work through. Ideally, students will refer to the editing sections as they proofread and edit their papers throughout the text. Grammar and punctuation study should be linked to the editing process students go through with each writing assignment.

Acknowledgments

The improvements in this fifth edition are the result of many helpful comments from instructors and students. I am especially grateful for the suggestions of Cedric Burden, Lawson State Community College; Sherie Coelho, Antelope Valley College; Sharon Kokaska, El Camino College; L. A. Norman, University of Central Arkansas; and Caroline Stern, Ferris State University.

Writing Voyage

Setting Sail

Writing is a voyage of discovery. As a writer, you are in charge of the voyage, the directions it takes, and the success of the journey. As you progress through this book, you will develop skills to express yourself most effectively and to make your writing travels more enjoyable.

Already an experienced writer, you bring to class considerable skills and knowledge from your previous experiences. As a result, you are ready to begin your writing voyage immediately and to continue learning as all writers do: by writing.

This unit introduces the writing process used throughout the book. The process includes basic steps that most writers use to reach their final writing destination. By the time you finish the book, you will have personally tailored this process for any writing you may do.

Why Write?

At this point in your life, you have probably already done some, or perhaps a great deal of, writing. Along with this course, you may take other writing courses in the future.

Throughout your writing experiences in school, however, you may never have asked yourself why you were writing. Perhaps your instructors never gave you a reason either. Like most students, you may have just accepted the fact that writing is something teachers assign and students dutifully do.

As a college student, you should understand the role that writing plays in a person's education. Since you will be writing during your college years and beyond, it is useful for you to understand how developing your writing skills will benefit you now and throughout your life.

The purpose of the upcoming activity is to get you thinking about the importance of writing and to begin your writing. The more you value writing as an essential part of your education, the more you will benefit from courses such as this.

Writing Activity 1.1

With a classmate, discuss some possible reasons why writing is a part of the educational curriculum. Why should students develop their writing skills? Consider both short-range and long-range reasons, and list all of the ideas that you and your partner generate.

When you finish, write a paper for your classmates that answers the question, "Why do I have to take a writing class?" Your purpose is to provide students with some good reasons for taking such a course, which may also provide incentive for their wanting to do well. Use the ideas that you and your partner have generated any way you wish. When you finish, share your paper with classmates.

Prewriting

When you write, what do you do before you actually put pen to paper or hands to the computer? Do you scratch your head for a while? Do you jot down some ideas? Do you have a ritual of sitting at the same desk at the same time of day with a favorite writing pad and pen? Do you like to take a walk and think before beginning?

Everything that writers do to help them get started is a part of their "prewriting" process. This process varies from writer to writer, and what works for one person doesn't necessarily work for another. Some writers prefer planning a paper in some detail, while others work best from a general idea or two percolating in their heads.

Each unit has a prewriting section with different options that writers use to help them get started. For example, the first "partner" activity you did was your prewriting work for the first writing assignment. By generating a list of ideas, you came up with some material to use in your paper.

As you try different prewriting strategies, you will undoubtedly find that some work better for you than others. You may also find that different strategies work for different types or lengths of writing. You may even take something from one strategy and something from another to devise your own approach.

Th purpose of the prewriting activities is to help you find ways to get started that will lead to productive writing. By trying different options, you will discover what works best for you. It is a trial-and-error process that will help define your own prewriting strategy.

THINKING BEFORE YOU WRITE

Sometimes students who sit and ponder when given a writing assignment feel that something is wrong with them. "Why can't I just start writing like other people?" they think. "I must have writer's block."

Thinking before writing is an important part of the prewriting process for many writers. Thinking about what to write and how to express it may be as important as anything you do for a paper. Whenever you are thinking about what to write or pondering your options, you have begun the process that leads to writing an effective paper.

SELECTING A TOPIC

Deciding what to write about is a task shared by all writers. For some, it is one of the most difficult parts of writing. Selection of a topic is a part of the prewriting process that often requires a good deal of thinking.

Thinking about writing involves asking yourself questions. Writers use the following types of questions to help them decide on a topic.

1. What topics interest me enough to write about?
2. What do I know enough about to write on?
3. What could I write that would interest readers?
4. What purpose would I have in writing to my readers?

These questions focus on the basic elements of writing: the writer's interest and knowledge and his or her desire to convey this knowledge to readers.

Prewriting Activity 1.2

Select a topic to write on from among your favorite interests, hobbies, and pastimes. Apply the questions presented for selecting a topic to help you, using your classmates as the reading audience for the paper.

*STUDENT SELECTION
PROCESS*

1. What topics interest me enough to write about?

I like to go to concerts, read, take road trips, and make jewelry. All of these things interest me, and I consider them hobbies.

2. What do I know enough about to write on?

I've been to a lot of concerts, so I could write about that. I don't know what I'd write about my interest in reading. I just like it. I haven't been on that many road trips—it's more that I'd like to do more traveling. I know a lot about basic jewelry making.

3. What could I write about that would interest readers?

I'm sure lots of classmates go to concerts, so there's probably not much new I could tell them. I guess the jewelry making could be interesting, at least for the girls in class. I'd be writing mainly for them, although I know guys who make jewelry too.

4. What purpose would I have in writing to my readers?

I could try to get classmates interested in jewelry making and show them that it isn't hard to do.

PLANNING THE FIRST DRAFT

Now that you have a topic, a reading audience (classmates), and a tentative purpose for writing, you are ready to think about your first draft. You may be in the habit of starting your writing by now. On the other hand, you may find that thinking about your topic before writing has some merit. This is a part of your trial-and-error prewriting process that will help you discover what works best for you.

The following questions will help you decide what you want to write about your topic.

1. What would readers want to know about the topic?

2. What examples could I give for interest?

3. How can I best accomplish my purpose?

Prewriting Activity 1.3

Spend some time thinking about your topic by answering the three questions just presented. You may either write down your answers or make mental notes.

*STUDENT RESPONSE
(TOPIC: MAKING
JEWELRY)*

1. What would readers want to know about the topic?

I think they'd be interested in how to make jewelry—in this case simple necklaces and bracelets. I can tell them what they need to buy and what the basic process is for making a necklace or bracelet. They might also want to know where to get the materials and what the costs are.

2. What examples could I give for interest?

I could include a few of the things that I've made to sell, give to friends, or wear myself.

3. How can I best accomplish my purpose?

If I explain the simple process clearly and convince them that the results can be really nice, I think I'll accomplish my purpose of getting at least a few people interested in the hobby.

Writing Your First Draft

Now that you have completed your prewriting work, you are ready to write the first draft of your paper. In the first draft, writers get their ideas on paper, and then they revise and polish their writing in subsequent drafts.

FIRST DRAFT GUIDELINES

The following suggestions will help you write your first draft.

1. *Make use of your prewriting plans.* From your prewriting, you have a basic idea of what you want to write, so take advantage of your planning. However, feel free to add things that come to mind and to revise plans as you go. Your prewriting plan provides a general direction to follow rather than an unalterable blueprint.

2. *Don't worry about perfect wording.* Get your ideas down in the wording that comes to you. You can revise and improve your wording in the next draft.

3. *Don't worry about making mistakes.* You can take care of a misspelled word or omitted comma when you edit your writing. Now is not the time to worry about mistakes.

Writing Activity 1.4

Write the first draft of your paper, keeping in mind the three suggestions just presented.

Making Jewelry

STUDENT FIRST DRAFT   In high school I had a friend who made her own bracelets and necklaces. She taught me how to do it, and I've been making them ever since. It's a very easy process to follow, something that anyone can learn to do. It can also save you some money.

No doubt there's one or more craft stores in your town that sell the materials that you will need: the bracelet or necklace strand, the "beads" to string on the strand, the spacers to separate the beads, and the coupler to latch the bracelet or necklace around your wrist, ankle, or neck. I like to select the "beads" first, which may be plastic, glass, or wooden beads, shells, charms, bone, wire rings, etc., and then find an appropriate strand to string them on.

The length, thickness and type of strand you select—string, yarn, leather, plastic, wire—depend on the size of the beads and the overall look that you want. I usually pick out the beads and then try them on different strands in the store until I find one they look best on. The beads have holes in them, so it is easy to slip them on and off the strands as you experiment. It is also good to hold the necklace or bracelet to your neck or wrist to check its length and get an idea of what it will look like on.

Other decisions you can make through experimenting include how many beads look best on the strand, what color combinations or different types of beads you may want to use, and whether or not the beads fit loosely enough on the strand that you need to buy the small rubber spacers to keep them separate. The artistry in necklace or bracelet making is in selecting the most attractive, interesting or unusual combinations and patterns of beads, strands, and colors to demonstrate your personal taste.

Once you buy the beads, strand, coupler, and spacers (if needed), take them home and experiment further by laying out the strand on a table and stringing your beads in different patterns and combinations. Don't separate the beads with spacers until you know the exact pattern you want. Finally, attach the two parts of the coupler to the ends of the strand to complete your necklace or bracelet. You have made a necklace or bracelet for under $5 that would cost $10 to $20 in a store, and you have something attractive to wear, to sell, or to give as a gift.

Revisions

After finishing your first draft, go back and take a good look at it. Think of your draft as a roughly sculptured figure that now requires a finely chiseled finish to be complete and presentable to viewers.

REVISION GUIDELINES

As you reread your first draft, apply the following suggestions.

1. *Additions:* Read your draft, looking for places where you might add something—an example, detail, or step—to make the paper clearer or more interesting for readers.

2. *Improved Wording:* Read each sentence to see if a change in wording would make it clearer or smoother, for example, replacing some words with more appropriate ones, deleting unnecessary words, or moving words or phrases to better locations. (See the section "Wording Problems" later in the unit.)

3. *Improved organization:* Read your draft to see if any sentences or paragraphs seem out of place. Decide where you might move them to improve the paper's organization.

4. *Paragraphing:* If your draft is at least a page long, it should be divided into paragraphs. Read your draft and begin a new paragraph when you move to something new about your topic—a different point, step, or example. (See the upcoming section "Paragraphing.")

5. *Purpose:* Review your purpose for writing this paper. Then read your draft to see what you might add, delete, or change to accomplish your purpose even better.

Revision Activity 1.5

With a classmate, evaluate the student draft on jewelry making by applying the five revision suggestions. What suggestions would you make to the student writer to improve her draft in any of those areas?

When you finish, evaluate your own draft following the revision suggestions. Make notes on your handwritten or printed draft, highlighting the changes you want to include in your next draft. If you would like a reader's opinion on something, ask one of your classmates for his or her input. If you want some direction on paragraphing or sentence wording, see the two sections following Activity 1.6.

Finally, rewrite your draft, including any revisions that you feel would improve the paper.

Draft Evaluation Activity 1.6

When you complete your second draft, compare it with the first draft and write a paragraph on the kinds of changes that you made in the second draft and how you feel they improved your paper. Then exchange paragraphs with a classmate or two to see the kinds of revisions other writers made.

PARAGRAPHING

If you don't have a lot of experience paragraphing your writing, you will want to go over this section before you write the second draft of your paper. As you work through this book, you will learn additional paragraphing techniques in each unit that you can apply to the different kinds of writing you will do.

Among students, experience with paragraphing varies greatly. You may already be quite sophisticated in your paragraphing skills, you may have some understanding of paragraphing but little experience, or you may vaguely recollect writing paragraphs in elementary or high school. As your instructor becomes more familiar with your writing, he or she can judge how much instruction you need on paragraphing.

Basic Paragraphing

Paragraphing is not an exact science. Two writers may paragraph the same paper in somewhat different ways. However, there are some general rules that apply to paragraphing:

1. *Develop one idea in a paragraph.* All of the sentences in a paragraph relate to one idea. For example, if a paragraph begins with the sentence, "Shoeing horses is hard work," the rest of the sentences should show us how hard the work is.

2. *Change paragraphs when you move to something new in a paper.* A different point, a different event, a new step, a different example, or a different aspect of your topic calls for a new paragraph.

3. *Although paragraphs vary in length, avoid writing extremely long or short paragraphs.* Readers get bogged down in paragraphs that run on for ten or fifteen sentences and get little out of paragraphs that contain only a sentence or two. Long paragraphs can usually be divided effectively, and short paragraphs can be combined with related paragraphs or lengthened with some development.

Paragraphing Activity 1.7

Following the suggestions just presented, divide each of the following papers into paragraphs. Compare your paragraphing decisions with classmates. Then reread the first draft of your paper (Activity 1.4) and make paragraphing decisions based on what you have learned.

Cruising Money

At least one Friday every couple of weeks, my friends and I pile into a car and cruise Mooney Boulevard in Vicksburg. Mooney is a wide four-lane street with malls, restaurants, and parking lots on each side along the three-mile cruising strip. When I tell my mom I'm going cruising, she always looks at me like I'm crazy. She'll say, "How can you spend the night driving up and down a street? Why don't you go to a movie or something?" Well, we do go to movies some weekends, and we also go to Zak's, a teenage nightclub. But on a lot of Friday nights, cruising is my favorite activity. The biggest kick in cruising is checking out all the new guys. At school you're stuck with the same faces every day, but when you're cruising, you never know who's going to drive up next to you. Guys from all over the area come to cruise Mooney. It's fun to see a load of good-looking guys heading the other direction and try to figure out a way to catch them. We'll flip a U-turn just about anyplace to go after a car of "hunks." Most of the time we just check the guys out, but sometimes we'll pull over and talk to them or split up and ride in each other's cars. Nothing much ever happens, but it's fun riding around and talking with guys I've never met. And you never know. Maybe the next car that pulls up beside me will have Mr. Right in it. Anything's possible when you're cruising. Another fun part of cruising is being with the gang. Patti, Marty, Charlotte, Vicki, and I have been pals since our freshman year in high school. We call ourselves the "Stubbs," and when we go cruising, we are very crazy. We turn the radio up full blast and sing our hearts out. We puff on cigarettes like real degenerates. We'll hang halfway out of the car to talk to guys, and we'll race them off the line when the light changes. And we laugh at anything and everything. Cruising brings out the craziness in us, and we have a blast together. Then there's the practical side of cruising. It's pretty cheap entertainment. We split the gas five ways each time we go, and that's about a dollar apiece. Then we stop at Mearle's Drive-in on the way home and buy milk shakes and fries, which is another dollar or two. That's a pretty cheap night compared to going to the movies or a concert. Even when we're short on money, we can always pool enough cash to head for Mooney's. Tomorrow night the Stubbs will head for Mooney's Boulevard in Marty's 1978 Monte Carlo. We may find some great-looking guys, or we may strike out. But either way we'll have a lot of fun because we enjoy cruising and being together. And we'll still have plenty of money left for next weekend. So even though we're in college now, we're not too old to enjoy cruising. Luckily, a lot of college guys like it too.

Apartment Hunting

Two weeks before school started, I started hunting for an apartment along with my future roommate. Actually, I ended up doing most of the looking because she was still working at an ice house. I went into Monroe at least five times looking for a two-bedroom apartment to rent, and I usually came home discouraged. Luckily, I found a pretty nice place to rent three days before school began. But shopping for an apartment with a limited budget is hard work. There are a lot of great apartments in Monroe, but they are all too expensive. I found a number of newer two-bedroom, two-bathroom apartments near the college with good-sized living rooms and kitchens, plenty of cupboard and closet space, and a swimming pool or Jacuzzi on the grounds. I'd ask the landlord the rental price, and it would always be somewhere from $375 to $450 a month. Since the maximum we could pay was $325 a month, the apartments were out of our range. It was depressing going through these nice apartments we couldn't afford. Then there's the problem of finding a good location. Obviously, the apartments nearer the college are the best located, but they are also the most expensive. Often when I'd find a decent-sounding apartment in the paper for $300, it would end up being halfway across town from the college or in some run-down neighborhood. The farther an apartment complex is away from the college, the less chance there is that it will have college students in it. We didn't want to end up in a complex with a bunch of older people or young married couples. I drove all over Monroe more than once tracking down a good-sounding deal, and usually the apartment ended up being beside a railroad track or a good twenty minutes from the campus. Then there's the problem of size. The larger apartments are naturally the more expensive ones. Many of the nicer apartments in our price range felt like doll houses: tiny rooms and low ceilings. We had quite a bit of old furniture to move into an apartment, and we both slept on queen-sized beds. We needed adequate closet space for a semester's worth of clothes. We also planned on doing all of our own cooking, so we wanted a good-sized kitchen. Many of the apartments that sounded really nice turned out to be too small to consider. But as time began running out, I figured we'd probably end up taking a small apartment and stuffing everything into it that we could. Luckily, all of the effort finally paid off. After looking at at least twenty-five different apartments and rejecting all of them, I found an apartment complex that was being remodeled. It was an old complex that didn't look too hot from the outside, but inside, the remodeled apartments were like new. The apartments were good-sized and rented for $310 a month, and they were only ten minutes from the college. I put down a deposit immediately, and my search was over. What I thought would be an easy task had turned into two weeks of driving around, making phone calls, scanning newspapers, and finding a lot of places I didn't like or couldn't afford. Finding an apartment is hard work when you can't spend much money, and you need to plan on spending a lot of time looking.

SENTENCE WORDING

For all writers, an important part of draft revision is improving their sentence wording. When they first struggle to express a thought, the words seldom come out as smoothly or clearly as they would like. Writers share the task of reworking sentences in a first draft, and the results are usually gratifying.

Wording Problems

The following wording problems are common in first draft sentences.

1. *Wordiness:* using more words than are necessary to express an idea.

   Example   I am late for school because of the fact that my car wouldn't start.

Revised	I am late for school because my car wouldn't start.
Example	The reason why I did well on my test was because I studied hard for my test.
Revised	I did well on my test because I studied hard.

2. *Awkward phrasing:* using words and phrases that don't fit together smoothly and logically.

Example	Lunch you could have in the cafeteria hours between eleven and two o'clock.
Revised	The cafeteria is open for lunch between eleven and two o'clock.
Example	Although we went to the swap meet, but we didn't buy anything.
Revised	Although we went to the swap meet, we didn't buy anything.

3. *Poor word choice:* not using the best word to express a thought.

Example	We were excited about doing things in the track meet.
Revised	We were excited about participating in the track meet.
Example	Jonathan had learned all his children to use a computer.
Revised	Jonathan had taught all his children to use a computer.

Sentence Activity 1.8

The following first draft sentences need revising. The sentences have problems with wordiness, awkward phrasing, and poor word choices. Revise and rewrite each sentence to make it smoother and clearer. Then reread your first draft (Activity 1.4) and revise sentences to make them smoother, clearer, and less wordy.

Examples

First draft	My goal is to lose six pounds of my body weight.
Revised	My goal is to lose six pounds.
First draft	On the left side of the ring has my name on it in initials.
Revised	On the left side of the ring are my initials.

1. It was a Wednesday afternoon, and I noticed in my computer class a number of foreign students.

2. Being an only child is a very lonely moment in your life.

3. John's friends envy him due to the fact of the attention he receives, the possessions he possesses, and the privileges he is privileged to have.

4. The day was a total learning process of inestimable value to myself.

5. You will get a lot of responsibility for college.

6. The tables are round and square and setting on a carpet that is indoor and outdoor.

7. The pier has three microscopes planted on it, so you can see across the bay with those microscopes.

8. Working outdoors makes welding a difficult place to work.

9. The feasts on, before, or around Christmas day can be very fulfilling.

10. My room is a fifteen-by-twenty-foot square, and it is white in color on the walls and ceiling.

Final Editing

Now that you have revised your paper to improve its content, organization, and wording, you are ready to give it a thorough proofreading to find and correct any errors in punctuation, spelling, or grammar. No matter how well organized or informative a paper is, if it is riddled with errors, readers may lose interest.

PROOFREADING GUIDELINES

When proofreading a draft for errors, cover the following general areas.

1. *Check to make sure that each sentence ends with a period.* A common problem among writers is to run pairs of sentences together rather than separating them with a period. (See the upcoming section "Run-on Sentences.")

2. *Check to make sure you haven't left off any word endings.* Occasionally, writers will leave off an *ed* on a past tense verb, an *s* or *es* on a plural word, an *s* on a present tense verb, or an *ly* on an adverb. A quick check of word endings may uncover some inadvertent omissions.

3. *Check your spelling carefully.* Misspelled words are the most common writing errors and the most troubling for readers. If you use a computer, learn to use the spelling checker on your word processor. Also make a list of words that you frequently misspell, and work on eliminating all the words on the list.

   If you struggle with spelling, your instructor may refer you to the "Spelling" section in the appendix at the back of this book. This section gives you some basic spelling rules and includes lists of frequently misspelled words.

4. *Check your "internal" punctuation.* Make sure you have inserted commas where you want readers to pause in your sentences and apostrophes (') in contractions (you're, isn't). (See the section "Comma Usage" later in the unit.)

5. *Check your use of subject pronouns (I, he, she, you, we, they).* Writers too often write "Me and my brother went fishing" instead of "My brother and I went fishing," or "Marie, Harriet, and me are friends" instead of "Marie, Harriet, and I are friends," or "Me and her went to the mall together" instead of "She and I went to the mall together."

Of course, this checklist doesn't cover all of the types of errors you may run across in your writing, and it doesn't provide you with the rules and practice you may need to eradicate certain tendencies. It does give you some direction in proofreading your drafts and correcting common errors. As you work through the book, you will learn the rules and get the practice you may need to write correctly and to proofread accurately.

Proofreading Activity 1.9

Following the guidelines just presented, proofread your latest draft and correct any errors that you find. Your instructor may have you work through the upcoming sections on run-on sentences and comma usage before you proofread your paper. When you finish correcting your paper, write or print out the final draft to share with classmates.

SENTENCE PROBLEMS

The most common problem with sentence structure comes from running pairs of sentences together. Two or more sentences run together are called a *run-on sentence*. In most cases, run-on sentences confuse readers and make writing hard to understand. The purpose of this section is to help you recognize the most common types of run-ons, to show you how to correct them, and to help you avoid them in your writing.

Run-on Sentences

Here are some common features of run-on sentences:

1. A run-on sentence is usually two sentences run together without a period ending the first sentence or a capital letter beginning the second.

    Example   June is a very spoiled child she expects to get her way at all times.

2. A run-on sentence with a comma between the two sentences is called a *comma splice*. A comma by itself does not separate sentences, and it does not replace a period.

Example   We never go into town during the week, it is too far from our farm.

3. The sentences within a run-on are usually closely related in meaning.

Example   Maria is doing well in algebra she has gotten B's on all her tests.

4. Most run-on sentences follow certain patterns. A *pronoun* often begins the second sentence within a run-on sentence: he, it, they, she, you, we, and I. The following t-words also begin the second sentence in a run-on sentence: the, then, there, that, this, these, and those.

   Here are some examples in which the underlined pronoun or t-word begins the second sentence within the run-on sentence:

   Examples   Ted's parents spoil him <u>they</u> give him money to brush his teeth.

   Sylvia came to class early <u>she</u> wanted to study her notes.

   The tides at the beach were unpredictable, <u>they</u> made swimming dangerous.

   John went for a walk <u>then</u> he took a nap before going to work.

   Getting to the museum isn't difficult <u>there</u> are many routes to take.

5. To correct run-on sentences, you either need to separate the sentences with a period or combine them with a joining word. Here are the run-on sentences correctly punctuated. When a joining word is added, it is underlined.

   Examples   Ted's parents spoil him <u>because</u> they give him money to brush his teeth.

   Sylvia came to class early. She wanted to study her notes.

   John went for a walk, <u>and</u> then he took a nap before going to work.

   Getting to the museum isn't difficult. There are many routes to take.

Run-on Activity 1.10

Most of the following sentences are run together. Correct the run-on sentences and comma splices by putting a period after the first sentence and capitalizing the second sentence or by combining the sentences with a joining word. *As a general rule, separate longer run-on sentences with periods and connect the shorter sentences with joining words.* When you finish, proofread your latest draft for run-on sentences and make the necessary corrections.

Example   The bear backed into its cave, it was frightened by the flames.

Revised   The bear backed into its cave because it was frightened by the flames.

Example   I have tried to ignore your annoying habit of cracking your toes in class I must now ask you to stop before I go crazy.

Revised   I have tried to ignore your annoying habit of cracking your toes in class. I must now ask you to stop before I go crazy.

1. The downtown bus is always late, I don't expect it to arrive for another twenty minutes.

2. Bill Clinton jogs regularly you couldn't tell by looking at him.

3. Fred and Hilda have something special in common they were born in the back of the same taxi cab exactly one year apart.

4. Howard is never late for work, for he has an alarm that plays reveille.

5. The hurricane hit at midnight it brought winds of eighty miles an hour.

6. Most children seem to perform best when praised they often don't do as well when they are criticized.

7. Fishing was slow on Sunday morning, the salmon had all been caught Saturday evening in the fishing derby.

8. Only five of the fifty contestants were selected to represent the college in the academic decathlon those five will compete on national television this spring.

9. The otter disappeared under the dam, then it surfaced fifty yards downstream in the middle of some lily pads.

10. The political science students were active in the gubernatorial election in their state there were over 500 students participating in phone banks.

COMMA USAGE

The purpose of using commas in your writing is to clarify the meaning of sentences for readers. Proper comma usage establishes the reading rhythm of a sentence by showing readers where to pause and by separating words or phrases whose meaning would be ambiguous if they were run together. Improper comma usage, on the other hand, can destroy sentence rhythm and confuse readers.

Basic Comma Rules

The following basic comma rules will serve you well for punctuating sentences effectively. A few additional rules will be covered later in the book.

1. *Commas in series:* Three or more words or groups of words in a series should be separated by commas. Words in a series are usually joined by *conjunctions,* such as *and, but,* or *or.*

   Examples   I enjoy hiking, fishing, and reading.

   Marie likes to jog in the morning, after lunch, after work, or in the early evening.

   Jorge is excited about the debate, prepared to argue his case, and determined to do well.

   Samantha works on Saturdays but relaxes on Sundays. (No comma needed because there are only *two* groups of words joined by *but:* "works on Saturdays" *but* "relaxes on Sundays."

2. *Commas in compound sentences:* In a sentence containing two complete sentences (*independent clauses*) joined by a *conjunction*—and, but, so, or, yet, for,—a comma goes after the word before the conjunction.

   Examples   Teddy is planning on going to the curriculum meeting after school, but she may change her plans if her tooth continues to ache.

   Those bugs on the ceiling are coming in through the broken window screen, so I think we'd better buy a new one.

   The rain has flooded all of the streets around the college, and it is impossible to park anywhere near campus.

   (Exception: If the compound sentence is short, no comma is needed since readers wouldn't pause in the middle: I walk to school but I take the bus home. Sarah enjoys algebra and she does well on her tests.)

3. *Introductory groups of words:* If a sentence begins with an introductory group of words, a comma sets off the introduction. Introductory phrases and clauses often begin with a *preposition* (in, on, by, with, between, through, for example), a *subordinate conjunction* (when, while, as, unless, although, because, if, after, before), or a word that ends in *ing* or *ed* (working, hoping, troubled, amazed).

   Examples   On your way out of the auditorium, please lock the double doors in the back.

   In the middle of her greatest season, Maribel broke her pitching hand.

   If you have finished mowing the lawn, please give me some help with the laundry.

Because I have over 100 pages of botany to read tonight, I can't go to the concert.

Looking at her watch every few minutes, Marcela waited impatiently for her date to arrive.

Alarmed at how quickly his hair was falling out, Marvin bought a wig.

Shouting at the top of her lungs, Sophia attracted the judge's attention.

Comma Activity 1.11

Insert commas in the following sentences where they are needed in series, in compound sentences, and after introductory groups of words. When you finish, proofread your latest draft for correct comma usage.

Example   In the back of the bus, we found snakes, frogs, and lizards.

1. Andretti barreled down the straightaway braked on the curve and punched the gas on entering the backstretch.

2. Stealing chickens trespassing hunting on private property and tying cats' tails together were charges brought against Akins.

3. In the back of my mind I remember having traveled this stretch of Texas before.

4. Judith wanted to go on a hayride but she was allergic to hay.

5. In spite of everything you've heard about Claudine she's really a dangerous person.

6. We can cut the firewood this afternoon after school or we can wait and cut it on Saturday morning.

7. Because you have been so faithful to the team you've earned the Most Inspirational Chess Player award.

8. It's raining too hard to pick strawberries behind the house so let's do it another time.

9. After we take the subway to Main Street let's walk up to 55th and Broadway.

10. Our plans are to meet at Maria's go to the dance in one car eat at Feducci's go back to Maria's for our cars and drive home.

11. That small mangy feisty flea-bitten cat is all mine.

12. Practicing for the piano concert on Friday Marian got blisters on her thumbs pinkies and index fingers but that didn't prevent her from playing beautifully at the concert.

Writing Review

At the end of each unit, you apply what you have learned to a second writing assignment. The prewriting, drafting, revision, and editing steps in the unit are summarized for your use.

WRITING PROCESS

ASSIGNMENT

1. Write a paper on *one thing* that is important in your life, for example: family, religion, education, becoming wealthy, being physically fit, marriage, becoming an accountant or physical therapist, traveling the world. Write this paper for your classmates so they can better understand your priorities.

TOPIC SELECTION

2. To choose a topic, answer the following questions.
   a. What topics interest me enough to write about?
   b. What do I know enough about to write a paper on?
   c. What would interest my readers (classmates)?
   d. What would my purpose be in writing to my readers?

PREWRITING

3. After you have selected a topic and a tentative purpose for writing, answer the following prewriting questions to help you plan your first draft.
   a. What would my readers (classmates) want to know about the topic, and what do I want to tell them?
   b. What examples might I include to clarify how I feel about the topic and add interest for readers?
   c. How can I best accomplish my purpose?

FIRST DRAFT

4. After you have done some prewriting planning, write the first draft of your paper following these suggestions.
   a. Make use of your prewriting plans, but feel free to make changes as other ideas come to you through the drafting process.
   b. Don't worry about perfect wording because you can revise your sentences later.
   c. Don't worry about making mistakes because you can correct them later.

REVISIONS

5. When you finish your first draft, pair with a classmate and evaluate the student draft in the book by applying the following revision suggestions. Then evaluate your own draft using the same guidelines, and get a second opinion from a classmate if you would like. Finally, write your second draft, including all revisions you have noted for improving the paper.
   a. Read the draft to see where adding something new—an example, a new point, some detail—could improve the paper for readers.
   b. Read each sentence to see how its wording might be improved by deleting unnecessary words, smoothing out awkward phrasing, and replacing questionable words.

c. Read the draft to see if anything seems out of place. Move sentences or even a paragraph to improve the paper's organization.

d. Check the paragraphing to make sure that you change paragraphs when you begin something new, that the sentences within a paragraph are all related, and that you don't have any overly long or short paragraphs.

e. Review the purpose of your paper and consider changes that will help you accomplish that purpose even better.

EDITING

6. Proofread your latest draft for errors using the following guidelines.

a. Make sure you have a period at the end of each sentence, and look in particular for run-on or comma splice sentences that need correcting.

b. Check your word endings to make sure you haven't left off any *s, ed, ing,* or *ly* endings.

c. Check your comma usage within series (three or more words or groups of words), compound sentences (before *and, but, so, yet, or,* or *for* that join two complete sentences), and after introductory groups of words. Make sure you don't insert commas where they aren't needed. Also check your use of apostrophes (') in contractions (you're, isn't).

d. Check your use of subject pronouns (I, he, she, we, they, you) to make sure you are writing "Joan and I are friends" instead of "Joan and me are friends," or "She and I went to the movies" instead of "Her and me went to the movies."

e. Check your spelling carefully to make sure you catch and correct any misspelled words. Use the spelling checker on your word processor to help you.

FINAL DRAFT

7. Write or print out the final draft of your paper and share it with classmates and your instructor.

STUDENT TOPIC SELECTION

The first thing that comes into my head is my family when I think of priorities. I know education is important to me, but I take that part for granted—it's something I've got to do. Getting married or making money or getting a great job are all out there somewhere, but they aren't priorities for me yet. So I return to my family—the one constant in my life. That's definitely what I'm going to write about.

PREWRITING PLAN

My mom and dad are really important to me. I want that to come across clearly. They've done a lot for me, and I'll provide examples of that. I also want to bring out how we enjoy being together and still do things together. Plenty of examples. Then I'd like to talk about the ways that I count or rely on them, knowing they're always there for me. I'll be revealing that I'm still pretty dependent on them for being in college, but that's the way it is and I want to be honest. I don't want the paper to sound too sappy but I want my feelings to come through. My purpose is to show my classmates how important my family is to me.

My Family

STUDENT DRAFT

When I think back through good memories of my life, most of them are in some way associated with my family. Family is the one constant that has always been a part of me, my rock against the storms of life. I can't imagine life without my mom and dad, and I hope they're around for a long, long time.

The one thing my folks always had for me, as well as for my brother, was time. I was on a swim team from the time I was ten years old through high school, and I don't ever remember them missing one of my meets. They were always there rooting me on, congratulating me when I did well and consoling me when I did poorly. It was the same with all my activities: volleyball, basketball, school plays, back-to-school nights, you name it. I never had to worry about my folks not showing up or not caring about what I was doing. I could count on them.

I've also done my share of leaning on their shoulders over the years. I never felt there was anything I couldn't tell my mom and dad, and I'm the kind who has to get it all out when I have a problem. Over the years they've heard it all: the time in junior high when one boy was constantly bugging me, the time in high school when I got caught drinking, the time I wrecked their Volkswagen Rabbit, rough times with my former boyfriend, and on and on. They always listened to me, helped me any way they could, gave me good advice when I needed it, and always showed they cared. Even getting through my freshman year of college away from home with a "roommate from hell" was something I couldn't have survived without many, many long-distance calls home and some timely visits from the folks.

We've had our share of fun too. The swim meets were weekend mini-vacations where we traveled all over the state and spent lots of good times together. We loved going to movies and eating out as a family, and we still do when I get home on breaks. We also have fun just sitting around the house watching TV and eating popcorn. My parents are fun-loving people, and I still have as much with them as I do with my friends, well almost as much.

The great thing about family, at least about mine, is I know nothing is going to change. Whether I'm twenty, thirty, or forty, I'll have two very special people who care for me and want the best for me. Friends may come and go, good times and bad times lie ahead, and there are lots of uncertainties in this world. Through all of this it's really great to know that family is forever, the one constant in my life. I hope I'm someday able to pass on the same sense of security and love to my own children.

Readings

The readings at the end of each unit parallel the student writing topics for that unit. You may use the readings to get ideas for your own writing as well as for your enjoyment and analysis.

Cross-Country Skiing

BY PAUL KASER

1   When I was a freshman in college, some friendly upperclassmen introduced me to the joys of downhill (sometimes called Alpine) skiing. They gave me no lessons. "Don't need them," they assured me. "Lessons are for wimps. Just get on the skis and go. You'll stop at the bottom." They took me to the top of the "pro" slope and let me go.

2   They were wrong about my not needing lessons, but they were right about my stopping at the bottom. While one of my skis headed off independently toward the parking lot, I gracefully crumpled myself and remaining ski around a light pole. This was just after I had bowled through a line of real skiers waiting for the ski lift, then through a semicircle of novices sensibly practicing their snowplow stops.

3   But did this early minor catastrophe stop me from pursuing the excellent thrills of downhill skiing ever again? Absolutely. I picked myself up, dusted myself off, and limped with dignity to the lodge bar where I sulked, sopped up cheap brandy, and swore off the deadly sport of downhill forever.

4   It was not till a decade or so later that I returned to skis, but not to those death-dealing downhill monsters. This time, I took up cross-country (sometimes called Nordic) skiing.

5   The very name "cross-country" was more comforting to me than "downhill." After all, isn't it better to go more or less horizontally as in Nordic skiing than to hurl yourself graveward at a 45 degree angle until a tree, light pole, or boulder stops you?

6   As a cross-country skier, I may occasionally descend for a few short yards, but that is my choice, not my obsession. I find an unassuming hill, introduce myself politely, clamber up its backside, and then drift down at a modest speed, coming to a civilized halt at its bottom—not *on* mine. There is none of that supersonic ascent into white hell that downhillers require of themselves.

7   Alpine skiers like to brag about "challenging nature" and "pushing the envelope," which seems to mean seeking the highest, most lethal slope and plunging down it toward their chiropractor.

8   We cross-country skiers understand that nature is to be appeased, not challenged, since we know that nature, when competed against, can be a very nasty mother who thinks nothing of littering her snowy flanks with the fractured femurs and shattered egos of envelope-pushing downhillers.

9   Cross-country skiers, by contrast, slide around quietly on clean snow, to linger now and then in order to compliment nature on a well-sculpted frozen waterfall or smoothly quilted snow-meadow, then slide inoffensively back to the station wagon.

10   Although some Nordic skiers like to exhaust themselves in more rigorous treks, most set more humble goals, like travelling a carefully plotted loop that gets them back to their station wagon before they have to answer a "call of nature." Nordic-type skiers, at least those of my ilk, never seek to push any envelope. We know downhillers who pushed their envelope right into traction.

11   Nordic skiing is also much cheaper. This is because cross-country skiers don't flock in swarms of expensively equipped and feathered show-offs.

12   Thus, the cross-country skier need not spend his children's college tuition money or sell his birthright in order to buy his skis and poles. Cross-country equipment costs about a third of what downhill equipment costs.

13   Because manufacturers of Alpine ski equipment continually "improve" their gear (moon-zombie boots, elegant French skis, soon-to-be-snapped poles), the downhiller has to keep remortgaging his house to keep up with the crowd.

14   And that's just the hardware. When it comes to clothes, the conscientious downhiller is required to make weekly trips to the bank, then to the ski boutique to deck himself out in the latest rainbow-splash Spandex glamour outfit. Not to do so would be to risk being ridiculed as a snow-nerd by the more fashionable peacocks of the slopes.

15   Cross-country types, on the other hand, practice their sport in any old outfit they please. I have seen them whisking along in old Levis and sweat shirts, even shorts and T-shirts on bright, windless days. Let the downhillers dress to impress. Cross-country types don't give a designer label how scruffy they look. If it's comfortable, they wear it.

16   Finally, cross-country skiers don't have to pay for lift tickets or entry fees because all they need to do is drive along till they see a fairly level stretch and get out and ski without lining up to ask the permission or pay the fees of some voracious corporation.

17   To sum up, cross-country (or Nordic) skiing is quieter, safer, and less expensive than is its first cousin downhill (or Alpine). It can also provide steady and efficient exercise and is a great family sport.

18   I like to think that many cross-country enthusiasts had their truth-in-skiing revelation in much the same manner as did I—while tallying up my downhill bruises and contemplating my flattened wallet.

19   I wonder if anyone ever found my other downhill ski?

QUESTIONS FOR DISCUSSION

1. Why do you think Kaser chose to contrast downhill skiing to his favored cross-country skiing rather than devoting the entire essay to his hobby?

2. If a person's hobby tells you something about him or her, how might you contrast downhill to cross-country skiing enthusiasts?

3. After reading the essay, do you agree with Kaser's viewpoint on the advantages of cross-country skiing? Why or why not?

4. Analyze the organization of the essay—Kaser's strategy for presenting his information on cross-country and downhill skiing. How effective is the organization? Why?

5. What did you learn or find of particular interest in the essay? What, if anything, could you relate to your life?

6. Locate descriptive passages you found particularly vivid or interesting. Analyze their appeal.

VOCABULARY

Novice (2), sopped (3), femurs (8), trek (10), ilk (10), voracious (16)

Still Just Writing

BY ANNE TYLER

1   I was standing in the schoolyard waiting for a child when another mother came up to me. "Have you found work yet?" she asked. "Or are you still just writing?"

2   Now, how am I supposed to answer that?

3   I could take offense, come to think of it. Maybe the reason I didn't is that I halfway share her attitude. They're *paying* me for this? For just writing down untruthful stories? I'd better look around for more permanent employment. For I do consider writing to be a finite job. I expect that any day now, I will have said all I have to say; I'll have used up all my characters, and then I'll be free to get on with my real life. When I make a note of new ideas on index cards, I imagine I'm clearing out my head, and that soon it will be empty and spacious. I file the cards in a little blue box, and I can picture myself using the final card one day—ah! through at last!—and throwing the blue box away. I'm like a dentist who continually fights tooth decay, working toward the time when he's conquered it altogether and done himself out of a job. But my head keeps loading up again; the little blue box stays crowded and messy. Even when I feel I have no ideas at all, and can't possibly start the next chapter, I have a sense of something still bottled in me, trying to get out.

4   People have always seemed funny and strange to me, and touching in unexpected ways. I can't shake off a sort of mist of irony that hangs over whatever I see. Probably that's what I'm trying to put across when I write; I may believe that I'm the one person who holds this view of things. And I'm always hurt when a reader says that I choose only bizarre or eccentric people to write about. It's not a matter of choice; it just seems to me that even the most ordinary person, in real life, will turn out to have something unusual at his center. I like to think that I might meet up with one of my past characters at the very next street corner. The odd thing is, sometimes I have. And if I were remotely religious, I'd believe that a little gathering of my characters

would be waiting for me in heaven when I died. "*Then* what happened?" I'd ask them. "How have things worked out, since the last time I saw you?"

5   I think I was born with the impression that what happened in books was much more reasonable, and interesting, and *real,* in some ways, than what happened in life. I hated childhood, and spent it sitting behind a book waiting for adulthood to arrive. When I ran out of books I made up my own. At night, when I couldn't sleep. I made up stories in the dark. Most of my plots involved girls going west in covered wagons. I was truly furious that I'd been born too late to go west in a covered wagon.

6   I know a poet who says that in order to be a writer, you have to have had rheumatic fever in your childhood. I've never had rheumatic fever, but I believe that any kind of setting-apart situation will do as well. In my case, it was emerging from that commune—really an experimental Quaker community in the wilderness—and trying to fit into the outside world. I was eleven. I had never used a telephone and could strike a match on the soles of my bare feet. All the children in my new school looked very peculiar to me, and I certainly must have looked peculiar to them. I am still surprised, to this day, to find myself where I am. My life is so streamlined and full of modern conveniences. How did I get here? I have given up hope, by now, of ever losing my sense of distance; in fact, I seem to have come to cherish it. Neither I nor any of my brothers can stand being out among a crowd of people for any length of time at all.

7   I spent my adolescence planning to be an artist, not a writer. After all, books had to be about major events, and none had ever happened to me. All I knew were tobacco workers, stringing the leaves I handed them and talking up a storm. Then I found a book of Eudora Welty's short stories in the high school library. She was writing about Edna Earle, who was so slow-witted she could sit all day just pondering how the tail of the *C* got through the loop of the *L* on the Coca-Cola sign. Why, I knew Edna Earle. You mean you could *write* about such people? I have always meant to send Eudora Welty a thank-you note, but I imagine she would find it a little strange.

8   I wanted to go to Swarthmore College, but my parents suggested Duke instead, where I had a full scholarship, because my three brothers were coming along right behind me and it was more important for boys to get a good education than for girls. That was the first and last time that my being female was ever a serious issue. I still don't think it was just, but I can't say it ruined my life. After all, Duke had Reynolds Price, who turned out to be the only person I ever knew who could actually teach writing. It all worked out, in the end.

9   I believe that for many writers, the hardest time is that dead spot after college (where they're wonder-children, made much of) and before their first published work. Luckily, I didn't notice that part; I was so vague about what I wanted to do that I could hardly chafe at not yet doing it. I went to graduate school in Russian studies; I scrubbed decks on a boat in Maine; I got a job ordering books from the Soviet Union. Writing was something that crept in around the edges. For a while I lived in New York, where I became addicted

to riding any kind of train or subway, and while I rode I often felt I was nothing but an enormous eye, taking things in and turning them over and sorting them out. But who would I tell them to, once I'd sorted them? I have never had more than three or four close friends, at any period of my life; and anyway, I don't talk well. I am the kind of person who wakes up at four in the morning and suddenly thinks of what she should have said yesterday at lunch. For me, writing something down was the only road out.

10   You would think, since I waited so long and so hopefully for adulthood, that it would prove to be a disappointment. Actually, I figure it was worth the wait. I like everything about it but the paperwork—the income tax and protesting the Sears bill and renewing the Triple-A membership. I always did count on having a husband and children, and here they are. I'm surprised to find myself a writer but have fitted it in fairly well, I think. The only real trouble that writing has ever brought me is an occasional sense of being invaded by the outside world. Why do people imagine that writers, having chosen the most private of professions, should be any good at performing in public, or should have the slightest desire to tell their secrets to interviewers from ladies' magazines? I feel I am only holding myself together by being extremely firm and decisive about what I will do and what I will not do. I will write my books and raise the children. Anything else just fritters me away. I know this makes me seem narrow, but in fact, I *am* narrow. I like routine and rituals and I hate leaving home; I have a sense of digging my heels in. I refuse to drive on freeways. I dread our annual vacation. Yet I'm continually prepared for travel: It is physically impossible for me to buy any necessity without buying a travel-sized version as well. I have a little toilet kit, with soap and a nightgown, forever packed and ready to go. How do you explain that?

11   As the outside world grows less dependable, I keep buttressing my inside world, where people go on meaning well and surprising other people with little touches of grace. There are days when I sink into my novel like a pool and emerge feeling blank and bemused and used up. Then I drift over to the schoolyard, and there's this mother wondering if I'm doing anything halfway useful yet. Am I working? Have I found a job? No, I tell her.

12   I'm still just writing.

QUESTIONS FOR DISCUSSION

1. How does Tyler view her career as a writer? Why is being a writer viewed by some people as less than a "real" job?

2. What aspects of Tyler's background and personality contributed to her interest in writing? What aspects of your own background have contributed to your adult interests?

3. How has being a woman affected Tyler's choices in life? How might her perspective on life differ from a male writer's?

4. As a writer, how does Tyler view the world around her differently than most people? What if anything can we learn from Tyler's perspective?

VOCABULARY

Eccentric (4), commune (6)

Gotta Dance!

BY ROB HOERBURGER

1   I walked into the confessional a repentant sinner and walked out a dancer. The priest who heard my sins half-jokingly suggested that for my penance I join the church's production of *West Side Story*, which he was directing. I was 27 at the time and hadn't performed on a stage since fourth grade, but I figured at the very least I could help out with the lights.

2   Instead, I ended up with the featured role of Riff, the leader of the Jets, mostly because of a lucky break (as in the ankle of the actor originally cast), and the usual dearth of male bodies in community-theater productions. After months of rehearsal, I was comfortable enough with the dialogue and the singing, but the dancing—and *West Side Story* is *mostly* dancing—petrified me. Right up to opening night, I was never sure which foot I would land on.

3   My anxiety was born of some taboo I had long ago internalized about dancing not being masculine. The typical after-school and after-supper pastimes for boys in my suburban neighborhood were baseball and football. Forget that dancing can actually develop the timing and coordination needed to play second base, or that dancers have physiques that gym rats only dream about. Any parent signing his or her son up for dance class instead of (or even in addition to) Little League was practically subject to child-abuse charges—because invariably that boy would be subject to the cruel taunts of his peers.

4   This unspoken prohibition was especially painful because secretly I loved to dance. Sports were O.K., but there were many nights when I would forgo the pickup game of baseball on the street, throw on some Motown and whirl around my room for a few hours. But always behind closed doors. Now here I was about to make a public spectacle of myself, and in *West Side Story* no less.

5   Most of the other men in the cast expressed similar anxiety, but we got a reprieve in that the choreography de-emphasized the more balletic turns in favor of macho posturing and finger-snapping and the climbing of fences. When the steps did get a little more complicated, I took the choreographer's advice to "show a lot of attitude" and chalked the rest up to the power of prayer. And I vowed to get better.

6   But childhood taboos die hard. It took me a year and a half to summon the courage to enroll in a dance class in Manhattan. As I signed my name for a year's worth of lessons, a lifetime of aversion—my own and my friends'—to dancing in public flashed through my head. I thought of linebackers in high school who took and gave poundings on the football field but sweated through the box step at the prom. And I knew firefighters and fleet-footed

detectives who had been in shootouts who cowered at the sight of a wood floor with a strobe light above it. Even after John Travolta gyrated through *Saturday Night Fever,* tough guys still didn't dance.

7   I had been assured that there would be other men in the class, but when I arrived for the first one I was surrounded by leggy women in tights and tutus. The only other man was the instructor, Jeff, a former Broadway dancer who had been in *A Chorus Line* early in its run. He wore makeup and several earrings. Would I have felt more comfortable if he looked like Cal Ripken? Probably, but then I didn't have time to dwell on it, because I was immediately barraged with not only new steps but a new language ("plié," "relevé," "jazz third") and lessons in attire. ("This is not aerobics," Jeff would say, casting gentle aspersions at my jock wear—sneakers and sweats, which I clung to as the last bastions of my maleness.)

8   I tried to hide in the back lines, but in dance studios even the support beams have mirrors. I heard my name a lot in those first weeks: "Keep your shoulders down." "Other hand." "Watch your head." Yet every time I was tempted to quit, I also heard Jeff's words of encouragement: "If you get only 25 percent of the routine, I'll be happy" or "Just showing up is the victory."

9   Eventually the routines seemed less tyrannical, and I started to relax. I even compromised on my attire—retaining my Nike T-shirt but trading the sweats and sneakers for black satin jazz pants and jazz shoes. ("Now those," Jeff said, "have style.") And the benefits of the class were instantaneous— walking to my train after each session, I felt a kind of honorable exhaustion, having coaxed into consciousness muscles I hadn't even known existed. It was the same sense of physical satisfaction that I'd felt hitting a bases-clearing double or finishing a half-marathon.

10   My lessons were interrupted when the next show came along: *Man of La Mancha,* which required me to age 30 years but hardly afforded me an opportunity to show off my new steps. When the show finished its run, I returned to the studio, only to find Jeff out sick and the class being taught by a drill-sergeant substitute. She demanded that each dancer cross the floor individually while she exhorted, "Kick that leg higher—and now *sell* it." Under Jeff's kid-gloves tutelage, I had imagined myself as Fred Astaire, but now, under this magnifying glass, I turned back into Fred Flintstone—stumbling, clumsy, self-conscious, as if all the inhibitions I had been whittling away suddenly gathered themselves back into an intractable whole. On my third or fourth solo flight across the floor I kept going into the locker room, up the stairs and out the door.

11   Jeff's absence turned out to be permanent—his illness was forcing him to retire—and the studio closed soon after that, a victim of the economy's own failing health. Then I got word of a cast call for a local production of *South Pacific,* a show whose feats are primarily vocal, at least for the men. Reluctantly, I auditioned and made the male chorus. It looked as if my dancing days would be indefinitely deferred.

12   The men did have one big number—*There Is Nothin' Like a Dame*— which basically involved animated marching. Posture and expression were

key, and, because Jeff had emphasized these in class, I had no trouble picking up the routine. The choreographer even singled me out to demonstrate a couple of steps, and the other men—most of whom had never danced on stage before and were wearing the same long faces I did during *West Side Story*—were saying things like "Obviously you've done this before." Now I was being celebrated for something that most of my life I had feared would bring me ridicule.

13   After much fine-tuning and many weeks of rehearsal, the other men came around, and by the time the show opened there was a buzz about *There Is Nothin' Like a Dame*. The women in the show had three times as many dance numbers and their steps were much fancier. But the novelty appeal of "men who can move" ran high, and when we successfully executed a kickline at the end of the song we brought down the house.

14   At moments like that, and the many since I've had dancing in public and private, I remember that trip to the confession booth, and realize that dance has in fact become a kind of physical and psychic redemption. But it isn't penance anymore.

QUESTIONS FOR DISCUSSION

1. Why was Hoerburger ashamed of his lifelong love of dancing? Why do many people view dancing as being "unmanly"?

2. Why did Hoerburger take his love for dancing "public"? How did this experience change his perspective?

3. Hoerburger said that dancing in public has become "a kind of physical and psychic redemption." What does he mean?

4. What, if any, interests have you had that run counter to stereotypical male or female roles? What male-female stereotypes are breaking down in our society?

VOCABULARY

Penance (1), prohibition (4), aversion (6), aspersions (7), exhorted (10), intractable (10), psychic (14), redemption (14)

Inner Voyage

One of your most valuable writing journeys is the inner voyage toward self-discovery. When you write and reflect on significant experiences in your life, you discover how they helped shape who you are and why you think and feel as you do.

Your writing for this unit focuses on personal experiences that remain vivid in your memory. You will recall these experiences for yourself, as well as for your classmates, and you will analyze them in order to understand the impact they have had on your life.

Sharing experiences through narrative writing is enjoyable and rewarding for both writer and readers. You learn to re-create your experiences to make them real and vivid for your readers. By reflecting on the significance of your experiences, you pass on to your readers what you learn about yourself, others, and life in general.

Prewriting

In this unit you write about a personal experience that occurred much earlier in your life. During your prewriting, you consider different experiences that you recall, select one that you would like to write about, and "play back" that experience in your mind before writing. Your writing goal is to recapture the experience for your classmates as vividly as you remember it.

TOPIC SELECTION

In selecting a personal experience to write about, writers often think about the following:

1. What experiences are particularly memorable? Consider experiences that may have been frightening, exciting, funny, sad, or joyous, or produced a combination of emotions.
2. What experiences do I remember well enough to write about in detail?
3. What experiences might my readers (classmates) be interested in?
4. What might my purpose be in writing about a particular experience for my classmates? What could they learn or gain from reading about it?

Topic Selection Activity 2.1

Considering the four questions just presented, choose an experience from your childhood to write about. Sift through memories from different times in your life before the age of twelve. The topic you finally select may not be readily apparent.

STUDENT TOPIC SELECTION

There's the incident in first grade when the dad of a girl I liked died and I got in trouble for making noise at her house a few days later. The memory is pretty fuzzy though. Then there was my first "fight" when I was in second grade. It really wasn't much of a fight, just a little wrestling match, but I remember I didn't enjoy it. Not sure I'd have much to write about. I don't even remember how it started.

Then there was the problem I had with a long-time friend in eighth grade, but I'd rather go back farther in my childhood. There was the time in first grade when I buried a neighbor kid's gun in a field and we never found it again. I remember that pretty well, including how mad the kid got and how scared I was. There were other neighbor kids around to see what was going on, and I remember my mom getting involved. Then I moved to another town and, of all things, this kid moves in right behind me. What a coincidence, like my big mistake had followed me to another town. I think I'd like to write about the gun experience because I remember it well, I remember the kid well, and I remember how I felt about my mom helping me. The experience bothered me for some time. It might be interesting to at least some of my classmates.

PREWRITING REFLECTION

Before writing a paper about a personal experience, many writers first reflect on their memorable experience. Here are some things they consider:

1. What actually happened? Try to visualize an experience as accurately as you can remember it: where it took place, who was involved, what occurred, and what was said. Run the experience through your mind like a movie.

2. What did you think and how did you feel? Try to recall your thoughts and feelings at the time of the experience. What different things were going through your mind as the experience unfolded? How did you feel at different times during the experience?

3. What were the results of the experience? How did it turn out for you and for others involved? How did it affect your life?

4. Why is the experience so memorable? What significance might it have? Did you learn anything about yourself, other people, or life in general? Did you gain or lose anything from the experience?

Prewriting Activity 2.2

Using the four questions just presented, reflect on the experience you have selected to write about. Take your time answering the questions. This will allow your memory to bring to the surface everything that it can. The more you can remember and put into perspective, the easier it will be to write your first draft.

STUDENT REFLECTION

I clearly remember I was just in kindergarten. There was the big dirt lot with the eucalyptus trees and the old rabbit hutches near the front. It was hot—summer vacation time—and the gang had gathered at the lot. Then I remember Brian coming with this big beautiful six-shooter and everything that happened afterwards—my burying it, trying to find it later, going home to Momma, Brian coming over, Momma digging in the lot, and so on. I can visualize everything.

I felt very envious when I saw that gun, and I didn't like Brian much anyway. Then I felt scared when I couldn't find the gun, and I felt embarrassed with Brian yelling at me in front of the others. Then I felt ashamed and sorry when I was home with Mom, and I felt awful when she was digging in the lot trying to find the gun. Then I was relieved when Mom bought Brian another gun, but I still felt ashamed of what happened. Then when we moved and Brian moved to the house behind us, I was shocked and dejected, like it was meant for me to suffer for what I did.

Everything turned out all right in the end for everyone, except that the experience stayed with me and made me feel ashamed and cowardly. I wasn't so sure of myself after that, and I knew what it was like to have an enemy. I think I learned that I'm sensitive to criticism and don't like people mad at me or making me look bad, and that has stayed with me my whole life.

First Drafts

Now that you have selected a topic and reflected on your experience, you are ready to write the first draft. When you write the draft, you are telling a story to your classmates. Keep in mind the following narrative elements to help make your paper most interesting.

NARRATIVE ELEMENTS

1. *Setting:* In order for readers to visualize the experience, let them see where and when it took place. Include such details in your draft wherever they will help readers picture a particular scene.

2. *Characters:* Include in your draft the people who are important to the experience. Help readers visualize these people, and tell readers what, if anything, they should know about each person.

3. *Story:* The most important thing is the story you have to tell your readers. Tell your story—whatever happened to you in this particular experience— in a way that you feel will be most interesting and realistic to readers.

4. *Resolution:* Conclude your paper by leaving readers with a sense of completion: How did things turn out? What came out of the experience? What, if anything, did you learn? Why did you relate this particular experience to them?

Drafting Activity 2.3

Read the following student draft and notice how the writer handles the elements of setting, character, story, and resolution as he relates his experience.

The Lost Gun

On Saturdays, the neighborhood gang gathered at the vacant lot to play cowboys. The open space was great for range wars, and the eucalyptus trees were used for hideouts. There were even some old rabbit hutches for locking up prisoners. As we gathered with our assortment of guns and holsters, Brian swaggered in with the biggest, shiniest six-shooter I'd ever seen. It had a ten-inch barrel and an ivory handle. It made my gun look like a peashooter. It wasn't fair that the youngest, brattiest kid in the gang had the best gun.

Before we started, I asked Brian to let me see the gun. He reluctantly handed it over, and I told him I wanted to borrow it for a while. Since I was the big leader of the gang, he couldn't refuse. As soon as we broke up for cowboys and Brian was out of view behind the trees, I ran to a far corner of the lot and buried the gun in the soft dirt. I wanted to give Brian a scare.

Before long, the bad guys were rounded up, and Brian was demanding his gun back. I let him squirm awhile, then laughed and said I'd hidden it. He didn't laugh and demanded I find it. We all trudged across the lot to the corner, and I dug where I thought I'd buried it. No gun. I dug some more, and then I dug deeper and faster. Still no gun. Brian started yelling, "Find my gun!" and I started getting sick. I knew it was there somewhere, but the whole corner was looking the same to me. Everyone stood around and watched as their big leader desperately pawed at the ground. No one helped. Brian finally screamed, "My dad's gonna get you, you bastard!" My eyes started burning, and I knew I was going to cry if I stayed around. I took off running across the lot with Brian yelling, "You bastard! My dad will get you!"

That afternoon, I lay down with my mom for a nap, but I couldn't sleep. I felt terrible about what I had done, and I was frightened about what would happen to me. I hadn't told Mom a thing, but when I heard Brian calling outside the window, I confessed everything to her. She calmly listened to me, then went out to the garage and got the shovel. We met Brian outside and the three of us returned to the lot.

By now it was very hot outside, and my mom dug in the heat for an hour. She turned up most of the dirt in that corner, but the gun was never found. I stood and watched her helplessly, and I felt worse and worse as she worked and sweated because of me. I'd never felt more worthless.

My parents bought Brian a new gun, so he was satisfied. But I wasn't the big shot of the gang any more. Little Brian had pushed me around that day, and the gang didn't forget. I was just one of the boys, and that was where I belonged. I wasn't particularly brave, and I still needed Mom to bail me out of trouble. We moved to another town the next year, and of all coincidences, Brian moved into the house behind the alley. His moving there reminded me I wasn't the big shot I had pretended to be. That one incident with the gun kept us from ever becoming friends although we were neighbors for five years.

Drafting Activity 2.4

Write the first draft of your personal experience, keeping in mind your pre-writing reflections and the four elements of storytelling just presented. As a general guideline, change paragraphs as you move to something new in your experience: a different time, place, or situation. (You may want to review the paragraphing in "The Lost Gun" draft.)

Revisions

First drafts of papers about personal experiences often have similar revision needs. The following suggestions will help you evaluate your draft and make effective revisions.

REVISION GUIDELINES

1. Read your draft to make sure that readers can visualize where the experience took place and understand when it occurred and how old you were. (See the section "Concrete Language," later in this unit.)

2. Evaluate your draft to see if you have related the experience in a way that highlights the most important parts and allows readers to know what you were *thinking* and *feeling*.

3. Evaluate your conclusion to see if readers can understand why this experience was significant enough for you to share with them.

4. Read each sentence to see if it could be made tighter, smoother, or clearer by deleting unnecessary words, rewording awkward phrases, or replacing questionable words.

5. Review your paragraphing to see if you have changed paragraphs as you move to different parts of the experience and if you have avoided overly long or short paragraphs. (See the upcoming section, "Paragraphing.")

Revision Activity 2.5

Read the following student draft, and with a classmate, evaluate it by applying the suggestions for revision. Notice what the writer does well along with making suggestions for revision.

Now evaluate your own draft in the same way, making revision plans for your next draft. For a second opinion, exchange drafts with a classmate.

When you are ready, write the second draft of your paper. Your instructor may have you go over the upcoming sections on paragraphing and concrete language before revising the draft. You may continue evaluating and rewriting drafts until you are satisfied. This may or may not occur after two drafts; there is no magic number of rewrites that satisfies every writer.

The Spelling Bee

I went to a small country school from the first through sixth grade. I was a pretty good student, but one thing I could really do was spell. In grades four and five, I went a year and a half without missing a word on weekly spelling tests based on our workbook lists, and I was usually the last one left standing in classroom "spell downs."

In the sixth grade, our state had a statewide spelling competition beginning with small regional contests and ending months later with the final
competitors competing for the state championship. Our teacher, a tall, dark-
haired woman who was married to a tax collector, announced the contest
and explained how a person got from step one to the state championship. I
figured if I ever was going to enter a contest, this would be it. I even imagined
myself having some success.

Things started out well. I won my room spelling bee when Billy Dayton,
my main competitor, misspelled a word and I spelled it correctly. That also
made me the school representative because we only had one sixth grade class.
I moved on to the district contest, which had the winners of the six schools
in our small district, and I won again. I received a winner's certificate, and
the superintendent of the district said something that made me feel so proud
that I had an emotional reaction, and the audience responded.

My confidence was high until I walked into the Laurel Community Center for the area competition. The building was bigger than our whole school,
and there were over a hundred people in the audience, including ten of my
relatives who, along with Mom and Dad, had come to cheer me on. Then I
saw my competitors, and the way they looked and acted and the places they
were from made me scared. I quietly made my way to the chair with my
number on it and sat staring at my feet, my confidence replaced by anxiety.

Finally, the spelling bee began, and one by one, the students walked up
to the microphone, were given a word, spelled it, and returned to their seats.
If a word was spelled incorrectly, a small bell was rung, but it hadn't rung
yet. The bell had made a high tinkling sound, not unlike the sound you hear
in an ear test. I was number eighteen out of twenty, and I was in agony waiting
my turn. When the moderator called my name, I walked to the microphone.
Then I looked out into the audience and saw all my relatives beaming at me.
Then I heard the moderator say, "Mary Sue, spell 'chauffeur.'" I knew what
the word meant, but I had never seen it in print. I had no visual image of the
word, so I started spelling it out like it sounded: "s-h-o-f-e-r." I heard a sym-
pathetic groan from the audience, then the little bell sounding my doom. I
walked back to my chair, and the next contestant spelled chauffeur correctly.

I sat for almost an hour in humiliation, the first person to go down and
the only person out in the first round. The only perverse pleasure I got was
watching others miss and join me in misery. I listened to kids spell wondrous
words that I couldn't have pronounced, much less spelled, and I realized this
was a whole new world. I didn't belong here with these smart kids; I belonged back at Tucker Elementary with my slow-witted friends.

When the contest was finally over, my relatives were kind, and my dad
said something that made me feel better and made me cry at the same time.
It was a long ride home, and all I could think of was how dumb I was and
how smart everyone else was. Even when I did well at school in the next
weeks, I'd think, "Big deal. You're the smartest of the dummies." It wasn't
until I moved up to the big high school in the tenth grade that I began to
realize that it really wasn't that the city kids were any smarter. By twelfth

grade I didn't feel inferior to many students, and I had gotten over the old feelings. But to this day, if someone wants to bring me off my high horse, all they have to do is say, "Spell 'chauffeur,' Mary Sue."

PARAGRAPHING

Effective paragraphing requires using common sense. Most readers don't enjoy wading through long paragraphs because they can lose important points or get bogged down. They don't enjoy reading strings of short paragraphs because they lose continuity by stopping and starting so frequently. Readers are also confused by a paragraph that jumps randomly from idea to idea because, from past reading experience, they expect sentences within a paragraph to be related.

If you remember these three common-sense points—don't run paragraphs on too long, don't string short paragraphs together, and make sure the sentences in a paragraph are related—you will avoid most paragraphing problems that trouble readers.

Paragraphing Activity 2.6

Mark the beginning of each new paragraph in the following papers about personal experiences. Change paragraphs as the writer moves to something new within the experience, and avoid overly long paragraphs or strings of short ones (a couple of sentences each). When you finish, review the paragraphing of your first draft (Activity 2.4).

Humiliation

I remember first grade was going along well. I was having fun in school. I liked my teacher, I got to play the wood block in the percussion band, and I even had a girlfriend. Then a string of events happened that ruined the year for me. My girlfriend's name was Karen, a quiet, dark-haired girl with a shy smile. After school, we'd go over to her house and sit on top of the slanted shingle roof, enjoying the sun, the view, and just being together. We'd sit there day after day, sometimes holding hands, and I was very happy. Then Karen was absent from school for a while, and the teacher, Mrs. Bray, told us Karen's father had been killed in an electrical accident. I remember being shocked by the news. I'd never heard of anyone's father being killed; it wasn't something that happened. I wondered how Karen was doing, but I was afraid to go and see her. Then one day the entire class walked together to Karen's garage to pick up some old hobby horses and props Karen's mother was lending our class for a play. We were all in the dusty old garage collecting the wooden stick horses and everyone was pretty quiet. Then I blurted out something loudly, I don't remember why. I liked to be the center of attention, but why I picked that time to say something stupid is beyond me. When I did, Mrs. Bray really jumped on me. "Shut up, Ben!" she hissed angrily. And I didn't open my mouth the rest of the day. Walking back to school, I felt awful. Mrs. Bray had never scolded me before, and I now had done something so terrible that she told me to shut up. On top of that, I had been acting stupid at Karen's house only a week after her father died. That made me a doubly evil person, and even though Karen hadn't been in the garage with us, I knew she'd find out. I felt miserable. I never saw Karen again. She stayed home from school for a long time, and then apparently she and her mother moved away. I walked by her house a couple of times before she moved, but I never had the courage to stop. I really never recovered that year from the incident. Things weren't right again between me and Mrs. Bray; I always felt I'd failed her. We moved that summer, and since I never saw Karen again, I assumed she thought the worst of me, and I'd never believe otherwise. Thinking back on that year, I still feel sad some fifteen years later. It's an awful feeling to do something you feel is terrible and never be able to make amends. I just wish I could have seen Karen one last time and said, "I'm sorry."

Piano Recital

I'd always enjoyed playing the piano until my first recital in the fifth grade. I didn't mind playing for my teacher, Mrs. Scott, and I didn't mind playing for my family. But playing for a roomful of strangers and piano students was more than I could handle. We all gathered in Mrs. Scott's living room. There were about twenty folding chairs in rows across the room with sofas lining the walls. All the chairs and sofas were filled with parents and other students, and it felt as though a hundred people were packed in the hot room. Since I was the fifth student on the program to play, I sat stiffly and listened to the others. I wasn't too nervous at first, but as my time came closer, I got tense. The students before me were playing like angels, and the audience applauded for each one. I knew I wasn't as good as the others, and the more I listened, the more I wanted to escape. Finally, my turn came. Mrs. Scott introduced me and told the audience I would be playing "Country Gardens," a song I'd practiced a hundred times. I put my hands to the piano, and before I knew it, they were playing "Country Gardens." I didn't feel in control, and I was moving through the song mindlessly. I started to panic. My hands kept playing but I was blanking out. Finally, I stopped playing. I couldn't play another note. I sat paralyzed at the piano having no idea what to do next. Finally, I felt Mrs. Scott's arm on my shoulder. She asked me quietly if I'd like to start the song again. I told her I didn't. She tried to encourage me by saying how beautifully I played it. The audience started applauding for me. I didn't move a finger to the keyboard. I don't know how long I sat there, but Mrs. Scott finally took me back to my seat. The next student went to the piano, and the recital continued. I sat in a daze. I don't remember much of the rest of the afternoon. There was punch, and everyone tried to console me. I just wanted to go home. I knew this was my last recital.

I did take lessons a couple more weeks, and then I quit. The recital had done me in. I still remember sitting at the piano like a zombie. That was the first experience I remember choking with the pressure on, and all my life I've tried to avoid situations where the pressure was more than I could handle.

Seeing Grandpa

A week after my grandfather died, my mother told me she saw him standing in our backyard. She said he had returned to speak to her and that he would be back again. Mother believed in dead relatives returning to visit loved ones before they finally rested, and she said he might visit me too. It scared me to think about it. Three nights later I awoke and saw Grandpa standing at the foot of my bed. There was no doubt that it was Grandpa: the tall, thin body, the tousled white hair, the big, watery eyes. He stood there and stared at me with those big, sad eyes, but he never spoke. It somehow seemed natural for him to be standing there, and he was such a kind, gentle man that I wasn't the least frightened. We just looked at each other for the longest time, and then he turned slowly and walked out my bedroom door. I crawled out of bed and followed him. He walked out the back door, and by the time I peeked out the back window, he was gone. It was the last time I ever saw my grandfather. I slept with my mother the rest of the night, and the next morning I told her about Grandpa. She wasn't at all surprised or concerned. She said he was probably contented now and wouldn't return. We talked about the incident as though it was the most natural thing in the world. No matter how absurd it sounds, it seems like the right thing for my grandfather to have come back one last time. It made me feel good, and it must have helped him. Since the incident, I have had more respect for some of my mother's beliefs that I once thought were nonsense. There are some things that happen that logic can't explain. Grandfather's return was one of them.

SENTENCE REVISION

All writers share the task of revising first draft sentences to make them smoother, clearer, and stronger. In this section, you learn to replace vague language with *concrete* wording, and you review revision considerations from Unit 1.

Concrete Language

As you reread your sentences, consider replacing vague, general language with more specific wording. Here are some suggestions for using concrete language in your writing:

1. Use the most specific term possible to refer to a particular thing. For example, you might use *German shepherd* instead of *dog, TWA 747* instead of *airplane, six-lane freeway* instead of *road, Buddhist temple* instead of *church,* and *lemon chiffon pie* instead of *dessert.*

2. Use vivid, descriptive verbs to make your sentences lively and interesting. For example, you might write, "The boxer *staggered* across the ring and then *crumpled* to the canvas" instead of "The boxer *moved unsteadily* across the ring and then *fell down* on the canvas."

3. Make your writing as visual as possible. Use language that allows the reader to see and feel what you are expressing. For example, compare "The huge man careened down the slope and crashed into a startled skier, knocking her head-first into a snow bank" to "The man raced down the slope and hit another skier, knocking her into the snow."

Here are some examples of vaguely worded first draft sentences followed by more descriptive revisions:

Vague	The tree in my yard is very colorful.
Better	The pear tree behind the house is covered with pink blossoms.
Vague	Liquid comes out of my dog's mouth at certain times.
Better	Slobber dribbles down my bulldog Murphy's mouth when he gets excited.
Vague	The girl moved across the ice in a nice fashion.
Better	The eight-year-old in pigtails glided smoothly across the ice.
Vague	The weather is terrible this morning.
Better	It's five degrees below zero with a wind of thirty miles an hour.
Vague	Bothered by a leg problem, the football player moved differently.
Better	Hobbled by a swollen ankle, the halfback ran at half speed.
Vague	That old person just left with my glasses.
Better	That blue-haired old lady just made off with my sunglasses.

Revision Activity 2.7

Revise the following vaguely worded sentences by replacing general terms with specific ones and weak verbs with vivid ones. Then review your first draft and make your sentences as concrete and visual as possible.

Example	We left to go downtown and take care of some business.
Revised	My best friend and I left school at noon to order our class rings from the jewelry store downtown.

1. There is a funny smell coming from one part of the garage.

   _____

2. Melissa has a very strange hairdo.

   _____

3. That man is strong for his age.

   _____

4. The horses left from the starting gate and moved down the track.

   _____

5. The moon is beautiful tonight.

   _____

6. The nervous, excited young teenage girl waited anxiously and expectantly for her evening's date to finally and unquestionably arrive.

   _____

7. The boxer put his right glove in the other boxer's face and then did it again with the other hand.

   _____

8. After a long hike, the boy didn't feel great at all.

   _____

9. Your relative is quite small for his age.

   _____

10. The bird went up to the top of the tree and sat on a piece of it.

    _____

Wording Problem Review

Here is a review of some basic wording problems to consider as you revise your first draft sentences.

1. *Wordiness:* using more words than necessary to express a thought.

   Example The hailstones that had collected on the lawn in front of the house gave the appearance of snow to anyone who saw them on the lawn.

   Revised The hailstones on the front lawn of the house looked like snow.

2. *Awkward phrasing:* using words and phrases that don't fit together smoothly or logically.

   Example Because we've lived in weather where the temperature is cold all our lives, so we are used to dressing the proper way.

Revised   Because we've lived with cold weather all our lives, we're used to dressing warmly.

3. *Poor word choice:* using an incorrect or questionable word to express a thought.

Example   Your speech on positive thinking transpired all of us.

Revised   Your speech on positive thinking inspired all of us.

Revision Activity 2.8

The following first draft sentences need revising because they have problems with wordiness, awkward phrasing, and poor word choices. Revise and re-write each sentence to make it smoother and clearer. Then evaluate your first draft sentences for wording revisions.

Example   John had a bald spot that parted his hair in the middle that was black.
(wordy, awkward, poor word choice)

Revised   John had a bald spot in the middle of his black hair.

1. The first thing is to let the oil settle down on the oil pan and let the oil cool down right there.
2. In football you don't have to have that good of an endurance to play it.
3. We went to a good show, and we saw it last weekend together.
4. Even though I am his cousin, but he doesn't let me borrow his notes.
5. From all of the dish washing, your hands are pruning and aging with rapidity.
6. It's hot outside tonight with very few breezes.
7. The doctor told my dad I was on time to stop the infection from spreading.
8. By looking at their patio from north to south, it is 12 feet by 12 feet.
9. The accident almost cost me to lose my life.
10. I was curious to see what a group of cat's behaviors were together, so I followed that group of cats.

Final Editing

Now that you have revised your paper for content and wording improvements, you are ready to proofread it for any errors that may remain. When proofreading, pay particular attention to those areas with which you typically have problems, for example, run-on sentences, misspellings, or comma omissions. Your goal is to locate and correct all errors so that the final draft that you share with readers is error free.

PROOFREADING GUIDELINES

As you check your paper for errors, be sure to cover the following areas.

1. *Make sure you have a period at the end of each sentence.* Look in particular for sentences that are run together without a period or that are separated by a comma instead of a period (comma splice). If you have problems with run-ons, review the upcoming section on run-on sentences before proofreading.

2. *Make sure you haven't left off any word endings.* Since your paper is probably written in the past tense, check to make sure you have an *ed* ending on all regular past tense verbs. Also check your irregular past tense verbs for spelling.

   If you need some work on *ed* endings with past tense verbs or on spelling irregular verbs correctly, refer to the "Correct Usage" section in the appendix at the back of the book, which deals with regular and irregular past tense verbs.

3. *Check each sentence carefully for misspelled words.* Check the spelling of any word that doesn't look right to you, and check your use of homonyms such as there/their/they're, its/it's, and your/you're.

4. *Check the internal punctuation of each sentence.* Make sure you have used commas in series of three or more words or groups of words; before conjunctions (and, so, but, or, for, yet) in a compound sentence; and after introductory groups of words. Also make sure you haven't inserted commas where they aren't needed. If you included any dialogue in your paper, check your use of quotation marks. (See the section on quotation marks a little later in the unit.)

5. *Check your use of subject pronouns.* Make sure you have used the proper subject pronouns (I, he, she, they, we, you) and haven't begun sentences with "My sister and me," "Me and my cousins," "France's mother and her," or "The Smiths and them." (See the section "Subject Pronouns," later in the unit.)

Editing Activity 2.9

Following the guidelines just presented, proofread your latest draft for errors and make the necessary corrections. Your instructor may have you cover the upcoming sections on punctuation and pronoun usage before proofreading.

When you have corrected all errors, write or print out the final draft of your paper about a personal experience, and share it with classmates and your instructor.

SENTENCE PROBLEMS

This section reviews what you learned about run-on sentences and comma splices in Unit 1. Since run-on sentences are an ongoing problem for many writers, they will be covered at different times throughout the book.

Run-on Sentences

Here is a summary of points on run-on sentences presented in Unit 1:

1. A run-on sentence is usually two sentences run together without a period.

2. A comma splice contains two sentences separated incorrectly by a comma. Wrong: Jules enjoys long walks in the morning, he usually takes his dog with him.

3. A pronoun (I, he, she, you, we, they, it) most frequently begins the second sentence within a run-on sentence or comma splice. The following t-words also begin the second sentence of many run-on sentences: there, then, the, that, this, those, these.

4. You can correct run-on sentences and comma splices by placing a period between sentences or by combining the sentences with a joining word, such as and, but, so, yet, because, until, before, although, unless. As a general rule, separate longer run-on sentences with a period and combine shorter ones with a joining word.

Run-on Activity 2.10

Most of the following sentences are run together. Correct the run-ons and comma splices by separating complete sentences with periods and capital letters and by combining sentences with joining words (and, or, but, so, for, yet, because, until, when, if, as, unless, since, while, where). Use your own judgment regarding when to separate sentences and when to join them. When you finish, proofread your latest draft for run-on sentences or comma splices.

Example   Freda tried out for the track team, she wanted to get in shape.

Revised   Freda tried out for the track team because she wanted to get in shape.

Example   I have tried to reason with Melissa about buying a new car that will put her in debt, she is determined to buy the car despite the consequences.

Revised   I have tried to reason with Melissa about buying a new car that will put her in debt. She is determined to buy the car despite the consequences.

1. Taxes are devouring middle-class incomes people are looking for tax shelters.

2. Please take your tools home today before you do, please clean them well.

3. Tad never stopped to ask the price of cantaloupes at the fruit stand he assumed they were very expensive, he was right.

4. Allie has thirty minutes to read and answer one hundred test questions, she'll have no trouble finishing her mind works like a computer.

5. The tamales in this restaurant are terrible they have a mushy potato filling.

6. Sometimes the combination to the vault works perfectly, it clicks open without a problem other times it doesn't work at all we have to call a locksmith.

7. I'd like to put down a large payment on the braces I'll be getting in October I have the money now I might not have it two years from now when the braces come off.

8. The doctor was weary after doing eight hours of open-heart surgery although he was scheduled to continue on the night shift, he was relieved by his supervisor.

9. Mira has the skill to be a great pianist many people question her dedication, she only practices an hour a day she should be practicing at least five.

10. Fred is always in trouble with his probation officer he continually forgets to check in, Nellie has no problems with hers.

11. Harvey is doing well in plant science although he originally intended to major in business, he may change his major to ag-business, his father, a cotton farmer, will be pleased.

12. The old high school gang broke up after graduation, some of them went away to different colleges others stayed home and went to the local community college others enlisted in the service or went to work at the garment factory.

PUNCTUATION

Since you may have included some dialogue in your paper about a personal experience for this unit, this section covers the proper use of quotation marks in dialogue.

Quotation Marks

In any paper you write, you may on occasion want to include the specific words that someone said to add interest to your essay. Another time, you may want to quote an expert on a subject to provide support for a position you've taken. To show that a person is talking in your paper, you need to do two things:

1. Put *quotation marks* (" ") around the spoken words.

2. Make reference to the person speaking.

Here are some examples of direct quotations correctly punctuated:

Examples   John said, "Where are you going with my hammer?"

"I don't want to go shopping in these curlers," said Harriet.

Alvin interrupted Mary by saying, "Stop telling those flattering lies about me."

My mother said, "You have always had a bad temper. Remember the time you threw your brother out the window?"

"I want you to go," Mike insisted. "We need you to liven up the party."

"Alice's biggest weakness," her sister admitted, "is that she can't say 'no.'"

Here are the basic rules for punctuating direct quotations, as demonstrated in the example sentences, and a word about indirect quotations.

1. Quotation marks go around only the spoken words: John said, "Where are you going?"
2. Quotation marks always go *outside* of end marks: Maria replied, "I am going home."
3. The reference to the speaker may come at the beginning, in the middle, or at the end of a quote. A comma always separates the reference to the speaker from the quote itself: "I don't believe," said Mark, "that we have met."
4. If a quote contains two or more sentences together, the quotation marks are placed in front of the first sentence and after the last sentence only: Juan said, "I am very tired. I am also hungry and thirsty."
5. A comma comes after the last word in a quote only if the sentence continues after the quote. Otherwise, an end mark is used: "You are a good friend," said Julia.
6. If the reference to the speaker is in the middle of a quote, the quoted words on both sides of the reference are in quotation marks. (See rule 3.)
7. When you change speakers in a paper, you usually begin a new paragraph.
8. Direct quotations are the exact words of the speaker. An *indirect quotation* tells what the speaker said *as told by the writer:* Jack said that he needs a second job. Mary told me that she was tired of school. Indirect quotations are *not put in quotation marks* because they are not the words of a speaker.

Quotation Activity 2.11

Most of the following sentences are direct quotations that need punctuating with quotation marks. Punctuate the quotations correctly following the rules just given. If a sentence is an indirect quotation, don't put it in quotes. When you finish, check your latest draft for correct usage of quotation marks.

Example   If you don't stop biting your nails, you'll draw blood said Claire.

Revised   "If you don't stop biting your nails, you'll draw blood," said Claire.

1. Hank said Please bring me a glass of Alka-Seltzer.
2. The trouble with school said Muriel is the classes.
3. I know what I'm going to do after my last final whispered Allyson.
4. Freda admitted I have very oily hair. I have to wash it twice a day.
5. That's a beautiful ring exclaimed Bob Where did you buy it?
6. No one said Millie is leaving this house. We have a mess to clean up!
7. Charlotte said that her nephew from Miami would arrive by bus.
8. Teddy said My niece will be on the same bus as your nephew.
9. Maria said that you would help me with my algebra.
10. Will you please help me with my lab report for botany? asked Freddie.

CORRECT USAGE

Each "Correct Usage" section presents some basic rules of grammar to help you eliminate any usage problems you may have in a paper. Since your paper for this unit probably involves people, this section covers the proper use of subject pronouns in your writing.

Subject Pronouns

The following basic rules will help you use subject pronouns correctly in your writing.

1. Subject pronouns are always the same: I, he, she, we, you, it, they.
2. The following pronouns are *not* used as subjects: me, him, her, us, them, myself, herself, himself, ourselves, yourself, themselves.
3. The most common subject pronoun errors involve compound subjects:

   Incorrect   John and me went skating. Mary and him are a couple. The Ludlow family and them met for brunch. Felix, Katerina, and her look great together.

4. A good technique for selecting the correct pronoun form with compound subjects is to consider the pronoun by itself. For example, in the sentence "John and me went skating," would you say, "Me went skating"? In the sentence "The Ludlow family and them met for brunch," would you say, "Them met for brunch"? The incorrect forms stand out badly by themselves, and the correct forms—*I* and *they*—sound correct.

Examples

Incorrect	Jonathan, Syd, and <u>me</u> like tuna sandwiches.
Correct	Jonathan, Syd, and <u>I</u> like tuna sandwiches.
Incorrect	Samantha and <u>him</u> are excellent mechanics.
Correct	Samantha and <u>he</u> are excellent mechanics.
Incorrect	Fran's mother and <u>her</u> don't want to go shopping in the rain.
Correct	Fran's mother and <u>she</u> don't want to go shopping in the rain.
Incorrect	Alice, Alex, and <u>them</u> did well on the fitness test.
Correct	Alice, Alex, and <u>they</u> did well on the fitness test.

Subject Pronoun Activity 2.12

Underline the correct subject pronoun in each of the following sentences. Then proofread your latest draft for correct usage of subject pronouns.

Examples   Sue and (<u>I</u>, me) belong to the same business sorority.

I don't think that you and (<u>she</u>, her) really hate each other.

1. The Smiths, the Gonzaleses, and (we, us) will meet at the bottom of the mountain.
2. Shirley, (he, him), and (I, me) are studying together tonight.
3. Fred and (they, them) quit their jobs on the same day.
4. Do you think that Gladys, Thelma, and (she, her) are triplets?
5. I'm tired of wandering around the museum, but Gwen and (they, them) certainly aren't.
6. Are you and (they, them) still obligated to attend the supermarket opening?
7. Matty and (I, me) don't have anything in common.
8. Phil, my brothers, and (I, me) went ice skating at Mill Pond.
9. (We, Us) and (they, them) are archrivals in bocci ball.
10. (She, Her) and (he, him) don't see eye to eye on anything.

Writing Review

At the end of each unit you apply what you have learned to a final writing assignment. For this unit, you write on another personal experience that occurred in the recent past.

To write your paper, follow the steps presented, which summarize the writing process for this unit.

WRITING PROCESS

TOPIC SELECTION

1. Select an experience from your recent past (the last few years) that taught you something of value that you could pass on to younger readers. Consider the following:

   a. What recent experiences do I remember well enough to write about in detail? Consider experiences related to school, work, family, personal relationships, social situations.

   b. What experiences did I learn something from that younger readers might also face in their future?

   c. Of the experiences I recall, which one stands out as being particularly significant in my life?

PREWRITING

2. When you have selected a topic, reflect on the experience before writing by considering the following:

   a. Picture the experience in your mind and recall as best you can when and where it occurred, who was involved, and what exactly happened.

   b. Try to remember your thoughts and feelings at different times in the experience so that you can relate them to your readers.

   c. Reflect on the significance of the experience. What did you learn that has helped you (or may help you in the future)? How can you best convey what you learned to younger readers?

FIRST DRAFT

3. After you have reflected on the experience, write the first draft of your paper following these guidelines.

   a. Decide who your primary reading audience will be: college freshmen? high school seniors? younger children? Select a specific reading audience, and keep them in mind as you write.

   b. Write about your experience without worrying greatly about wording or making mistakes.

   c. Keep the four elements of storytelling in mind as you write: providing a setting, including and bringing to life the significant characters, telling the story with your audience in mind, and concluding with your resolution (in this case, what you learned).

   d. Change paragraphs as you move to different parts of the experience: different times, places, or incidents.

REVISIONS

4. When you finish your first draft, evaluate it for possible revisions by applying the following guidelines. Then write the second draft of your paper, including any revisions you feel will improve it for readers.

   a. Can readers clearly picture where and when the experience took place?

b. Have you highlighted for readers the most important parts of the experience and shared with them your thoughts and feelings during the experience?

c. In the conclusion, have you revealed the significance of the experience to your readers and passed on what you learned?

d. Can you improve some of your first draft sentences by making them more concrete (visually descriptive), more concise, smoother, or clearer?

e. Does your paragraphing help readers move smoothly through the experience? Do you change paragraphs as you move to different aspects of the experience, and have you avoided extremely long or short paragraphs?

EDITING

5. When you have written your second draft, proofread it carefully for errors by covering the following areas.

a. Read each sentence to make sure you have a period at the end. Check in particular for run-on sentences or comma splices that need correcting.

b. Check your word endings, and in particular the *ed* ending on all regular past tense verbs.

c. Check your spelling carefully, and look up the spelling of any words you are uncertain of.

d. Check your use of commas in words in series, in compound sentences, and after introductory groups of words; and make sure you have used apostrophes in contractions (don't, it's). If you have included dialogue, make sure you have introduced the speakers (Julia said, Mike shouted) and put quotation marks (" ") around the spoken words.

e. Check your use of subject pronouns (I, he, she, we, they, you), and make sure you haven't begun any sentences incorrectly with "Me and my mother" or "The Gomez twins and me," or "Ralph and her," or "The Williamses and them."

FINAL DRAFT

6. When you have proofread your paper and corrected all errors, write or print out your final draft. Share copies of it with classmates, your instructor, and people within your specific reading audience.

STUDENT TOPIC SELECTION

I think I'll write about my freshman year in college. I'll actually have to include a few experiences within my freshman year, all of which I learned a similar lesson from. I'll have to tie all of these experiences together so they seem like parts of one bigger learning experience, which they were.

TOPIC REFLECTION

The experiences that stand out include a meeting in my dormitory, the first day of swim practice, a discussion in English class, and a freshman queen competition. All had the same effect on me: humbling. It was really hard discovering I wasn't as popular, smart, talented, or good looking as I thought, and it was a hard lesson to learn. I think it would be good to share with upcoming college students who may have similar experiences.

College Experience

I went from a high school of one hundred and fifty graduating seniors to a college of twenty thousand students my freshman year. I had been something of a big wheel in high school, and I was about to get a real shock coming out of the shelter of my small-town life.

The first defining experience I recall was a meeting of my classmates on the same dormitory floor. We got together to elect floor officers and discuss rules and regulations. I was surprised by how confident and articulate many of the girls were. I felt overmatched by their brains and good looks, so I sat in a corner and kept quiet. Needless to say, I wasn't nominated for any office, and I left the meeting a bit shaken. I sure didn't feel like the former student body president of my high school.

A similar experience occurred in an English class. We had all read the same short story by Flannery O'Conner, but students in the class came up with insights and connections I hadn't begun to make. It was a lively and interesting discussion, but I was frightened stiff that the instructor would call on me. No one would have recognized me as a top ten student at Grimly High School.

The old swimming pool was one place I could regain my confidence, I thought. No way. Being an all-league swimmer where I came from was nothing compared to the talent on the college team. Some of these girls were the best in the state. I was put in a lane with about ten other "B" level swimmers, and that was clearly where I belonged.

A final humbling experience was something I'd always looked forward to in high school—popularity contests. A number of freshman girls were nominated for something called "Dream Court" to be a part of college homecoming activities. Posters of girls nominated by different clubs and dorms started going up around campus, and needless to say, my face wasn't among them. I wasn't nominated or, to my knowledge, even considered for nomination by anyone. I wasn't that pretty or popular.

Needless to say, my freshman year was rough. My whole life I felt I had a pretty good idea of who I was, and one semester in college changed all of that. I lost all confidence, and for a long time I went into a shell. No one got to know me because I didn't know who I was myself.

Then after feeling sorry for myself for a long time, I went the other direction and foolishly decided to make a name for myself. I joined everything that I could, kissed up to every popular girl and boy, tried to talk and laugh louder than anyone, and tried to be the life of the party by outdrinking everyone. After a couple months of this, one of the few friends I had on campus asked me the question that needed asking: "Who are you trying to be?" That really got me thinking.

My freshman year was a mess, and I'd never want to relive it. However, it was a year I had to go through to understand a few things. No matter where I'd gone to college, there would be people who were smarter, better looking, and more talented than me. My first two reactions to that realization—first, to go into a shell, and second, to try to be something that I wasn't—were I think pretty natural reactions. I don't fault myself for either because I learned from both.

What I learned were a few basic things that have helped me rediscover myself. First, I know I'm basically a pretty good person, and that's the most important thing. Second, although I'll never be the smartest, prettiest, or most talented, I know I have what it takes to be successful as long as I work at it. Third, I know I can be myself and make friends and enjoy life. It takes time to get to know people and make friends in a new environment, and I had wanted it all to happen overnight.

As a sophomore, I am a different person than as a freshman. Actually, I'm the same person with a year's experience and understanding. I may now appear as confident and sound as articulate as the girls that I met at the first meeting a year ago. I may even intimidate some of them as I was intimidated. Thousands of freshmen surely go through experiences similar to mine, and like me, most of them will have to learn the hard way. Maybe that's why I've become a peer counselor at the college. When I talk to a freshman who is down in the dumps, I can say to her in all honesty, "Hey, I've been there. I know how you're feeling. It's going to get better."

Readings

My Mother Never Worked

BY DONNA SMITH-YACKEL

1   "Social Security Office." (The voice answering the telephone sounds very self-assured.)

2   "I'm calling about . . . I . . . my mother just died . . . I was told to call you and see about a . . . death-benefit check, I think they call it . . ."

3   "I see. Was your mother on Social Security? How old was she?"

4   "Yes . . . she was seventy-eight . . ."

5   "Do you know her number?"

6   "No . . . I, ah . . . don't you have a record?"

7   "Certainly. I'll look it up. Her name?"

8   "Smith. Martha Smith. Or maybe she used Martha Ruth Smith? . . . Sometimes she used her maiden name . . . Martha Jerabek Smith."

9   "If you'd care to hold on, I'll check our records—it'll be a few minutes."

10   "Yes. . . ."

11   Her love letters—to and from Daddy—were in an old box, tied with ribbons and stiff, rigid-with-age leather thongs: 1918 through 1920; hers written on stationery from the general store she had worked in full-time and managed, single-handed, after her graduation from high school in 1913; and his, at first, on YMCA or Soldiers and Sailors Club stationery dispensed to the fighting men of World War I. He wooed her thoroughly and persistently by mail, and though she reciprocated all his feelings for her, she dreaded marriage. . . .

12   "It's so hard for me to decide when to have my wedding day—that's all I've thought about these last two days. I have told you dozens of times that I won't be afraid of married life, but when it comes down to setting the date and then picturing myself a married woman with half a dozen or more kids to look after, it just makes me sick. . . . I am weeping right now—I hope that some day I can look back and say how foolish I was to dread it all."

13   They married in February, 1921, and began farming. Their first baby, a daughter, was born in January, 1922, when my mother was 26 years old. The second baby, a son, was born in March, 1923. They were renting farms; my father, besides working his own fields, also was a hired man for two other farmers. They had no capital initially, and had to gain it slowly, working from dawn until midnight every day. My town-bred mother learned to set hens and raise chickens, feed pigs, milk cows, plant and harvest a garden, and can every fruit and vegetable she could scrounge. She carried water nearly a quarter of a mile from the well to fill her wash boilers in order to do her laundry on a scrub board. She learned to shuck grain, feed threshers, shock and husk corn, feed corn pickers. In September, 1925, the third baby

came, and in June, 1927, the fourth child—both daughters. In 1930, my parents had enough money to buy their own farm, and that March they moved all their livestock and belongings themselves, 55 miles over rutted, muddy roads.

14   In the summer of 1930 my mother and her two eldest children reclaimed a 40-acre field from Canadian thistles, by chopping them all out with a hoe. In the other fields, when the oats and flax began to head out, the green and blue of the crops were hidden by the bright yellow of wild mustard. My mother walked the fields day after day, pulling each mustard plant. She raised a new flock of baby chicks—500—and she spaded up, planted, hoed, and harvested a half-acre garden.

15   During the next spring their hogs caught cholera and died. No cash that fall.

16   And in the next year the drought hit. My mother and father trudged from the well to the chickens, the well to the calf pasture, the well to the barn, and from the well to the garden. The sun came out hot and bright, endlessly, day after day. The crops shriveled and died. They harvested half the corn, and ground the other half, stalks and all, and fed it to the cattle as fodder. With the price at four cents a bushel for the harvested crop, they couldn't afford to haul it into town. They burned it in the furnace for fuel that winter.

17   In 1934, in February, when the dust was still so thick in the Minnesota air that my parents couldn't always see from the house to the barn, their fifth child—a fourth daughter—was born. My father hunted rabbits daily, and my mother stewed them, fried them, canned them, and wished out loud that she could taste hamburger once more. In the fall the shotgun brought prairie chickens, ducks, pheasant, and grouse. My mother plucked each bird, carefully reserving the breast feathers for pillows.

18   In the winter she sewed night after night, endlessly, begging cast-off clothing from relatives, ripping apart coats, dresses, blouses, and trousers to remake them to fit her four daughters and son. Every morning and every evening she milked cows, fed pigs and calves, cared for chickens, picked eggs, cooked meals, washed dishes, scrubbed floors, and tended and loved her children. In the spring she planted a garden once more, dragging pails of water to nourish and sustain the vegetables for the family. In 1936 she lost a baby in her sixth month.

19   In 1937 her fifth daughter was born. She was 42 years old. In 1939 a second son, and in 1941 her eighth child—and third son.

20   But the war had come, and prosperity of a sort. The herd of cattle had grown to 30 head: she still milked morning and evening. Her garden was more than a half acre—the rains had come, and by now the Rural Electricity Administration and indoor plumbing. Still she sewed—dresses and jackets for the children, housedresses and aprons for herself, weekly patching of jeans, overalls, and denim shirts. She still made pillows, using feathers she had plucked, and quilts every year—intricate patterns as well as patchwork, stitched as well as tied—all necessary bedding for her family. Every scrap of

cloth too small to be used in quilts was carefully saved and painstakingly sewed together in strips to make rugs. She still went out in the fields to help with the haying whenever there was a threat of rain.

21   In 1959 my mother's last child graduated from high school. A year later the cows were sold. She still raised chickens and ducks, plucked feathers, made pillows, baked her own bread, and every year made a new quilt—now for a married child or for a grandchild. And her garden, that huge, undying symbol of sustenance, was as large and cared for as in all the years before. The canning, and now freezing, continued.

22   In 1969, on a June afternoon, mother and father started out for town so that she could buy sugar to make rhubarb jam for a daughter who lived in Texas. The car crashed into a ditch. She was paralyzed from the waist down.

23   In 1970 her husband, my father, died. My mother struggled to regain some competence and dignity and order in her life. At the rehabilitation institute, where they gave her physical therapy and trained her to live usefully in a wheelchair, the therapist told me: "She did fifteen pushups today—fifteen! She's almost seventy-five years old! I've never known a woman so strong!"

24   From her wheelchair she canned pickles, baked bread, ironed clothes, wrote dozens of letters weekly to her friends and her "half dozen or more kids," and made three patchwork housecoats and one quilt. She made balls and balls of carpet rags—enough for five rugs. And kept all her love letters.

25   "I think I've found your mother's records—Martha Ruth Smith; married to Ben F. Smith?

26   "Yes, that's right."

27   "Well, I see that she was getting a widow's pension. . . ."

28   "Yes, that's right."

29   "Well, your mother isn't entitled to our $255 death benefit."

30   "Not entitled! But why?"

31   The voice on the telephone explains patiently:

32   "Well, you see—your mother never worked."

QUESTIONS FOR DISCUSSION

1. What do you learn about Smith-Yackel's mother in the essay? What can you infer about the author's feelings toward her mother?

2. Social Security obviously has a narrower connotation of "work" than most of us have. Discuss the fairness of the mother not receiving benefits because she never "worked" by Social Security's definition.

3. Why do you think the author chose to write about this experience? What might you learn from it?

4. Is being a housewife an acceptable form of "work" for women? Is it an option that young women still have in our society?

VOCABULARY

Reciprocated (11), flax (14), sustenance (21)

Science

BY DAVID R. C. GOOD

1   This morning at breakfast my ten-year-old daughter said that mockingbirds make one hundred seventeen different sounds. She was working in her science book, doing her last-minute homework. "One hundred seventeen?" I asked. It seemed impossible at first; then the more I thought about it, the more I listened to the chatter-boxes (I could hear them right there from the sink), the more I began to believe it was true. I've always thought they were amazing birds.

2   "So what else does it say about them?" I asked.

3   "About what?"

4   "About mockingbirds and how many sounds they make."

5   "No, Dad," she said. "While I was lying in bed this morning, I counted them." She said what she was studying was intestines, large and small, and did I know that my small ones would unravel to equal my height.

6   I didn't know that.

7   Science has always baffled me. I took Earth Science, a general science class, when I was sixteen. Earth Science was the science required for those of us who weren't going to go anywhere. Most of my friends were going to go to Berkeley or UCLA to work in plastics and electricity, so they took chemistry and physics. As for the rest of us, those in Earth Science, I guess we were going to be working in dirt. Anyway, my complete memory of Earth Science is the day I had the class under my control. It was early in the spring semester and one of those rare moments in my life. I mean I could not make a bad joke. *No duds.* Of course the teacher didn't see it that way. You see he made the mistake of laughing at first. I don't remember his name, but I do remember he was young and inexperienced enough.

8   Anyway, we were studying astronomy, and things had gotten so bad that he finally had to stop the class to straighten me out. He threatened me with a trip to the dean or worse, and I could sense the guy was serious. I really never meant him any harm, and I knew when to quit. So I said I would and I meant it. Then he did the inexperienced thing and tried to draw me back into the discussion by asking in a most serious tone of voice a question related to his astronomy lesson.

9   "Now, David," he said. "What do we call the path a satellite follows around a planet when the path swings out wider at one end than the other?" He had me there, of course. I knew it was one of those questions to which he had just given the answer, an easy one, I guessed, but of course I hadn't been paying attention. I had been laying down one-liners. I had been preoccupied, and now the whole class was waiting, large gulps of laughter wallowing deep in their throats. They knew I was faced with the choice—give the simple answer and save my hide, or give the smart-assed one and see the dean.

10   "I can't say for sure," I said most seriously. The teacher was eyeing me for any sign of indiscretion, ready to cut me off at the first sign of a joke, "but I

do remember you said it went around, not in a circle, but in the shape of a *frog's butt*." The moment was there, then. It was that perfect one, that moment of absolute stunned silence, that moment when everybody in the room knew the right answer, and I had led them all right up to it, so close that it took that special moment to realize what I'd said. Then the laughter began, and I walked out of the room to spend the rest of that day and every fifth period for the rest of the year in the dean's office. There I got to know the dean's secretary by name and within a week I was handling special deliveries of emergency passes, passes to counselors, and passes for athletes to be released early for away games.

11   As for science, I was given credit (for staying away?) and allowed to pass to the next grade. Of course I was glad at the time. However, in the years since, there have been times when I've wondered what I missed out on while running summons for the dean: elliptical orbits, the length of intestines, the number of songs a mockingbird can sing.

QUESTIONS FOR DISCUSSION

1. How does the opening of the essay tie in with the school experience the author relates? Why do you think he opened the essay as he did?

2. What things do we learn about the author from his behavior in Earth Science class? Why was he such a "wiseguy"?

3. Students have two audiences to consider: the teacher and the class. How do the two audiences create a conflict for Good?

4. Relate a school experience in which you were more interested in the class's reaction than the teacher's. What was the result?

5. Reflecting on his experience in the last paragraph, what regrets does Good have? How does the concluding paragraph relate to the opening?

6. What, if anything, do you regret about some aspect of your high school experience?

VOCABULARY

Intestines (5), astronomy (8)

The Woman Warrior

BY MAXINE HONG KINGSTON

1   My American life has been such a disappointment.

2   "I got straight A's, Mama."

3   "Let me tell you a true story about a girl who saved her village."

4   I could not figure out what was my village. And it was important that I do something big and fine, or else my parents would sell me when we made our way back to China. In China there were solutions for what to do with little girls who ate up food and threw tantrums. You can't eat straight A's.

5   When one of my parents or the emigrant villagers said, "Feeding girls is feeding cow-birds," I would thrash on the floor and scream so hard I couldn't talk. I couldn't stop.

6   "What's the matter with her?"

7   "I don't know. Bad, I guess. You know how girls are. 'There's no profit in raising girls. Better to raise geese than girls.'"

8   "I would hit her if she were mine. But then there's no use wasting all that discipline on a girl. 'When you raise girls, you're raising children for strangers.'"

9   "Stop that crying!" my mother would yell. "I'm going to hit you if you don't stop. Bad girl! Stop!" I'm going to remember never to hit or to scold my children for crying, I thought, because then they will only cry more.

10   "I'm not a bad girl," I would scream. "I'm not a bad girl. I'm not a bad girl." I might as well have said, "I'm not a girl."

11   "When you were little, all you had to say was 'I'm not a bad girl,' and you could make yourself cry," my mother says, talking-story about my childhood.

12   I minded that the emigrant villagers shook their heads at my sister and me. "One girl—and another girl," they said, and made our parents ashamed to take us out together. The good part about my brothers being born was that people stopped saying, "All girls," but I learned new grievances. "Did you roll an egg on my face like that when I was born?" "Did you have a full-month party for me?" "Did you turn on all the lights?" "Did you send my picture to Grandmother?" "Why not? Because I'm a girl? Is that why not?" "Why didn't you teach me English?" "You like having me beaten up at school, don't you?"

13   "She is very mean, isn't she?" the emigrant villagers would say.

14   "Come, children. Hurry. Hurry. Who wants to go out with Great-Uncle?" On Saturday mornings my great-uncle, the ex-river pirate, did the shopping. "Get your coats, whoever's coming."

15   "I'm coming. I'm coming. Wait for me."

16   When he heard girls' voices, he turned on us and roared, "No girls!" and left my sisters and me hanging our coats back up, not looking at one another. The boys came back with candy and new toys. When they walked through Chinatown, the people must have said, "a boy—and another boy—and another boy!" At my great-uncle's funeral I secretly tested out feeling glad that he was dead—the six-foot bearish masculinity of him.

17   I went away to college—Berkeley in the sixties—and I studied, and I marched to change the world, but I did not turn into a boy. I would have liked to bring myself back as a boy for my parents to welcome with chickens and pigs. That was for my brother, who returned alive from Vietnam.

18   If I went to Vietnam, I would not come back; females desert families. It was said, "There is an outward tendency in females," which meant that I was getting straight A's for the good of my future husband's family, not my own. I did not plan ever to have a husband. I would show my mother and father and the nosey emigrant villagers that girls have no outward tendency. I stopped getting straight A's.

QUESTIONS FOR DISCUSSION

1. What particular incidences in the narrator's life make up the essay? How are they related?

2. When Kingston told her mother she got straight A's, why did her mother say, "Let me tell you a true story about a girl who saved her village"?

3. Why were girls treated differently than boys in Chinese families? What effect did this have on Kingston?

4. Why did Kingston decide not ever to have a husband? Why did she stop getting straight A's?

5. Why do you think the author wrote about her life as a Chinese girl? How do you think her childhood affected her?

6. Are girls treated differently than boys within your ethnic group? In what ways, if at all?

VOCABULARY

Emigrant (5)

Clear Direction

Successful writing voyages often depend on knowing where you are going and how you will get there. If you know the direction that you want a paper to take and have a plan for getting there, you have an excellent start in accomplishing your purpose.

The direction for a paper is provided by its *thesis*: the main idea you convey about your topic. When readers ask themselves the point of a particular piece of writing, they are asking, "What is the thesis?" A paper without a thesis is like a voyage without a destination; with no course to follow, your writing may drift aimlessly, leaving readers puzzled or disappointed.

The emphasis in this unit is on thesis-directed writing, which you will find useful for any paper you may write. As in earlier units, you follow a process of prewriting, drafting, revising, and editing to reach your destination: an effective final draft. Within those basic steps, you are provided the flexibility to shape the process to suit your personal writing needs.

Prewriting

For most writers, prewriting involves coming up with a topic and deciding what to do with it. It can also include generating ideas for the paper and a plan for presenting them. If this were a neat four-step process, it would answer these questions:

1. What am I going to write about?
2. What approach do I want to take?
3. What do I want to include in the paper?
4. How can I best organize my thoughts?

While most writers consider variations of these questions during prewriting, they don't necessarily do so in a linear fashion. Instead, they may start anywhere within the process and work backward or forward, deal with questions in tandem (such as considering topic and approach simultaneously), give some questions (such as topic selection) much thought and others (such as organization) little or none; or they may not deal with all considerations consciously (for example, discovering a topic approach while drafting).

For your prewriting activities in this unit, you learn how to generate a potential thesis statement, and you devise a plan for your paper by listing your ideas. Rather than providing you a rigid how-to formula for writing preparation, the prewriting activities give you options to try and then apply in ways you find useful for your writing.

THESIS STATEMENT

When you read the term *thesis statement,* you may think of some elevated, formal writing. However, if someone asks questions about a paper you've written such as, "So what's your point?" or "What are you getting at?", they are asking thesis-related questions. In reality, *thesis* is a simple writing concept that provides direction for all of us, whether we are writing an informal letter ("Just writing to let you know what happened at school last week") or a twenty-page research paper ("This paper will show that the hole in the ozone layer over the North Pole does not pose an environmental threat").

With the kinds of writing you will be doing throughout college, it is important to decide what you want to do with a topic: the approach or the direction you'd like a paper to take. To help you accomplish this, it is useful to come up with a tentative thesis statement early in the writing process.

The following points clarify the thesis concept.

1. A thesis expresses the main idea you want to develop in a paper. It usually expresses your *viewpoint* on the topic.
2. Your thesis determines the way in which you develop a topic in an essay. You write your essay *in support* of your thesis.
3. Without a thesis, an essay lacks direction. There is no *controlling idea* to tie the paragraphs together and to help the reader understand your intent.

4. There is no right or wrong thesis; it reflects the way you view a particular topic. The *effectiveness* of the thesis is usually determined by how well it is supported in the paper.

Here are examples of thesis statements students have used for a variety of topics. Notice that writers use varied approaches to the same topic. These approaches would produce very different papers on the same topics.

Topic	water beds
Thesis	Water beds are a health hazard to millions of users.
Thesis	Within ten years, water beds will make mattresses obsolete.
Thesis	For a healthy night's sleep, buy a water bed.
Topic	daylight saving time
Thesis	I'd like to live on daylight saving time all year around.
Thesis	For a nocturnal person, daylight saving is a disaster.
Thesis	Daylight saving has both advantages and disadvantages.
Topic	gun control
Thesis	Gun control laws are a threat to every law-abiding American.
Thesis	Gun control is the only way to reduce violent crime in America.
Thesis	The only effective gun control is the total elimination of handguns.
Topic	"Fresh Prince" TV program
Thesis	"Fresh Prince" is the best family comedy of the decade.
Thesis	"Fresh Prince" is a fantasy representation of life for black Americans.
Thesis	"Fresh Prince" is a great showcase for young black actors.

Deciding on a thesis for a particular paper is an important part of the writing process. Not only does the thesis direct your writing, it shapes your readers' perception of how you think or feel about a topic. Whatever time you spend coming up with the best thesis for a particular paper is worth it.

Thesis Consideration

When thinking about a thesis for a specific topic, consider the following:

1. *How do I really feel about the topic?* Don't worry about how other people feel, or how you think you *should* react, or what approach might sound best to readers. Your thesis should develop from your honest feelings about the topic.

2. *What is most important or most interesting about a topic?* For example, what is the most important thing that readers should learn from a paper

you write on selecting a college major? Or what might interest readers most in a paper you are doing on great white sharks (their threat to humans? their voracious eating habits?)?

3. *What thesis could I you do the best job of supporting in a paper?* No matter how strongly you feel about a particular viewpoint, your paper will run out of gas if you can't support your thesis effectively. For example, although you may feel strongly that there are forms of human life on other planets besides earth, you may find little evidence that would convince readers or help you write an effective paper.

Thesis Activity 3.1

Applying the three questions just presented, write a thesis statement for any five of the following topics. Select a statement that you believe in and feel you could support in a paper. (Fill in each blank with your specific choice of topics.)

Example

Topic   a particular hobby (writing songs)

Thesis   It takes little talent to write lyrics for country songs.

1. Topic   a particular town (_____)

   Thesis _____

2. Topic   a particular team (_____)

   Thesis _____

3. Topic   a particular TV program (_____)

   Thesis _____

4. Topic   a particular job (_____)

   Thesis _____

5. Topic   a particular holiday (_____)

   Thesis _____

6. Topic   a particular school (_____)

   Thesis _____

7. Topic   a particular type of music (_____)

   Thesis _____

8. Topic   a particular pet (_____)

   Thesis _____

9. Topic   a particular restaurant (_____)

Thesis _____

10. Topic   a particular book or movie (_____)

Thesis _____

Topic Selection Activity 3.2

Select a topic to write on following these guidelines.

1. Choose a topic that really interests you. It may be one of the topics from Activity 3.1 or another of your choice.

2. Choose a topic that you know enough about to write a paper on.

3. Choose a topic that you think might interest your classmates, who are the reading audience for your paper.

4. When you have selected a topic, generate a tentative thesis for your paper: the main point about your topic that you want to convey to readers.

STUDENT TOPIC AND THESIS SELECTION

Since I returned to college after many years being away, I was interested in what college would be like twenty years later. I think I'd like to write about what college is like from my perspective as an older returning student. It might interest my classmates to view college through my eyes and compare it with their own perceptions.

My thesis for the paper is pretty clear to me: in my opinion, college hasn't changed that much in twenty years. That is the main idea that I would support in my paper.

MAKING LISTS

Now that you have selected a topic and a tentative thesis, you can consider what kind of support you may want to include in your paper. One way that writers generate support for a thesis is to make a list of supporting ideas.

For example, the older returning student who is writing about what college is like might list the following points in support of her thesis:

Thesis   College hasn't changed that much in twenty years.

Supporting Points

1. Students are similar.

2. Teaching methods are similar.

3. Cafeteria is the same.

4. Students hang out in the same places.

5. Teachers haven't changed much.

A list of supporting points is beneficial in different ways:

1. You have a number of points to develop in separate paragraphs in your draft.

2. You can look at your list and decide on the best organization for your paper: the order you want to present your points in the draft. For example, the returning student might reorder her points to write about them in the following way: students haven't changed, student hangouts are the same, teachers haven't changed, teaching methods haven't changed, the cafeteria is the same. Her points follow the order: student/student/teacher/teacher/cafeteria.

3. You can add some details after your supporting points to generate more material for your draft.

> **Examples**   Students haven't changed (some work hard, most do enough to get by, some do nothing; some are stuck up, some friendly, some shy).
>
> Teaching methods are the same (lots of lecturing, similar tests, lots of chalkboard notes).

As you can see, by making a list of points, you are likely to support your thesis well, you have the main ideas for your individual paragraphs, you have a general organizational plan for your paper, and you can add detail after each point to make your writing easier. That is good mileage to get from a simple prewriting technique.

Prewriting Activity 3.3

For your writing topic, do the following prewriting work:

1. Make a list of four or five supporting points for your thesis.

2. Decide on the best order to present these points in your paper.

3. For each point, generate some details that you might include in your draft.

First Drafts

After selecting a topic, deciding on a thesis for your paper, and generating some supportive material, you are ready to write your first draft. To write a thesis-directed paper, consider the suggestions given next.

THESIS-DIRECTED DRAFT

1. Organize your draft into three basic areas: beginning, middle, and ending.

    Beginning   In a paragraph or two, introduce your topic, state your thesis, and create some interest for readers.

    Middle   Present and develop the supporting points for your thesis in separate paragraphs.

    Ending   In a paragraph or two, conclude your paper by leaving readers with a sense of completion. You might reinforce your thesis in some way, summarize your main points, clarify your purpose for writing the paper, or leave your readers with a topic-related thought to ponder.

2. As you write your draft, feel free to add ideas you didn't think of during prewriting and to revise your writing plans as you go. Drafting is a process of discovery, and your prewriting plan is a rough outline, not a final blueprint.

3. Keep your thesis in mind as you write. Everything in your draft should in some way be related to supporting your thesis.

4. As with all first drafts, your goal is to get your ideas on paper with some sense of organization. Don't waste time worrying about perfect wording or an occasional error.

Drafting Activity 3.4

Before writing your draft, read the following student draft and the one entitled "Down with Jogging" in Activity 3.5, and analyze the beginning, middle, and ending organization of the papers. What did the writers accomplish in each part? Then write the first draft of your paper following the four suggestions on drafting just presented.

Returning to College

After twenty years of mothering and being a housewife, I returned to college to finish up my degree and then go after a teaching credential. I hadn't been in college since 1975, nor had I set foot on a college campus. Now I was returning to the same college I'd left at the end of my sophomore year twenty years ago. I figured that there would be a lot of changes in college in the past twenty years, and I was preparing to enter a strange and alien world. Now that I'm over five weeks into the first semester, what really strikes me as strange is how little anything has changed.

Sure, there have been a few changes. There are more foreign students on campus than in the 1970s, and there are more people my age and older returning to school. Some buildings have been added (a new library wing, two new dorms, a new administration building), plus two new parking lots and a baseball stadium. And walking has replaced bicycles as the main mode of transport around campus. But other than that, I could be back in the seventies as easily as being on campus in the nineties.

First, the students have changed very little. A minority of students in my classes work really hard and are grade oriented, and a majority do what they must to slide by, just like in the seventies. There are still the cliquish fraternity and sorority types, the down-to-earth, friendly students, the oversized athletes, and the bookish loners.

Students still hang out in the same places: downstairs in the student union, in the study sections of the library, in the upstairs cafeteria, or on warm days, in the square between the cafeteria and bookstore. They even dress similarly to the seventies: guys in T-shirts, Levi's, and tennis shoes, and girls in culottes, stretch pants, Bermuda shorts, and short straight skirts. Most of the students seem nonpolitical and bent mainly on enjoying themselves, similar to the campus attitude during the early seventies.

But it's not just the students who are similar to their seventies counterparts. Teachers and teaching methods haven't changed much either.

For example, I have a biology lecture section in the main science lecture hall. When I enrolled for the course, the instructor was just listed as "staff," so I was shocked when Dr. Darmby strode up to his lectern and began lecturing nonstop, lickety-split for a full fifty minutes. This was the same Darmby I'd had twenty years ago, and neither he nor his teaching method had changed much. I was surprised to find that a number of the faculty were still teaching twenty years later, and it appeared that those who had stayed had hired clones of themselves to replace the retirees. The faculty was depressingly similar to the none-too-energetic group I'd remembered.

Earlier in the semester, I'd gone upstairs to eat in the cafeteria, and I even sat at the old table where our "gang" sat twenty years ago. I selected chicken-fried steak, potatoes, a green salad, and milk, not really thinking about what the food had been like before. Well, the chicken-fried steak was full of gristle, the potatoes were watery, the salad had wilted, and the milk was barely cool. I ended up leaving three-fourths of everything on my plate and kicking myself for not remembering how bad the food had been in the seventies. Another déjà vu experience.

With so much unchanged at Tabor College in twenty years, my adjustment to college life has been rather easy. In some ways I'm rather disappointed. I guess I was somehow hoping that everything would be elevated with time: brighter, more involved students, challenging, enthusiastic instructors, an electric political atmosphere, and even gristle-free chicken-fried steak. But things seem just about the same, except of course for me, who's now looking at life through forty-year-old eyes instead of twenty-year-old. And maybe that's the problem. As a twenty-year-old, I remember thinking college life was pretty wonderful and exciting, and I'm sure it feels the same for most of the first-time students here. Maybe all of the old excitement of being a college student is still here, but I'm too old to catch it.

Revisions

After writing your first draft, set it aside for a while before starting the revision process. When you put some time between writing and evaluating your draft, you view it more objectively and make more perceptive revisions. Set your draft aside for an hour or overnight, and you will find things to improve that you wouldn't otherwise notice.

REVISION GUIDELINES

As you go over your draft, apply the following revision guidelines.

1. Evaluate your beginning. Have you introduced your topic and thesis effectively and created interest for readers? Evaluate your conclusion. Does it "wrap up" your paper in a meaningful way for readers? (See the section "Openings and Conclusions" later in the unit.)

2. Evaluate your middle paragraphs. Do they provide strong supporting points for your thesis? What explanations, details, or examples might you add to develop a particular point more effectively?

3. Evaluate the order in which you have presented your ideas. Would any sentence(s) or paragraph(s) fit more logically in a different location within the draft?

4. Read each sentence to see how you might revise the wording to improve its smoothness, clarity, or conciseness. Evaluate your sentence variety and make appropriate revisions. (See the section "Sentence Variety" later in the unit.)

5. Evaluate your paragraphing to make sure that you have a distinct opening, middle, and ending to your draft; that you have developed your supporting points in separate paragraphs; that the sentences within each paragraph are related; and that you don't have any extremely long or short paragraphs.

6. Evaluate the overall effectiveness with which you have supported your thesis. What can you do to convey your point even more clearly or persuasively?

Revision Activity 3.5

With a partner, read and evaluate the following student draft by applying the revision guidelines. Then evaluate your own draft in the same way, and exchange drafts with a classmate if you want a second opinion. Your instructor may have you go over the upcoming sections on paragraphing and sentence revision before evaluating your draft.

When you are ready, write the second draft of your paper, including all of the revisions you have noted to improve it.

Down with Jogging

For a while, my neighborhood was taken over by an army of joggers. They were there all the time: early morning, noon, and evenings. There were little old ladies in gray sweats, sleek couples in matching White Stag sweats and Adidas shoes, pot-bellied, middle-aged men with red faces, and even my friend Alex, who'd never exercised more than his beer-hoisting elbow. "Come on!" Alex urged me as he jogged by my house every evening. "You'll feel great."

Well, I had nothing against feeling great, and I figured if Alex could jog every day, anyone could. So I took up jogging seriously and gave it a good two months of my life, and not a day more. Based on my experience, jogging is the most overrated form of exercise around, and judging from the number of defectors from our neighborhood jogging army, I'm not alone in my opinion.

First of all, jogging is very hard on the body. Your legs and feet take a real pounding running around a track or down a paved road for two or three miles. I developed shin splints in my lower legs and stone bruises in my heels that are still tender. Some of my old lower-back problems that had been dormant for years also started flaring up. Then I read about a nationally famous jogger who died of a heart attack while jogging, and I had something else to worry about. I'm sure everyone doesn't develop the foot, leg, and back problems I did, and jogging doesn't kill hundreds of people, but if you have any physical weaknesses, jogging will surely bring them out, as they did with me.

Secondly, I got no enjoyment out of jogging, and few people stick with an exercise they don't enjoy. Jogging is boring. Putting one foot in front of the other for forty-five minutes isn't my idea of fun. Jogging is also a lonely pastime. Some joggers say, "I love being out there with just my thoughts." Well, my thoughts began to bore me, and most of them were on how much my legs hurt. If I can't exercise and socialize at the same time, I'm not interested.

And how could I enjoy something that brought me pain? What's fun about burning eyes, aching lungs, rubbery legs, and heavy arms? And that wasn't just the first week; it was practically every day for two months. I never got past the pain level, and pain isn't fun.

Jogging can have other negative spin-offs, too. It can be very bad on relationships. Husbands and wives start out as friendly jogging mates until hubby runs away from wife in a macho surge and thereafter only runs grudgingly at a "woman's" pace. Then there's the time involvement. Joggers run once or twice a day, thirty minutes to an hour at a time, along with the jogathons that take up the weekends. You've heard of golfing widows? Try jogging widows.

A friend of mine named Mildred started out as a three-time-a-week jogger three years ago. Harmless exercise. Today, she jogs thirty miles a week, runs in jogathons twice a month, subscribes to <u>Jogger's Weekly,</u> spends thousands a year on equipment and travel, and, not coincidentally, is no longer married.

But forget everything I've said. What about the great benefits of jogging, the ones that allow you to live longer, lighter, and happier than any nonjogger?

From my perspective, jogging is really overrated in those areas. I ran for two months and didn't lose a pound. The calories burn off very slowly when jogging, and the appetite, in my case, increased. I got my heart and respiratory system in better shape, but what a torturous way to do it. So many other exercises, including walking, accomplish almost the same results painlessly, so why jog? And the happier part? Jogging did not make me feel better, period. I didn't have more energy, I didn't look forward to the next day any more, I didn't spring up wide awake each morning. Jogging made me tired, sore, and irritable. And I can be all of those things <u>without</u> jogging.

I don't jog any more, and I don't think I ever will. I'm walking two miles three times a week at a brisk pace, and that feels good. I also play tennis and racquetball occasionally, and I bicycle to work when the weather is good. I'm getting exercise, and I'm enjoying it at the same time. I could never say the same for jogging, and I've found a lot better way to stay in shape. Anyone care to buy a pair of slightly worn size-six jogging shoes?

PARAGRAPHING

Each unit presents some paragraphing tips to apply to the paper you are currently working on. Since you are writing opening and concluding paragraphs as part of your thesis-directed paper, this section will help you begin and end your paper effectively.

Openings and Conclusions

Perhaps the two most important parts of a paper are its opening and conclusion. If you don't get off to a good start with readers, they may read your paper half-heartedly or not at all. If you don't conclude strongly, they are left with a weak final impression.

The following suggestions, along with continued writing practice, will help you begin and conclude your papers effectively. The first four are for *openings:*

1. Motivate readers to read further by introducing your topic in an interesting way: through a brief personal experience, an anecdote, an interesting quotation, a provoking fact, or an example of how readers are affected (by the topic).

2. Let readers know what lies ahead by presenting your thesis: the main idea you are going to develop in your paper.

3. Keep your opening relatively short—a paragraph or two—since it is an introduction, not the heart of your paper.

4. Through your opening, you will either "hook" or "lose" your readers' attention. Write it solely for their interest and understanding.

Here are some suggestions for *conclusions:*

1. In your conclusion, leave readers with something you want them to remember: the importance of the topic, the importance of their involvement in something, your purpose for writing, a crucial point, a memorable example, a prediction for the future, a provoking thought to ponder, a possible solution to a problem, a suggestion for readers to follow.

2. Your conclusion should fit logically and appropriately with what has come before. Therefore, you may not want to decide how you will end a paper until you've written everything but the conclusion.

3. Give readers something new in the conclusion—more than just a summary of what has come before. Make the conclusion worth their reading.

4. Think of the conclusion as the "last shot" at your readers. If they remember little else other than what they read in the conclusion, what will you leave them with?

OPENINGS AND
CONCLUSIONS

The following sample openings and conclusions give you some idea of the variety of ways that writers begin and end their papers.

Buying Furnishings for a House
(written for future homeowners)

OPENING

When my husband and I bought our first house, we were excited about getting rid of some of our junk furnishings and replacing them with nicer things. Our first acquisition was a beautiful entertainment center that we bought on sale.

When we put the three-piece unit in our family room, it swallowed up a lot of space. It made the room look tiny and took away from our seating space. Unfortunately, we were stuck with it because it was a "no return" sales item. That was one of many lessons we learned as we began to furnish our house. There are a lot of things to keep in mind when undertaking the costly task of furnishing a house.

(Middle paragraphs cover a number of points on furnishing a house wisely: taking measurements, taking into account the whole room, considering color schemes, considering decor themes, weighing deferred payment options, never purchasing nonreturnables.)

CONCLUSION

Above all else, make sure to take your time in furnishing your home. Most of what you buy may be with you for twenty years or more, so taking a few months to find just the right chair or picture is worth the effort. Furnishing a home is also expensive, so it makes sense to spread out your acquisitions over a few years rather than building up a huge debt. My husband and I now view furnishing our home as a longtime project; something that we will enjoy doing for many years. What a difference from those first months when we made hurried and ill-advised decisions. We learned the hard way.

Recycling Paper
(written to college audience)

OPENING

Americans throw away millions of tons of paper a year: newspapers, magazines, paper bags, letters, and envelopes. All of this paper represents thousands of trees that are cut annually from our dwindling U.S. forest lands. Our national forests don't have to be devastated, however, if we recycle our paper instead of throwing it away. With the recycling programs that are available today throughout the country, no American should ever throw away a piece of paper again.

(Middle paragraphs cover a number of different paper recycling programs available in most towns, the profits individuals can make by recycling their paper products, and ways to start up paper recycling programs in towns that don't have them.)

CONCLUSION

College students can make as big a contribution to saving our forests as anyone. Too often we throw away our notes, papers, handouts, returned tests, flyers, and student newspapers. Every college should have a number of paper "drop" stations on campus for recycling. The student council could be in charge of the program, and profits from selling the recycled paper could go to the student body. If your college doesn't have a recycling program, take the lead in getting one started, and once it is in place, carry the message to local K-12 school districts. Students can play a big role in helping to preserve U.S. forests for future generations.

Time for a Change
(letter to the editor of local newspaper)

OPENING

Coach Mabry has had three years to turn the college basketball program around, and the team isn't any better than when he came in 1992. The last two years he has had his own recruits to work with, so he can't blame the "carry-over" players that Coach Forney recruited previously. It's time for a change in basketball coaches because the current situation is producing some negative ramifications.

(Middle paragraphs cover the negative ramifications: poor attendance at games, disinterest in the program among students, lack of financial support from boosters, program in the red, program losing its previous national reputation.)

CONCLUSION

Division I coaches are hired with the understanding that losing seasons bring about firings. That's the nature of the business and one reason that they are paid considerably more than other college instructors. No one should feel sorry for Coach Mabry. He has had his chance, he's made over $100,000 a year, and he hasn't produced. It's time to give someone else a chance before the college basketball program goes into cardiac arrest. There are plenty of excellent coaches in the country who would love the chance to revive our once outstanding program. It can be outstanding again, but not with Coach Mabry at the helm.

New College Drop Date
(written to board of trustees)

OPENING

The change in the college's semester drop date from the twelfth week to the sixth week was instituted quietly this fall and went practically unnoticed by students. Then when the sixth week of the new semester crept closer and teachers began notifying their classes, it began to sink in with students that the new date was going to create some serious problems. The six-week drop date is clearly not in the best interests of most students, and it should be changed back to the original twelve-week date.

(Middle paragraphs cover the reasons why the writer opposes the new drop date: not enough time for students to make up their minds; not enough testing at that point for students to evaluate their standing; negative effects on financial aid for students who drop classes that early; will lead to higher college dropout rate; will lead to poorer GPAs and hinder students' chances of transferring successfully.)

CONCLUSION

For all of these reasons, the six-week drop date is bad for most students and should be changed. It is not surprising that students were not involved in discussions on changing the drop date or on its effects. If we had been, I don't believe the date would have been changed.

True, the six-week drop date may make life easier for instructors, but does the board make decisions based on what is easy for instructors or what is best for students? Please reconsider this hastily made change and do what is best for students: return the drop date to the twelfth week. There is plenty of time to make that change for the fall semester of 1997. Thank you.

Paragraphing Activity 3.6

Review the opening and concluding paragraphs of your latest draft, and revise them to be more informative and interesting and to improve their overall impact on readers.

SENTENCE REVISION

In the first two units, you worked on improving first draft sentences by eliminating unnecessary words, smoothing out awkward phrasing, replacing questionable word choices, and using concrete, visual language. Another consideration in sentence revision is *sentence variety:* using a variety of sentence structures and joining words to express your thoughts most effectively. In this section you begin working with a number of different sentence structures.

Guidelines for Improving Sentence Variety

By using a variety of sentence structures and joining words, you make your writing interesting for readers and express yourself most effectively. Some of the most common sentence problems are described here, with suggestions for solving them.

1. *Overreliance on a particular sentence structure:* You may find that you are using simple sentences (one subject, one verb) to the exclusion of other types.

   Example   At 7:00 a.m. it was cool and breezy in Turlock. However, by 10:00 a.m. the breeze had stopped. The temperature began rising slowly. By 3:00 p.m. the temperature had reached 100 degrees. Then the breeze came up again at about 7:00 p.m. By 10:00 p.m. it was cool and windy. There was a 40-degree difference between the high and low for the day.

   Check your sentences to see if you have relied on a particular sentence structure to the exclusion of others: simple (one subject, one verb); compound (two sentences joined by *and, but, so, or, yet, for*); or complex (sentences joined or beginning with *because, if, while, unless, although, before, after*). Revise sentences to include a variety of simple, compound, and complex sentences.

2. *Overreliance on one or two joining words:* You may be using *and* to the exclusion of other options.

   Example   A blue jay built her nest in a hanging plant on our apartment patio, and we inspected it occasionally, and a couple neighborhood cats also kept watch. The nest was about six feet above the ground, and we didn't worry about the cats. The blue jay would return regularly, and she would dive-bomb the cats and scare them away. One day the blue jay didn't return to the nest, and we never saw her again after that. After a couple months we took down the nest and threw the unhatched eggs away.

   Check your sentences to see if you have relied on one or two joining words exclusively, such as *and, so,* or *because.* If you have, replace the overused word with other appropriate word choices.

3. *Overreliance on short or long sentences:* You may be using too many long sentences. (For overreliance on short sentences, see the paragraph example from number 1 about the weather.)

Example   I feel very uncomfortable in my Psychology II class this semester because it is a small class and everyone is expected to participate in discussions. There are a number of older students in the class, some of whom have obviously taken a few psychology courses, and they frequently talk in jargon that I can't understand and make references to books I haven't read and psychological experiments that I've never heard of. When I do speak up in class, my observations and opinions sound pretty weak to me, and I'm sure these older students feel the same way although they don't reveal it and are always very considerate of the other students like myself, which is the one thing that makes the class tolerable.

Check the lengths of your sentences to see if you have too many short sentences (which hurts the flow of your paper) or overly long sentences (which readers can get lost in). Revise groups of short sentences by combining them with joining words or developing their content. Revise overly long sentences by dividing them into two or three complete sentences.

Sentence Revision Activity 3.7

Revise the following first draft paragraphs by varying sentence structures, replacing overused joining words, combining very short sentences, and dividing overly long sentences. Add, delete, and move words around any way you wish. Possible wording options: coordinate conjunctions (and, but, so, for, or, yet), subordinate conjunctions (although, because, since, if, unless, until, when, before, after, while, who, which, that).

Gretchen wanted to move out of the dorms, but she didn't know anyone to share an apartment with. She decided to look in the paper for "roommates wanted" ads, but she was leery about living with strangers. She finally decided to check out one ad because the apartment was in walking distance to the school, and because there were three girls who needed one roommate, and that would mean dividing the rent four ways, which was the cheapest way to go.

Gretchen went to the apartment and met the girls. They were a year older than her and seemed nice. Their apartment looked clean and was nicely furnished. Her rent would be $150 a month and her share of the utility bill $50. Although she knew little about the girls, Gretchen decided to move in with them although she would have to buy a bicycle to go to and from classes. Although her mother was concerned about the move, Gretchen felt she had made the right decision. She moved her belongings from the dorm.

She got her cleaning deposit back. She said farewell to her dormitory friends. She said good-bye to her floor supervisor.

Sentence Revision Activity 3.8

Review the sentences in your latest draft and, if necessary, make revisions to include more sentence variety, replace overused joining words, combine pairs or groups of short sentences, and divide overly long sentences.

Combining Sentences

Practice in combining sentences has proven successful in helping students enhance their sentence writing skills. The appendix includes a number of combining activities for students who could benefit from working with a variety of simple, compound, and complex sentence structures. Your instructor may assign these activities throughout the course to give you regular practice in building your sentence repertoire.

Final Editing

The last step in the writing process is to proofread your paper for any errors that might remain. By this time in the course you are probably well aware of your error tendencies, so pay particular attention to those areas.

This section introduces two new considerations that give some writers problems: sentence fragments and subject-verb agreement. You may want to cover these topics before proofreading your latest draft.

PROOFREADING GUIDELINES

1. Make sure you have a period at the end of each complete sentence. Check in particular for run-on sentences and comma splices, or for sentence fragments that need correcting. (See the section "Fragments," a little later in the Unit.)

2. Check your word endings to make sure you haven't inadvertently left off an *s* on a plural word, an *ed* on a past tense verb, or an *ly* on an adverb. Also make sure that your present tense verb endings agree with their subjects. (See the section "Subjects and Verbs" later in the Unit.)

3. Check your spelling carefully, and look up any words you are uncertain of. Also make sure you have made the correct homonym choices among words such as there/their/they're, your/you're, no/know, its/it's, and through/threw. (See the sections on these confusing homonyms under "Spelling" in the appendix.)

4. Check your internal punctuation, including comma usage in series of words, compound sentences, and after introductory groups of words; apostrophes in contractions; and quotation marks with dialogue. (If you have any problems with contractions, see the "Spelling" section in the appendix.)

5. Check your use of pronouns in compound subjects (Marsha and I, Ross and she, my mother and I, he and I, the Williamses and they).

Editing Activity 3.9

Following the guidelines just presented, proofread your latest draft for errors and make the necessary corrections. (Your instructor may have you cover the upcoming sections on fragments and subjects and verbs before you ¬roof-read.) Then write or print out the final error-free draft of your paper, and share it with your instructor and classmates.

SENTENCE PROBLEMS

In the first units, you worked on identifying and correcting run-on sentences and comma splices in your writing. A less frequent but equally troublesome problem is the sentence *fragment,* which is covered in this section.

Fragments

Here are some common features of sentence fragments to be aware of:

1. A fragment is an incomplete sentence. A sentence expresses a complete idea and makes sense by itself; a fragment makes little sense on its own.

   Examples   The man walking down the freeway.

   Because it has been snowing all weekend.

   Driving to school in an old Volkswagen bus.

2. A fragment often leaves the reader with an unanswered question.

   Examples   The girl standing in the fountain. *(What happened to her?)*

   If you do all your homework tonight. *(What will happen?)*

   Whenever I start to apologize to you. *(What happens?)*

3. Fragments often separate thoughts that belong together in one sentence.

   Examples   *(fragments underlined)*

   <u>If you want a ride to school tomorrow.</u> You can give me a call.

   I hope the game is over. <u>Before it starts raining hard.</u>

4. Since fragments are incorrect sentence structures that confuse readers, they should be revised to form complete sentences.

Example	The girl standing in the fountain.
Revised	The girl standing in the fountain is cooling her feet.
Example	After we pay this month's bills. We'll have little money left for entertainment.
Revised	After we pay this month's bills, we'll have little money left for entertainment.

Fragment Activity 3.10

The following paragraph contains a number of fragments. Some are the result of a split sentence, and others have a missing part. Rewrite the paragraph and correct all fragments by uniting split sentences and by adding words to fragments that are incomplete. When you finish, check your latest draft for fragments and make the necessary corrections.

Example	Mabel was interested in fashion merchandising. Because she loved to buy clothes. Expensive clothes in particular.
Revised	Mabel was interested in fashion merchandising because she loved to buy clothes. She was attracted to expensive clothes in particular.

It was a bad time to be looking for apartments. Because they were scarce and rent was high. A one-bedroom apartment $300 a month. Maria and Henry were hoping to find a two-bedroom apartment. Since she was expecting a baby in April. They needed to live closer to the campus. Because Henry didn't own a car. The only two-bedroom place they found was renting for $350. They decided to take it. Although the payments would be difficult. Could survive until Henry graduated in June. They moved their belongings into the apartment. They felt everything would work out. Unless Henry's grant application was not accepted.

CORRECT USAGE

Writers sometimes make grammatical errors within a sentence that distract readers. Knowledge of the basic rules of grammar help writers eliminate such errors. This section introduces you to the rules that govern subject-verb agreement.

Subjects and Verbs

As a general rule, every sentence you write contains a subject and a verb. The *subject* is who or what the sentence is about, and the *verb* tells what the subject is doing or joins the subject with words that describe it. To understand subject-verb agreement, you need to be able to identify these main sentence parts.

Subject-Verb Identification

The following sentences have their subjects underlined once and the verbs twice. Notice that in each sentence, the *subject* is who or what the sentence is about, and the *verb* tells what the subject is doing.

Examples   The <u>dolphin</u> <u>leaped</u> through the air. (*The sentence is about* a dolphin. Leaped *tells what the dolphin did.*)

The <u>doctor</u> <u>made</u> house calls. (*The sentence is about* a doctor. Made *house calls tells what he did.*)

The <u>boulders</u> <u>tumbled</u> down the mountain. (*The sentence is about* boulders. Tumbled *tells what they did.*)

A second way of finding the subject and verb is to locate the verb first and then the subject. To find the verb, look for the *action* in the sentence: running, thinking, talking, looking, touching, and so on. To find the subject, ask, "Who or what is doing the action?" Here are more examples.

Examples   The <u>raisins</u> <u>shrivel</u> in the sun. (*The action is* shrivel. *What is shriveling? The* raisins.)

<u>Jogging</u> <u>builds</u> Jolene's stamina. (*The action is* builds. *What builds stamina?* Jogging.)

<u>Clyde</u> <u>hates</u> sardines and anchovies. (*The action is* hates. *Who hates?* Clyde.)

Subject-Verb Activity 3.11

Underline the subject once and the verb twice in the following sentences. Either find out what the sentence is about (the subject) and what the subject is doing (the verb), or look for the action in the sentence (the verb) and find who or what is doing it (the subject).

Examples   The <u>noose</u> <u>tightened</u> around his neck.

The <u>skier</u> <u>fell</u> off the ski lift.

1. Juanita's ankle aches from roller skating.
2. The tarantula crawled inside Felix's sleeping bag.
3. Aunt Lottie from Toledo cracks walnuts on her head.
4. Ashes from the volcano covered the city.

5. Knitting relaxes Jose.
6. Today the stock market dropped to a record low.
7. Sal often thinks about joining the circus.
8. A fire spreading from a tool shed destroyed the family's belongings.
9. The countries in the Middle East negotiated a new peace treaty.
10. The rats chewed through the pantry wall.
11. High interest rates in March and April killed Fred's chances for a loan.
12. The hockey team from Calgary practices at 4:00 a.m. every day.
13. The opportunity for fame escaped Alice.
14. The poetry competition between classes ends today.
15. Ink blots from his fountain pen stained Rasheed's shirt pocket.

Subject-Verb Agreement

The following information will help you understand subject-verb agreement.

1. The subject of a sentence can be *singular* (one of anything) or *plural* (more than one of anything). The plural of most words is formed by adding *s* or *es*: cats, dogs, dresses, boxes.

2. There are two forms of present tense verbs: one ends in *s* and one does not (ride/rides, fight/fights, sing/sings).

3. When you use a present tense verb, you must select the correct form of the verb to agree with the subject. If the subject of the sentence is *singular*, use the form that ends in *s*. If the subject is *plural*, use the form that does *not* end in *s*.

   a. *Singular subject:* present tense verb ends in *s*.

   b. *Plural subject:* present tense verb does not end in *s*.

   Examples   *(subject underlined once, verb underlined twice)*

   Singular subject   The elm tree sheds its leaves in early December.

   Plural subject   The elm trees shed their leaves in early December.

   Singular subject   Your aunt believes in reincarnation.

   Plural subject   Your aunts believe in reincarnation.

4. Here are the exceptions to the basic subject-verb agreement rules. With the singular subject pronouns *I* and *you*, the verb does *not* end in *s*: I enjoy roller-skating; you prefer skateboarding. Verbs such as *dress, press,*

regress, and *impress* end in *s* despite the presence of a plural subject: The Johnson girls dress alike.

Subject-Verb Agreement Activity 3.12

Circle the correct form of the present tense verb in parentheses that agrees with the subject of the sentence.

Examples   Your uncle (build, (builds)) huge sand castles.

Your uncles ((build,) builds) huge sand castles.

1. Juanita often (practice, practices) her baton twirling three nights a week.
2. The girls (practice, practices) karate in the school's gymnastics room.
3. My nephew from New Orleans (believe, believes) in extraterrestrial beings.
4. My nieces (believe, believes) that my nephew is crazy.
5. The pole-vaulters from Central College (warm, warms) up for their event by using a trampoline.
6. The high jumper from Drake University (warm, warms) up for her event by doing stretching exercises.
7. The city newspapers that I subscribe to (do, does) a lousy job of covering campus activities.
8. The college newspaper (do, does) a great job of covering city events.
9. That pickle on your hamburger (look, looks) like it's been nibbled on by a rat.
10. Those olives (look, looks) like they've been dehydrated.
11. Your dentist (need, needs) braces on his lower teeth.
12. Most physicians that I know (need, needs) to take better care of their own health.
13. Your success (prove, proves) that hard work sometimes pays off.
14. My recent failures in math (prove, proves) that hard work isn't always enough.
15. A savings account (are, is) one thing I need to open immediately.
16. Savings accounts (are, is) great if you have anything to put into them.

Subject-Verb Variations

Here are some variations in the subject-verb pattern that often create agreement problems for writers:

1. *Separated subject and verb:* The subject and verb are separated by a group of words, most often a *prepositional phrase,* that confuses the agreement situation. *Solution:* Ignore any words between a subject and verb when making decisions about agreement.

   Prepositional Phrases *(prepositions italicized)*

after the game	*from* his room
against his will	*in* the boat
among the roses	*into* the water
around the house	*of* the three churches
before the test	*on* the table
behind the batter	*to* the ground
between the lines	*through* the mail
for good mileage	*with* her friends

   Examples   *(subject and verb underlined, prepositional phrases crossed out)*

   One ~~of the women teachers~~ smokes a pipe in the lounge.

   The aroma ~~of barbecuing steaks~~ nauseates Herman.

   Men ~~in the back of the room by the pencil sharpener~~ look threatening.

   Each ~~of the sixteen yellow raincoats~~ has a flaw in it.

2. *Sentences beginning with* there *plus a form of* to be: Sentences beginning with there is, there are, there was, and there were cause writers problems because the subject comes *after* the verb. *Solution:* Because *there* is never the subject in a *there + to be* sentence, locate the subject after the verb and use *is* or *was* with singular subjects and *are* or *were* with plural subjects.

   Examples   *(subjects and verbs underlined)*

   There is a snake in the basement.

   There are sixteen ways to cook potatoes.

   There was no one home at the Garcias'.

   There were no Christmas trees left in the lot when I went shopping.

3. *Compound verbs:* If a sentence has a single subject and two or more main verbs (compound verb), each main verb must agree with the subject.

Examples *(subjects and verbs underlined)*

<u>Mavis</u> <u>jogs</u> to work, <u>does</u> aerobics on her lunch hour, and <u>lifts</u> weights at night.

My <u>uncles</u> <u>make</u> great chili and <u>serve</u> it in old tin cans.

<u>G Street</u> <u>winds</u> around our suburb and then <u>dead-ends</u> by the canal.

<u>Sarah and Clyde</u> <u>love</u> to fight and <u>love</u> to make up even more.

Subject-Verb Agreement Activity 3.13

Underline the subject in each of the following sentences, and then circle the verb in parentheses that *agrees* with the subject. When you finish, proofread your latest draft for any subject-verb agreement problems.

Example   <u>One</u> of my goldfish (look, (looks)) ill.

1. Sarah and Jesus (dances, dance) smoothly together.
2. No one in the audience (understand, understands) the plot of the Fellini movie.
3. The huge planes (circles, circle) the runway in the fog.
4. The french fries from the Happy Hamburger (is, are) greasy.
5. The children from Grant School (appears, appear) bored after Act One of The Great Anchovy.
6. There (is, are) something about you that I like.
7. Before the election, the mayor (hires, hire) his campaign manager and (prepares, prepare) his speech.
8. Tryouts for the philharmonic orchestra (begins, begin) on Monday.
9. Julia and Fred (seems, seem) surprised by the attention from the press.
10. The students from Sweden and Israel (speaks, speak) and (writes, write) excellent English.
11. In the back of your locker (lies, lie) a pair of stinky sweat socks.
12. The view across the bay from the middle of the bridge (was, were) magnificent.
13. There (is, are) one of the Daffney twins, but I (don't, doesn't) know the whereabouts of her sister.
14. There (is, are) no good reason for you to miss the farewell party for Gonzo.
15. From the looks of your car, it (needs, need) a good wash and wax job.

Writing Review

Write a second thesis-directed paper following the writing process provided here. Apply what you have learned so far in the course.

WRITING PROCESS

TOPIC SELECTION

1. Select a writing topic, a thesis, and a reading audience following these suggestions:

    a. Choose a topic that you have a definite opinion on, that you are interested in, and that you know a lot about. Spend some time thinking about a topic you would really like to write on.

    b. Select a tentative thesis: the main point you want to convey to readers and support throughout your paper. Your thesis should reflect your viewpoint on the topic.

    c. Select the primary reading audience: the people who might benefit from or be most interested in reading it.

PREWRITING

2. To generate ideas for your paper, use the following listing techniques:

    a. List four or five supporting points for your thesis: the main reasons why you feel the way you do.

    b. Reorder your points the way you want to present them in your draft. You might go from most to least important point or from least to most important point, present your strongest points first and last, or present related points in succession.

    c. For each supporting point, note (mentally or in writing) details, examples, and other information you might include to develop that point in your draft.

FIRST DRAFT

3. When you have completed your prewriting work, write the first draft of your paper following these guidelines:

    a. Include a beginning, middle, and ending to your paper. Apply what you have learned about effective openings and conclusions, and develop your supporting points in the middle paragraphs.

    b. Follow your prewriting plan from the listing activity, but feel free to add things you didn't think of or to make changes in your plan as you work through the draft.

    c. Keep your thesis in mind to provide direction for the entire paper.

    d. Don't worry about perfect wording or an occasional error. Draft revision and editing lie ahead.

REVISIONS

4. When you finish your first draft, set it aside for a while before evaluating it. Then read the draft carefully for possible revisions, following

these guidelines. When you are ready, write the second draft of your paper.

a. Are your opening and conclusion strong points of your paper? In the opening, do you introduce your topic in an interesting way and reveal your thesis? In the conclusion, do you wrap up the paper effectively and leave readers with something new?

b. Do you support your thesis well in the middle paragraphs? Is each supporting point developed through appropriate details, explanations, and/or examples? Will readers clearly understand why you believe what you do about the topic?

c. Is your paper paragraphed effectively? Are the opening, middle, and ending paragraphed separately? Do you develop each supporting point in a separate paragraph? Are the sentences within each paragraph related? Do you have any overly long paragraphs that need dividing or short paragraphs that need combining or developing further?

d. Is your paper organized effectively? Have you presented your supporting points in the best possible order? Are there any sentences or paragraphs that would fit more logically in a different location?

e. Revise the wording of individual sentences to make them clearer, smoother, more concise, and more concrete (visual). Check your sentences to see if you need to improve their structural variety, replace overused joining words, combine pairs or groups of short sentences, or divide overly long sentences.

f. Evaluate the overall impact of your paper on your reading audience. What can you do to make it more interesting, more informative, or more persuasive?

EDITING

5. Using the proofreading guidelines on page 75, proofread your draft carefully for errors and make the necessary corrections.

FINAL DRAFT

6. Write or print out the final draft of your paper, and share it with your instructor, classmates, and members of the reading audience that you wrote it for.

STUDENT WRITING PROCESS

I'd like to write about selecting a major in college because it was something I had a problem with. I'd never rush into it again. That was a mistake, and I think I got some bad advice.

TOPIC

Choosing a college major.

THESIS

Choosing a major before you are ready is a big mistake.

AUDIENCE

Incoming college freshmen who haven't declared a major yet.

PREWRITING LIST (SUPPORTING POINTS FOR THESIS)

May take unnecessary courses (provide personal examples)
Will probably change mind later (provide personal example)
Waste time and money (provide personal examples)
Don't need major (take basic general ed classes first)

Selecting a Major

STUDENT FIRST DRAFT

Everyone tells you to get a major in college as soon as possible: counselors, advisors, parents. That way you'll have direction throughout your college career, and you won't waste time taking classes you don't need.

Like a good freshman, I listened to people and selected a major as soon as I got to college: pre-optometry. My girlfriend's father recommended it. I liked the idea of being called "doctor," and I wouldn't have to go to school nearly as long as an MD. Did I have any idea what optometrists really did? Not actually. Choosing a major before I was really ready was a big mistake.

As I progressed through my first two years, I dutifully took every math and chemistry class required and ignored most of the general ed requirements since I wouldn't need them for a BS degree to transfer to the optometry school I wanted to go to. I stuck to my pre-optometry schedule, happy to have a major and the "direction" that many of my friends still lacked.

However, something happened near the end of my sophomore year. I started thinking for myself a little. I began wondering what optometrists really did, and I arranged to meet an optometrist friend and spend a day with him at an eye clinic. I'd never been so bored in my life. The work was very routine, and there appeared to be no challenge or excitement to the job. I began to have real doubts about my major, and I felt guilty about that.

During this same time, I was taking a biology class that had me excited. I was learning a lot about DNA, genetic research, and the career opportunities for doing really meaningful work in medical research. I was getting excited about genetics from the work I was doing in the lab and from talking to researchers rather than from some vague career notion that I'd had as a seventeen-year-old. For the first time, I was ready to declare a major.

So how did a change in major affect me? First, it cost me an extra undergraduate year and an extra year of expense. I have to take two semesters of general ed requirements I'll need to graduate, and then in my fifth year I'll take biology major courses exclusively. I was also made to feel guilty by my dad, who tried to talk me out of changing majors, and my counselor, who told me, "Most students have doubts about their majors from time to time. Hang in there!" Bad advice that I didn't take.

From this experience, I'd say the worst thing a person can do is to declare a major because he or she feels pressured to do it. Many seventeen- and eighteen-year-old college freshmen aren't ready to make this decision, and counselors and parents should accept this. It makes a lot more sense for undecided students to get their general ed requirements out of the way and take that time to find out more about what interests them. Sometimes taking a lot of courses from different disciplines is the best way to "shop" for a possible major.

The one positive thing from the experience is that I did change majors to something I liked rather than stick out my first choice. I feel really good about my schooling and my future for the first time. So if someone does feel stuck in a prematurely selected major, my advice is that it's better to change majors and spend another year in school than to stick with a major you don't feel good about.

In the end, I was the only person who could ultimately decide what I wanted in a major and a career, and I was the only one who had to live with my decision. So don't let anyone pressure you into selecting a major before you're ready, and if you feel at some point like changing majors, don't feel guilty about it. It may be the best decision you ever make.

Readings

What's Your Best Time of Day?

BY SUSAN PERRY AND JIM DAWSON

1   Every fall, Jane, a young mother and part-time librarian, begins to eat more and often feels sleepy. Her mood is also darker, especially when she awakens in the morning; it takes all her energy just to drag herself out of bed. These symptoms persist until April, when warmer weather and longer days seem to lighten her mood and alleviate her cravings for food and sleep.

2   Joseph, a 48-year-old engineer for a Midwestern computer company, feels cranky early in the morning. But as the day progresses, he becomes friendlier and more accommodating.

3   All living organisms, from mollusks to men and women, exhibit biological rhythms. Some are short and can be measured in minutes or hours. Others last days or months. The peaking of body temperature, which occurs in most people every evening, is a daily rhythm. The menstrual cycle is a monthly rhythm. The increase in sexual drive in the autumn—not in the spring, as poets would have us believe—is a seasonal, or yearly, rhythm.

4   The idea that our bodies are in constant flux is fairly new—and goes against traditional medical training. In the past, many doctors were taught to believe the body has a relatively stable, or homeostatic, internal environment. Any fluctuations were considered random and not meaningful enough to be studied.

5   As early as the 1940s, however, some scientists questioned the homeostatic view of the body. Franz Halberg, a young European scientist working in the United States, noticed that the number of white blood cells in laboratory mice was dramatically higher and lower at different times of day. Gradually, such research spread to the study of other rhythms in other life forms, and the findings were sometimes startling. For example, the time of day when a person receives X-ray or drug treatment for cancer can affect treatment benefits and ultimately mean the difference between life and death.

6   This new science is called chronobiology, and the evidence supporting it has become increasingly persuasive. Along the way, the scientific and medical communities are beginning to rethink their ideas about how the human body works, and gradually what had been considered a minor science just a few years ago is being studied in major universities and medical centers around the world. There are even chronobiologists working for the National Aeronautics and Space Administration, as well as for the National Institutes of Health and other government laboratories.

7   With their new findings, they are teaching us things that can literally change our lives—by helping us organize ourselves so we can work *with* our natural rhythms rather than against them. This can enhance our outlook on life as well as our performance at work and play.

8   Because they are easy to detect and measure, more is known of daily—or circadian (Latin for "about a day")—rhythms than other types. The most obvious daily rhythm is the sleep/wake cycle. But there are other daily cycles as well: temperature, blood pressure, hormone levels. Amid these and the body's other changing rhythms, you are simply a different person at 9 A.M. than you are at 3 P.M. How you feel, how well you work, your level of alertness, your sensitivity to taste and smell, the degree with which you enjoy food or take pleasure in music—all are changing throughout the day.

9   Most of us seem to reach our peak of alertness around noon. Soon after that, alertness declines, and sleepiness may set in by midafternoon.

10   Your short-term memory is best during the morning—in fact, about 15 percent more efficient than at any other time of day. So, students, take heed: when faced with a morning exam, it really does pay to review your notes right before the test is given.

11   Long-term memory is different. Afternoon is the best time for learning material that you want to recall days, weeks or months later. Politicians, business executives or others who must learn speeches would be smart to do their memorizing during that time of day. If you are a student, you would be wise to schedule your more difficult classes in the afternoon, rather than in the morning. You should also try to do most of your studying in the afternoon, rather than late at night. Many students believe they memorize better while burning the midnight oil because their short-term recall is better during the wee hours of the morning than in the afternoon. But short-term memory won't help them much several days later, when they face the exam.

12   By contrast, we tend to do best on cognitive tasks—things that require the juggling of words and figures in one's head—during the morning hours. This might be a good time, say, to balance a checkbook.

13   Your manual dexterity—the speed and coordination with which you perform complicated tasks with your hands—peaks during the afternoon hours. Such work as carpentry, typing or sewing will be a little easier at this time of day.

14   What about sports? During afternoon and early evening, your coordination is at its peak, and you're able to react the quickest to an outside stimulus—like a baseball speeding toward you at home plate. Studies have also shown that late in the day, when your body temperature is peaking, you will *perceive* a physical workout to be easier and less fatiguing—whether it actually is or not. That means you are more likely to work harder during a late-afternoon or early-evening workout, and therefore benefit more from it. Studies involving swimmers, runners, shot-putters and rowing crews have shown consistently that performance is better in the evening than in the morning.

15   In fact, all of your senses—taste, sight, hearing, touch and smell—may be at their keenest during late afternoon and early evening. That could be why dinner usually tastes better to us than breakfast and why bright lights irritate us at night.

16   Even our perception of time changes from hour to hour. Not only does time seem to fly when you're having fun, but it also seems to fly even faster

if you are having that fun in the late afternoon or early evening, when your body temperature is also peaking.

17   While all of us follow the same general pattern of ups and downs, the exact timing varies from person to person. It all depends on how your "biological" day is structured—how much of a morning or night person you are. The earlier your biological day gets going, the earlier you are likely to enter—and exit—the peak times for performing various tasks. An extreme morning person and an extreme night person may have circadian cycles that are a few hours apart.

18   Each of us can increase our knowledge about our individual rhythms. Learn how to listen to the inner beats of your body; let them set the pace of your day. You will live a healthier—and happier—life. As no less an authority than the Bible tells us, "To every thing there is a season, and a time to every purpose under heaven."

QUESTIONS FOR DISCUSSION

1. What is the thesis of the essay? What are the implications of the thesis that could interest readers?

2. Analyze the opening and conclusion of the essay. What is presented in each? How effectively do the author's introduce and wrap up their topic?

3. What support is presented for the thesis? How convincing is the support?

4. How might you apply a knowledge of biorhythms to your everyday life? Do your own experiences confirm the authors' findings on the optimal times for various activities?

5. If you were structuring a daily educational schedule for elementary school children, how might you apply your knowledge of biorhythms to help plan it?

6. What do you think the authors' purpose was in writing this essay?

VOCABULARY

Alleviate (1), mollusks (3), homeostatic (4), chronobiology (6), dexterity (13), circadian (17)

Black Wasn't Beautiful

by Mary Mebane

1   In the fall of 1951 during my first week at North Carolina College, a black school in Durham, the chairman's wife, who was indistinguishable from a white woman, stopped me one day in the hall. She wanted to see me, she said.

2   When I went to her office, she greeted me with a big smile. "You know," she said, "you made the highest mark on the verbal part of the examination." She was referring to the examination that the entire freshman class took

upon entering the college. In spite of her smile, her eyes and tone of voice were saying, "How could this black-skinned girl score higher on the verbal than some of the students who've had more advantages than she? It must be some sort of fluke." I felt it, but I managed to smile my thanks and back off. For here at North Carolina College, social class and color were the primary criteria used in deciding status. The faculty assumed light-skinned students were more intelligent, and they were always a bit nonplussed when a dark-skinned student did well, especially if she was a girl.

3   I don't know whether African men recently transported to the New World considered themselves handsome or, more important, whether they considered African women beautiful in comparison with native American Indian women or immigrant European women. But one thing I know for sure: by the 20th century, really black skin on a woman was considered ugly in this country. In the 1950s this was particularly true among those who were exposed to college. Black skin was to be disguised at all costs. Since a black face is rather hard to disguise, many women took refuge in ludicrous makeup.

4   I observed all through elementary and high school, in various entertainments, the girls were placed on the stage in order of color. And very black ones didn't get into the front row. If they were past caramel-brown, to the back row they would go. Nobody questioned the justice of this—neither the students nor the teachers.

5   Oddly enough, the lighter-skinned black male did not seem to feel so much prejudice toward the black black woman. It was no accident, I felt, that Mr. Harrison, the eighth-grade teacher, who was reddish-yellow himself, once protested to the science and math teacher about the fact that he always assigned sweeping duties to Doris and Ruby, two black black girls. Mr. Harrison said to them one day in the other teacher's presence, "You must be some bad girls. Every day I come down here you all are sweeping." The science and math teacher got the point and didn't ask them to sweep any more. Uneducated black males, too, sometimes related very well to the black black woman. They had been less indoctrinated by the white society around them.

6   Because of the stigma attached to having dark skin, a black black woman had to do many things to find a place for herself. One possibility was to attach herself to a light-skinned woman, hoping that some of the magic would rub off on her. A second was to make herself sexually available, hoping thereby to attract a mate. Third, she could resign herself to a more chaste life-style—either (for the professional woman) teaching and work in established churches or (for the uneducated woman) domestic work and zealous service in "holy and sanctified" churches.

7   Lucy had chosen the first route. Lucy was short, skinny, short-haired and black black, and thus unacceptable. So she made her choice. She selected Patricia, the lightest-skinned girl in the school, as her friend and followed her around. Patricia and her friends barely tolerated Lucy, but Lucy smiled and doggedly hung on, hoping that those who noticed Patricia might notice her also. Though I felt shame for her behavior, even then I understood.

8   A fourth avenue open to the black black woman is excellence in a career. Since in the South the field most accessible to such women is education, a great many of them prepared to become teachers. But here, too, the black black woman had problems. Grades weren't given to her lightly in school, nor were promotions on the job. She had to pass examinations with flying colors or be left behind. She had to be overqualified for a job because otherwise she didn't stand a chance of getting it—and she was competing only with other blacks.

9   The black woman's training would pay off in the 1970s. With the arrival of integration, the black black woman would find, paradoxically enough, that her skin color in an integrated situation was not the handicap it had been in an all-black situation. But it wasn't until the middle and late 1960s, when the post-1945 generation of black males arrived in college that I noticed any change in the situation at all. *He* wore an Afro and *she* wore an Afro, and sometimes the only way you could tell them apart was when his Afro was taller than hers. Black had become beautiful. It was then that the dread I felt at dealing with the college-educated black male began to ease. Even now, though, when I have occasion to engage in any transaction with a college-educated black man, I gauge his age. If I guess he was born after 1945, I feel confident that the transaction will turn out all right. If he probably was born before 1945, my stomach tightens. I find myself taking shallow breaths, and I try to state my business and escape as soon as possible.

10   When the grades for the first quarter at North Carolina College came out, I had the highest average in the freshman class. The chairman's wife called me into her office again. We did a replay of the same scene we had played during the first week of the term. She complimented me on my grades. Then she reached into a drawer and pulled out a copy of the freshman English final examination. She asked me to take the exam over again.

11   At first I couldn't believe what she was saying. I had taken the course under another teacher; and it was so incredible to her that I should have made the highest score in the class that she was trying to test me again personally. For a few moments I knew rage so intense that I wanted to take my fists and start punching her. I have seldom hated anyone so deeply. I handed the examination back to her and walked out.

QUESTIONS FOR DISCUSSION

1. What is the topic of the essay? What is the essay's thesis? Where is it located?

2. How is the thesis supported? What are the main points of support? What evidence is provided for each point?

3. What sources does Mebane rely on for her thesis and support? How credible are they?

4. Analyze the opening and conclusion of the essay. What is accomplished in each? What effect(s) do they have on you?

5. What audience might the essay be intended for? What is Mebane's purpose for writing the essay? How well is the purpose accomplished?

6. What discrimination have you experienced because of your race, ethnicity, background, looks, or behavior? How did you deal with it?

7. Do you agree with the essay's thesis? Why?

VOCABULARY

Nonplussed (2), indoctrinated (5), stigma (6), chaste (6), zealous (6), doggedly (7), paradoxically (9)

Long Live High School Rebels

BY THOMAS FRENCH

1   Ten years ago I was in high school. It was the most absurd and savage place I have ever been.

2   To listen to the morning announcements, you'd have thought the most pressing crisis in the world was our student body's lack of school spirit. Seniors were grabbing freshmen, dragging them into the bathrooms and dunking their heads in the toilets—a ritual called "flushing." Basketball players were treated like royalty; smart kids were treated like peasants. And the administrators worshipped the word "immature." Inevitably, they pronounced it "imma-tour." Inevitably, they used it to describe us.

3   The principal and his assistants told us to act like adults, but they treated us like children. Stupid children. They told us what we could wear, when we could move, how close we could stand to our girlfriends, how fast we could walk to lunch and what topics were forbidden to write about in our school newspaper.

4   When I went out for the tennis team, I remember, the coach told me to cut my hair. It was down to my shoulders and looked terrible, but I loved it. I asked the coach what was the point. Just do it, he said.

5   If we were taught anything, it was that high school is not about learning but about keeping quiet. The easiest way to graduate was to do what you were told, all of what you were told, and nothing but what you were told. Most of us did just that. I smiled at the principal, stayed out of trouble, avoided writing articles critical of the administration, asked only a few smart-alecky questions and cut my hair as ordered. I was so embarrassed afterwards that I wore a blue ski cap all day every day for weeks.

6   I admit to some lingering bitterness over the whole affair. I'd still like to know, for one thing, what the length of my hair had to do with my forehand. Maybe that's why, to this day, I almost always root for high school students when they clash intelligently with administrators. High school needs a good dose of dissension. If you've been there in recent years, and I have because I work with student newspapers around Pinellas County, you'd know it needs dissension more than ever.

7   A reminder of this came with the news that one day last month an assistant principal at St. Petersburg High was rummaging through a student's car in a school parking lot. When the assistant principal found three empty wine-cooler bottles and what was suspected to be some spiked eggnog inside the car, the student was suspended for five days.

8   Though the student has argued that the search was an unconstitutional violation of his rights, the incident should not have come as any huge surprise. High school officials around this country have been searching through kids' cars and lockers for some time. One day a couple of years ago, a teacher tells me, officials at Lakewood High allowed police to search for drugs with dogs. At the time, students were gathered at an assembly on God and patriotism.

9   Searches tell students plainly enough what administrators think of them. But in this county, such incidents are only part of a larger tradition of control. Some memorable moments over the years:

10 ■ In 1983, a group of boys at Lakewood High decided it was unfair that they weren't allowed to wear shorts to school but that girls were allowed to wear miniskirts. The rationale for the rule was shorts—but not miniskirts—were too "distracting." To make fun of the rule, the boys began wearing miniskirts to school.

11   Administrators laughed at first, but once the rebellion began attracting publicity, the principal suspended the ringleader. When dozens of students staged further protest in front of the school and refused to go to class, the principal suspended 37 of them, too. Later, although close to 1,400 signatures were gathered on a petition against the rule, the Pinellas County School Board bore down and decided to ban shorts from all middle and high schools. Miniskirts, however, were still allowed.

12   "We need to set a moral standard for our children," explained board member Gerald Castellanos.

13 ■ Last year, William Grey, the principal of St. Petersburg High, suspended a ninth-grader who dyed her hair purple. "I just don't think school is the place for multi-colored heads," Grey said. He did acknowledge that he allowed students to dye their hair green for special events—the school's colors are green and white—but he insisted that was different because it was "promoting school spirit."

14 ■ Earlier this year at Pinellas Park High, two of the school's top students—they're number one and two in their class academically—were criticized by the principal when they wrote articles in the student newspaper pointing out that many of the school's students are sexually active and do not use birth control. I was working with the staff that year, and I know the two students wrote the articles in an effort to prevent teen-age pregnancies. But the principal called their work irresponsible—he disagreed with their methodology—and told the newspaper staff it should write more "positive" articles.

15 ■ This fall, says a teacher at Pinellas Park, the administration cracked down on cafeteria infractions by warning that anyone caught leaving a lunch tray on a table would be suspended.

16 ■ Last year, 16-year-old Manny Sferios and a group of other students from public and private high schools put together an underground magazine called *Not For Profit* and distributed several issues to students around the county. The magazine ridiculed apartheid, protested the proliferation of nuclear weapons and tried to prod students into thinking about something more than their next pair of designer jeans.

17   *Not For Profit* also contained a variety of swear words and ridiculed the small-mindedness of many school officials, and when administrators saw it, they began confiscating copies from kids and warning that those caught with the publication risked suspension.

18   Though the officials said their main objection to *Not For Profit* was its language, the magazine's activist stance also came under fire. Gerald Castellanos, the school board member, said he did not believe students were sophisticated enough to put together such a magazine.

19   "I sincerely sense the hand of some very anti-American, anti-free enterprise types in here," he said. "And I don't believe they're students."

20   Castellanos' attitude was not surprising. Too often the people who run our high schools and sit on our school boards are not prepared to accept or deal with students who think for themselves and stand up for themselves. It would mean a loss of some control, increased resistance to petty rules and a slew of hard questions for those officials who'd rather present a "positive image" than openly confront the real problems in our schools.

21   There are plenty of real problems that need confronting. Alcohol. Drugs. Broken families. Teen-age pregnancies. Not to mention what's happening in some of our classrooms.

22   While working on an article published earlier this year, I sat in a couple of classes at St. Petersburg High—the school run by William Grey, the principal who took a stand on purple hair—and what I saw were rows and rows of kids who were bored beyond description. They were trading jokes while the teachers tried to speak. They were literally falling asleep at their desks. One boy who had no interest in the subject matter—it was American history, by the way—was allowed to get up and leave. Another sat in his seat, strumming his finger across his lips, making baby noises.

23   Dealing with apathy as deep as this is challenge enough for anyone. It requires more teachers, more money, inspiration, real change—all of which are hard to come by. Throw that in with the other problems in our high schools, and the task becomes monumental.

24   I'm not saying that administrators aren't trying to cope with that task. I know they are. But frequently they waste time and distance themselves from students by exerting their authority in other ways. Make sure the kids don't wear shorts. See to it they put away their lunch trays. Bring in the dogs every once in a while and let them sniff around the lockers. In the face of everything

else, keep the school quiet. It's a way the adults tell themselves they're in charge. It's a way they tell themselves they're making a difference.

25   In the meantime, the ideas that our high schools should promote—freedom of thought and expression, for one—get shoved aside. And the students whom we should be encouraging—the ones who have the brains and spirit to start their own magazine, to protest silly rules, to ask what the color of one's hair has to do with an education—are lectured, suspended and told to get back in line.

26   Kids know it stinks. Once in a while, they find the guts to step forward and say so, even if it means getting in trouble. I think they should do it more often. Because if there's anything I regret about my own days in high school, it's that more of us didn't fight against the absurdity with every ounce of adolescent ingenuity and irreverence we had.

27   We should have commandeered the p.a. system one morning and read aloud from Thoreau's *Civil Disobedience*. We should have boycotted the food in the cafeteria for a solid week. We should have sent a note home to the principal's parents informing them he was suspended until he grew up. We should have boned up on our rights in a law library and published what we found in the school paper. And every time an adult said "imma-tour," we should have pulled kazoos out of our pockets and blown on them to our heart's content.

QUESTIONS FOR DISCUSSION

1. What is the topic of the essay? What is the essay's thesis? Where is it located?

2. How is the essay's thesis supported? What are the main points of support, and what evidence is provided for each point?

3. What sources does French draw on in the essay for his support? How credible are they?

4. Analyze the opening and conclusion of the essay. What is accomplished in each? What effect(s) do they have on you?

5. What audience might the essay be intended for? What is French's purpose for writing the essay? How well is the purpose accomplished?

6. How does your high school experience compare to the experiences provided in the essay? What specific examples can you recall?

7. Do you agree with the essay's thesis? Why?

VOCABULARY

Inevitably (2), dissension (6), methodology (14), apartheid (16), proliferation (16), monumental (23), irreverence (26)

Drawing Conclusions

Writers often help readers make decisions on topics that interest them: whom to vote for, where to vacation, what kind of car to buy, when to plant bulbs, what movie to see. As a writer, you help readers understand their options and make decisions based on the information you present.

A valuable writing skill is learning to draw reasonable conclusions from the information you present to readers. For example, if you compare three or four midpriced cars in a paper, readers will be interested in your conclusion: which car you might recommend. Drawing conclusions involves weighing different factors (such as price, performance, looks, durability) and making a decision based on your best judgment.

The emphasis in this unit is on making comparisons and drawing conclusions in your writing that will help readers make decisions. Obviously, the more knowledgeable you are about your writing topic, the more readers can rely on your information and the conclusions you draw from it.

Prewriting

Making comparisons and drawing conclusions are common experiences for most people: we make decisions every day on what to wear, where to eat dinner, what to watch on television, whom to vote for, what pair of tennis shoes to buy. In this unit, you transfer this experience to your writing to help other people make similar decisions.

TOPIC SELECTION

To select your writing topic for the unit, consider these suggestions:

1. What subject areas am I most knowledgeable in? Cars? Sports? Music equipment? Computer programs? Politics? Clothes?

2. What, specifically, could I compare in a particular area that might help readers make a decision or judgment? Different majors? Different teachers teaching the same course? Different stereo systems? Different colleges? Different pro basketball centers? Different college football programs? Different cars? Different clothing stores? Different living situations? Different politicians running for office?

3. What specific subjects would I compare within my topic? What three or four restaurants? What brands of jogging shoes? What specific colleges? What specific instructors? What specific stores? What brands of stereos? What specific word processing programs? What specific economy cars? What specific ways of cooking chicken?

4. What would my purpose be in making this particular comparison? To help readers decide what to buy? where to shop? where to enroll? where to work? what teacher or course to take? what to believe? what course of action to take? where to eat?

5. Who would I write the comparison for? What group of readers would be most interested in it? What group of readers would probably be less knowledgeable than I am about the subject?

Topic Selection Activity 4.1

Applying the suggestions just presented, select a topic for your comparison paper. Take your time and come up with a topic that interests you and that would interest some group of readers. Also decide what specific subjects you want to compare within your topic.

STUDENT TOPIC SELECTION

What shall I compare? I know a lot about car stereos. I've owned enough of them, and I could compare two or three different brands that people might consider buying. This might interest readers who own cars and are into music. I've taken three different math teachers at the college, and they are very different. I could compare them for other students so they would know what to expect when they had them. This might interest freshmen who have their math ahead of them.

I could compare college to high school because they are very different, but I'm not sure what my purpose would be. Students can find that out for themselves. I could compare two or three movies that I've seen recently and recommend them to people who haven't seen them, but that could be pretty hard. The movies were so different. What about comparing dorms and apartments? I've lived in both places. That doesn't sound too exciting to write about though.

I keep going back to my first topic: comparing car stereos. That topic interests me, and I know there are always people who are shopping for car stereo systems.

TOPIC	Comparing three brands of car stereo systems (Alpine, Pioneer, Sanyo)
AUDIENCE	Anyone interested in buying a car stereo
PURPOSE	Help readers decide on the best car stereo to buy

WRITING CRITERIA

When you make comparisons and draw conclusions, you consciously or unconsciously apply some *criteria* on which to judge your subjects. You base your criteria on what you feel is most important in forming a judgment.

For example, if you were considering different options in buying a house someday, your criteria might be the following:

cost

size

location

building quality

The house you ultimately select would probably meet your expectations in these four crucial areas better than the houses you compared it to. Without using such criteria to judge the houses, you might end up with a house that is overpriced, badly constructed, oversized for your needs, or in a neighborhood where home values are dropping.

To establish criteria for comparing the subjects in your paper, follow these guidelines:

1. Your criteria are the critical areas of comparison that readers should consider. For example, in comparing used pianos, your criteria might include price, brand, condition, touch, and tone. In comparing breeds of dogs, your criteria might include price, looks, temperament, size, and sex.

2. For your criteria, select a few major areas of comparison that you can cover in a paper. For example, in buying a house, there might be thirty different factors a couple could compare, but you couldn't cover them all

in a paper. Focus on the primary factors that would be most critical to readers in forming a judgment.

3. All criteria may not be of equal weight. For example, some people are willing to spend a little extra or give up some back seat space for a Honda Prelude that they love the looks of. Consider the relative value of your criteria before you write.

Criteria Activity 4.2

Applying the suggestions for criteria selection, come up with criteria for comparing the subjects of your paper by doing the following:

1. Select three to five critical areas of comparison that readers should consider before making a decision or judgment.

2. Consider the relative value of each criterion. Are some more important than others? Should some receive more emphasis in your paper?

3. Spend some time evaluating your subjects in each area of comparison. For example, let's say your topic is jogging shoes, and your subjects are Nike, Adidas, and Reebok jogging shoes. If your criteria are looks, comfort, durability, and price, evaluate Nike in each of those four areas, and then do the same with Adidas and Reebok. This will help prepare you for writing your first draft.

4. Based on your evaluation, what conclusion(s) might you draw for readers to help them make a decision or judgment? That Reebok jogging shoes are the best buy for their money? That Hakeem Olajuwon is the best NBA center, but because of his young age, Shaquille O'Neal may become even better? That apartment living is superior to dormitory living, if you can affort it? That ice plant is the most durable and colorful ground cover for warm weather climates? That Burger King gives you the best hamburger, coke, and fries for the money?

STUDENT CRITERIA

TOPIC   Car stereo systems

SUBJECTS OF   Alpine, Pioneer, and Sanyo systems
COMPARISON

CRITERIA   quality of sound
                          price
                          features
                          warranty

CONCLUSION   For a good quality stereo that you can afford, the Pioneer pullout with cassette and CD player is the best buy for your money.

First Drafts

After selecting a writing topic, deciding on the subjects to compare and the areas of comparison (criteria), and evaluating each subject in each area, you are ready to write your first draft. Keep the following suggestions in mind.

DRAFTING GUIDELINES

1. Include an opening, middle, and ending to your paper as you did in the previous unit. In the opening, introduce your topic in a way that allows readers to understand your purpose: to help them make a particular decision or judgment regarding the topic. In the middle, compare your subjects in the areas you have selected for comparison. In the ending, draw your conclusion for readers: what you would recommend based on the comparative information.

2. Organize your comparison either by comparing your subjects within one area at a time (how Alpine, Pioneer, and Sanyo stereos compare in sound; how they compare in price; how they compare in features, and so on), or by evaluating one subject at a time in all areas (how Alpine fares regarding sound, price, features, quality; how Pioneer fares regarding sound, price, features, quality; how Sanyo fares regarding sound, price, features, quality).

3. Draw your conclusion for readers based on the comparative information you provide in the middle paragraphs. You might draw an *unqualified* conclusion—meaning you would recommend the same choice to all readers:

    No one can go wrong in taking Mr. Allen for Calculus I at Kings College.

    The best place to buy boots in Clovis is Western Wear.

    You might draw a *qualified* conclusion—giving readers choices based on their means and needs:

    If you are a math major, take Mr. Allen's Calculus I class, but if you are a nonmajor filling a requirement, take Dr. Fillmore.

    If money is no object, buy your boots at Western Wear. If you are on a tight budget, go across the street to Boot World.

4. Keep your purpose in mind as you write: to present the best comparative information and to draw the best conclusion for readers so they can make a wise decision or judgment.

Drafting Activity 4.3

Write the first draft of your paper with the suggestions just presented in mind. You may want to read the following student draft before you begin.

Car Stereo Systems

If you are in the market for a car stereo, there are a lot of options available. I've put in a few systems myself over the years, and basically you get what you pay for. However, there are some good buys out there, depending on what your particular needs are.

Three car stereo brands that represent the high-price to low-price range are Alpine, Pioneer, and Sanyo. Nakamichi ranks with Alpine in the high range; Kenwood, Panasonic, and Sony are in the medium range with Pioneer; and Kraco, Craig, and Realistic join Sanyo in the lower-priced range.

In sound quality, there's not much difference between Alpine and Pioneer. Their frequency response, sound/noise ratio, and dynamic range are similar. If I listened to one and then the other using the same speakers, I couldn't tell which was which. The Sanyo, however, and its lower-priced cousins, don't sound as good. You get more noise with them as the volume increases, and their sound range isn't as great as the others.

In terms of features, all of the stereos offer cassette decks and CD player. Digital display and programming are standard on the Alpine and Pioneer, but not on the Sanyo. Alpine and Pioneer also offer pull-out models, remote control, and channel memory, not available with Sanyo and other cheaper brands.

The warranty on the different brands has to do with the quality of components and construction. As might be expected, the Alpine has the longest warranty of three years on parts and service while the Pioneer has a one-year parts-and-service warranty and Sanyo a 90 day to one year parts-only warranty. Clearly, the Alpine is better constructed, whereas the Pioneer and Sanyo are not going to hold up as well for as long a time.

The prices on the three models differ considerably. The Alpine models are priced from $500 to $1,500, Pioneer from $200 to $500, and Sanyo from $50 to $200. The range of prices within each brand reflects the different quality of models each offers. A $1,500 Alpine model would represent a state-of-the-art stereo of the finest craftsmanship, highest quality components, and the optimal number of features.

If I had money to burn, it would be great to have the $1,500 Alpine, knowing I've got about the best car stereo money can buy. However, not many people I know can afford one. For the money, I believe the best buy would be a midpriced brand like the Pioneer pull-out model with cassette and CD player, which you could get for under $300. You'd have good quality sound, the option to use tapes or CDs, and the security of being able to remove your stereo when you're parked. You could get the Pioneer even cheaper if you went with just a cassette or CD player and without the pull-out feature, if security isn't a problem.

Personally, I wouldn't recommend one of the lower-priced stereos like the Sanyo unless you aren't going to be in your car much or you really don't care about the quality of sound. Given the short warranty and lack of quality construction, you probably aren't going to be better off financially in the long run than if you'd bought a midpriced stereo.

Finally, whatever you decide on, I'd recommend shopping around and looking for a good sale. Sale prices are more common on the midpriced stereos since people who buy the more expensive ones aren't that price conscious and the cheaper stereos don't have much of a profit margin to discount. The only other consideration is whether you buy an American or foreign brand stereo—both are available at every price range—and that's an individual choice. Happy shopping.

Revisions

During the revision process, you look at your paper through "new" eyes to evaluate what you've done well and what you might do better. Though you may write your first draft with little thought to readers, you evaluate and revise the draft with one underlying concern: how your readers will respond to every word, sentence, and paragraph you have written. The shift in emphasis from first to second draft is from getting your ideas on paper to presenting them most effectively to your readers.

REVISION GUIDELINES

As you read and evaluate your draft, consider these suggestions:

1. Evaluate the strength of your opening. Have you introduced your topic in an interesting way? Do readers know you are writing a comparison that may eventually help them make a decision?

2. Evaluate the effectiveness of your comparisons. Can readers clearly see the differences (and similarities) among subjects in the important areas of comparison? Have you evaluated each subject in each area? Does your organization help readers follow the comparisons easily?

3. Evaluate your ending. Do you draw a clear conclusion for readers based on your comparative information and on what you think is the wisest advice? Have you drawn a qualified (one recommendation for everyone) or unqualified (choices based on readers' situation) conclusion, and does it make the most sense for your topic and readers?

4. Have you paragraphed your paper so that your opening, your areas of comparison, and your conclusion stand out for readers? Have you avoided extremely long or short paragraphs? Have you used *transitions* to tie your sentences and paragraphs together? (See the upcoming section "Transitions.")

5. Read each sentence carefully to see how you might make it clearer, tighter, smoother, or more concrete (visual). Check to see if you have

varied your sentence structures, joining words, and sentence lengths. (See the review sections on sentence revision later in the unit.)

Revision Activity 4.4

With a partner, read and evaluate the following first draft by applying the revision suggestions just presented. Then evaluate your own draft similarly, noting revisions you may want to make. (Your instructor may have you cover the upcoming sections on transitions and sentence revision before evaluating your draft.) If you'd like a second opinion, exchange drafts with a classmate.

When you are ready, write your second draft, including all revisions you have noted for improving its content, organization, and wording.

Dorms and Apartments

STUDENT FIRST DRAFT

The first semester of college, I lived in the dorms. The next semester I moved out into an apartment with a friend. I've lived in the dorms, and I've lived in apartments.

Dormitories are definitely cheaper than apartments. When you pay for a dorm room, you pay for an entire semester including your room, three meals a day, and laundry service. You get five months of room and board for about $1,000, or about $200 a month. Apartment living is much more expensive. You also have a lot more room in apartments. You have a living room, a kitchen, a couple of bedrooms, and a bathroom. You have more space to move around in and to be by yourself. Dorm space is less. But three paid meals a day really help.

I really enjoy the freedom of apartment living. I can come and go whenever I want to, and I can eat when I want. I'm entirely on my own. In the dorms, I had to be in at curfew, I had to eat each meal at a certain time, and I was watched by a dorm attendant who acted like a warden. The dorms were like a minimum security prison. And the dorm rooms were really small—a twelve-foot-by-twelve-foot cell.

I also prefer the quiet and privacy of apartment life. In the dorms, people stream in and out of the rooms constantly. There is no privacy. And it's always noisy because of the small rooms and thin walls. Sometimes it feels like living with one hundred girls in one big room. You also have to share a bathroom and shower at the end of the hall with twenty others. If you want privacy or quiet, you have to go elsewhere. An apartment is sure different.

All in all, the dorms and apartments both have their good points and their bad points. Which would you choose? I think I'll take the dorms.

PARAGRAPH TRANSITIONS

Writers use a variety of words and phrases to tie their sentences and paragraphs together effectively. A catch-all term for such wording is *transitions*.

You undoubtedly already use some transitions in your own writing. The purpose of this section is to make you more aware of their value and to introduce the range of options for transitional wording that is available to you.

Useful Transitions

The following transitional words and phrases will be useful for most writing you do.

1. Transitions that show movement in time, place, or sequence: first, second, next, then, after, before, while, now, in the meantime, finally, last.
2. Transitions that connect supporting points, ideas, or examples: first, second, also, another, in addition, additionally, furthermore, moreover.
3. Transitions that show relationships between thoughts: however, therefore, nevertheless, thus, despite, in spite of, on the contrary, on the other hand, for example, for instance, consequently.

Transitions such as *however, therefore, furthermore,* and *nevertheless* are often preceded by a semicolon (;). The semicolon indicates the beginning of a new sentence closely related to the sentence preceding it. When you use a semicolon to separate two sentences, you do *not* capitalize the first letter of the second sentence.

Examples   I need to go Christmas shopping; however, I don't know when I will find time.

Louise is living at home this semester; therefore, she'll save the cost of renting an apartment.

Alicia got an A on her English final; furthermore, she passed biology after two previous attempts.

Felix bowled a score of 23 his first game; nevertheless, he had a good time.

Transition Activity 4.5

Fill in the following paragraphs with transitional words to tie sentences and paragraphs together. Fill each blank with the word or phrase that makes the most appropriate connection. Then check your latest draft for transitional wording.

Example   <u>Before</u> buying a new typewriter, shop around for a used one.

<u>Then</u> look for reasonably priced typing paper.

Buying a used car is a complicated business. _____ , decide the make and year of car you're interested in. _____ look through the newspaper to see what's available. You will find the largest number of cars in the ads for used car lots. _____ , you may find your best buy under the private owner ads since these cars aren't marked up for profits as much as lot cars are. _____ , pick out a few cars that look interesting and spend a day looking at them. Take along pen and paper so you can take notes on each car and make comparisons.

_____ you look at a car, check the odometer for mileage, and confirm that the reading is accurate. The fewer miles on the car, the longer life it will have. _____ check the tires for wear and the body for dents or indications of body work done for accident repair. If the body looks good, the miles are reasonably low, and the tires are safe, take the car for a test drive.

_____ , test the brakes. _____ see how the car handles. Does it veer to the right or left when you release the wheel? Does it vibrate as you increase speed? Does the engine make any suspicious noises? Are there bothersome rattles inside the car? Does everything work: lights, radio, windshield wipers, heater, turn signals? Any combination of negative signs could indicate serious problems for the future. _____ , some problems are easily curable, and if you like the car except for a problem or two, don't completely write it off.

_____ you finish with one car, check out the other cars similarly. _____ compare all the cars to see which one you prefer. You may not like any of them; _____ , you should wait for new cars to surface in the paper and try again instead of settling for a car you don't want.

_____ , if there is a car you are interested in, take one last step. Take the car to a professional mechanic to give it a thorough inspection. For about $30, a mechanic can check it over carefully and test drive it to give you an expert's viewpoint. _____ you have done all you can to ensure you're getting a good car. _____ all your precautions, you may still have some trouble, but you've gone a long way toward buying a reliable used car.

SENTENCE REVISION

For most writers, sentence revision is an important part of the writing process. You revise sentences to help readers understand your ideas better and to achieve the best wording possible. To do this, you might change a word or two in one sentence, move a phrase in another, and completely reword a third.

In this section, you continue to hone your revision skills by working the "bugs" out of first draft sentences. Then you apply what you learn to revising the current draft of your comparison paper.

Wording Problems Review

A big part of draft revision is improving the wording of individual sentences. Not only are you making your sentences more readable in the process, you are also clarifying your ideas for both yourself and your readers.

Revision Review Activity 4.6

The following first draft sentences have problems with wordiness, awkward phrasing, weak word choices, and vagueness. Rewrite each sentence to make it smoother, clearer, and more concise. Then read the first draft of your comparison paper for possible sentence revisions.

Example   When I work this summer at a job, I'm going to save my money for a car that is used.

Revised   When I work this summer, I'm going to save my money for a used car.

1. One person I'll always remember and never forget is a girl named Cloretta.
2. It takes a special person who can deal with the many problems faced daily by an automotive mechanic to be one.
3. I have been learning my boys, two of them, to swim, but they haven't learned yet.
4. My best friend I ever had was not a person that I even liked to begin with.
5. The trees are easy to see if you go through the sidewalk.
6. The tree is full of golden leaves, and there are some leaves that are about to fall and about to announce that fall is almost upon us.
7. When buying a used car, the first thing you do is to find a lot of used cars to look at.
8. The game of golf can be conducted with the whole family in assemblage.
9. She is the type of person whom you can tell secrets to and not worry about spreading of those secrets.
10. In the profession of boxing, the price of successfulness is often physical damage that could last a lifetime or even less.
11. The taillights and turn signals are together, red being the taillights and yellow the turn signals, the taillight above the turn signal.
12. The Volkswagen was a vast growth in Germany in the 1940s.
13. The next step is for you to go over every one of your sentences and try to find different ways that you can improve each one to make better sentences.
14. It was with immense difficulty that we affirmatively located the establishment selling foods of a fried nature.
15. Lonette couldn't find a way that was best for her to study for the biology test that covered over four chapters and over a hundred pages of material.

Sentence Variety

Writers who use a variety of sentence structures express themselves most effectively and create the most readable prose. The more structural options you can draw upon, the better equipped you are to express yourself, and the more readers can appreciate your work.

Relative Clauses

A sentence structure that many writers find useful is the complex sentence with a *relative clause*. A relative clause begins with a relative pronoun—*who, whom, whose, which,* or *that*—that modifies the word that precedes it.

Examples
The man <u>who borrowed your lawn mower</u> moved to Alaska.

Here on the table are the books <u>that you left at my house</u>.

The math problem <u>that Joan had trouble with</u> is puzzling everyone.

The men <u>who own the fruit stand</u> are selling some beautiful nectarines.

That blue Mazda is the car <u>that I'd like to own someday</u>.

Ralph picked the watermelon <u>that was the largest and ripest</u>.

The woman <u>whose money you found</u> lives in Paris.

Hanna's umbrella, <u>which she bought for $30</u>, has a hole in it.

The students <u>who did well on the geology final</u> all studied together.

As you can see, the underlined clauses beginning with *who, which, that,* and *whose* describe or identify the word directly before them. Here is how the relative pronouns are used:

Who	used with *people*	The child <u>who</u> ate the gooseberries got sick.
Whom	used with *people**	The plumber <u>whom</u> you sent to my house was expensive.
Whose	used with *people*	The girl <u>whose</u> book was lost is in the library.
	used with *things*	The textbook <u>whose</u> cover is torn was sold at half price.

---

* *Whom* is used instead of *who* when it is followed by the subject of the clause: The man whom *you* introduced is famous. The speaker whom *we* met was very arrogant. The teacher whom *the students* admire is Ms. Alvarado. When *who* is used, it is the subject of the clause: The man *who* bought our car was from Italy. The girl *who* took your seat doesn't intend to move.

That	used with *people*	The family <u>that</u> lives next door moved.
	used with *things*	The magazine <u>that</u> you subscribe to is terrific.
Which	used with *things*	The "L" Street route, <u>which</u> is lined with trees, is very direct.

Relative Clause Activity 4.7

Complete the following complex sentences with your own words.

Example   The man who lives behind us _____ *mows his lawn at night*

1. The alligator that _____
2. She was the actress who _____
3. The only students who _____
4. Your new toaster, which _____
5. That new teacher whom you _____
6. The rock group that _____
7. I like a hamburger that _____
8. Please return my stamp collection, which _____
9. The kind of dog that _____
10. The movie star whose _____
11. I really prefer a doctor who _____

Relative Clause Activity 4.8

Combine each of the following pairs of sentences to form a single sentence with a relative clause beginning with *who, whom, whose, which,* or *that.*

Example   Maria Gomez works at Bank of America. She lives down the street from me.

Example   Maria Gomez, who works at Bank of America, lives down the street from me.

Revised (option) Maria Gomez, who lives down the street from me, works at Bank of America.

1. The boy sat behind me in Algebra. He dropped the class after two weeks.
2. You took the woman's seat on the bus. She is very mad.
3. The Kings River flooded its banks yesterday. It is often dry this time of year.

4. The foreign students are from Laos and Cambodia. I met them at the student union yesterday.

5. Glen and Elvira are good students. They will do very well in graduate school.

6. *The Congo* by Michael Crichton was an intriguing book. I couldn't put it down.

7. I found a man's wallet at the supermarket yesterday. He gave me a $25 reward.

8. I tried to buy concert tickets from a scalper. They would have cost me $100 apiece.

9. Melissa Guthridge contributes to numerous charities for children. She is very generous with her money.

10. The Bay Bridge is over five miles long. It is the longest bridge in the western United States.

Revision Activity 4.9

Read the first draft of your comparison paper and revise sentences to vary your sentence structures, to replace any overused joining words (such as *and, but, so,* or *because*), to combine short sentences or divide overly long ones, or to combine pairs of sentences by inserting relative clauses.

Final Editing

The last step in the writing process is to give your latest draft a final check for errors. If you are using a computer, print out the draft rather than proof-reading off of the screen. You will often find errors on the printed page that you overlook on the screen.

PROOFREADING GUIDELINES

When you proofread your latest draft, make sure to cover the following areas, and pay particular attention to the kinds of errors you tend to make.

1. Make sure you have a period at the end of each sentence. Check for run-on sentences and comma splices that need periods, and check for sentence fragments that should be attached to the sentences they belong with. (See the upcoming review sections on run-on sentences and fragments.)

2. Check word endings to make sure you have an *s* on plural words and an *ed* on regular past tense verbs, and that your subjects and verbs agree. (See the review section on subject-verb agreement later in the unit.)

3. Check your spelling carefully, including homonyms such as there/their/they're, know/no, its/it's, your/you're, and threw/through.

4. Check your internal punctuation, including comma usage in words in series, in compound sentences, after introductory groups of words, and to set off relative clauses, "interrupters," and ending phrases. (See the section a little later on comma usage with relative clauses, interrupters, and ending phrases.) Make sure you have apostrophes in contractions and possessive words (John's dog, the pencil's eraser, the legislature's schedule) and quotation marks around direct quotations. (See the section on possessives in the "Spelling" section of the appendix.)

5. Check your use of subject pronouns (Martha and I; my mother, father, and I; Gretchen and she; the Joneses and they), and make sure all pronouns agree with their antecedents. (Covered under "Correct Usage" later in the unit.)

Proofreading Activity 4.10

Proofread your latest draft for errors following the revision guidelines presented. (Your instructor may have you cover the upcoming sections on punctuation and grammar before proofreading.) Correct any remaining errors, and then write or print out your final draft to share with classmates, your instructor, and members of your specified reading audience.

SENTENCE PROBLEMS

The most common sentence problems—run-on sentences, comma splices, and fragments—have been introduced in earlier units. However, for students who have recurring problems, they will be reviewed in this section and throughout the text. You seldom eliminate a longtime error tendency after a brief lesson or two, but by working on it throughout the text, you can make great progress.

Run-on Sentence Review Activity 4.11

The following passage contains some run-on sentences and comma splices. Rewrite the passage and correct the run-on sentences by separating complete sentences or joining them with coordinate or subordinate conjunctions. Separate longer sentences and join shorter, related sentences.

Example   The teachers were upset. They had received no raise for three years they decided not to return to school in the fall without a decent contract.

Revised	The teachers were upset. They had received no raise for three years, so they decided not to return to school in the fall without a decent contract.

Joe was placed in the state penitentiary, he had served time in other places. His first trouble came in grade school. He was caught sniffing glue. He stayed in detention for a night his parents refused to pick him up until morning. Six months later he was back in juvy for stabbing a boy in the shoulder with an ice pick. He got into three more fights with inmates while in detention, he was finally released, his parents had split up neither of them wanted Joe. He was sent to live with an aunt in Grace Falls. He kept out of trouble for over a year until he got involved with some older men. They robbed a liquor store, he drove the car, later they had him delivering drugs because he was a minor. He finally got caught and was sent to detention for two more years. When he got out, he ran away and melted into the street life of the city. His aunt didn't hear about him for two years until she got a call that he had been arrested for assaulting a junkie. He was a month over eighteen, so when he was convicted, he was sent to the state penitentiary, no one from his family visited him.

Fragments

As you learned in Unit 3, fragments are caused by separating a clause from the sentence it belongs with or by leaving out words that would complete the sentence.

Example	I'm very tired this morning. Because I only got three hours of sleep last night.
Corrected	I'm very tired this morning because I only got three hours of sleep last night. (because *fragment joined to sentence it belongs with*)
Example	Walking to school this morning in the driving rain.
Corrected	I was miserable walking to school this morning in the driving rain. (*words added to form complete sentence*)

Fragments are most commonly created through punctuation errors and can be remedied by eliminating the period that separates them from the sentence they belong with.

Fragment Review Activity 4.12

Each of the following groups of sentences contains one fragment. Correct the fragment by adding it to the sentence that it belongs with.

Example	Joe was late for work. Since others were also late. Joe had no problem.

Revised   Joe was late for work. Since others were also late, Joe had no problem.

1. People are traveling more. Because gas prices aren't increasing. Hopefully, prices won't go up this summer.

2. Before you buy a car at Happy Harry's. Check it out carefully. He sells some real junk.

3. A nuclear accident is always possible. Unless nuclear energy plants are dismantled. Environmental groups continue to protest their existence.

4. Clean out your closet. When you finish. Give me the shirts you've outgrown.

5. The crowds used to be sparse at Minneapolis stadium. People are returning in large numbers. Because the Twins have started winning again.

6. Although the current recession is tough. It doesn't compare to the Great Depression. Ask people who have been through both.

7. Hanna is trusting. Because she believes in people. Her brother is the suspicious one.

8. Thanks for the great breakfast. Before I leave. Can I do the dishes for you?

9. The trip is on. Unless it snows. We'll go if it rains.

10. The choir practiced for hours. They sang the <u>Messiah</u> five times. Before they had finished for the night.

PUNCTUATION

Earlier units introduced the three most common situations for using commas: within series of words, before conjunctions in compound sentences, and after introductory groups of words. In this section, you learn three new uses for commas: to set off relative clauses (which were introduced earlier in this unit), interrupters, and ending phrases.

Comma Usage

Add the following rules for comma usage to the ones you are already using.

1. *Relative clauses:* To punctuate relative clauses correctly, follow these basic rules:

   a. If the word modified by a *who* or *which* clause is clearly named or identified, the clause is set off by commas.

   Mary Garcia, <u>who owns the dress shop on "G" Street</u>, is my neighbor. *(Mary Garcia clearly names the person.)*

   The Golden Gate Bridge, <u>which spans San Francisco Bay</u>, is painted annually. *(*Golden Gate Bridge *clearly names the bridge.)*

The new fish market on Oliver Avenue, <u>which opened its doors last Friday</u>, specializes in shellfish. *(*New fish market on Oliver Avenue *clearly identifies the market.)*

Matt Golden, <u>who drives a milk truck</u>, married Emma Blue, <u>who lives on his route</u>. *(*Matt Golden *and* Emma Blue *clearly name the people.)*

b. If a *who* or *which* clause is needed to identify clearly the word it modifies, don't set it off with commas.

The men <u>who work for my aunt</u> live in Trenton. *(*Who work for my aunt *identifies the men.)*

The directions <u>which you gave us</u> were easy to follow. *(*Which you gave us *identifies the directions.)*

I'd like to meet the woman <u>who painted that strange picture</u>. *(*Who painted that strange picture *identifies the woman.)*

c. Never use commas with relative clauses beginning with *that.*

The students <u>that sit in back of the room</u> are very talkative.

I'd like to see the watermelon <u>that weighs over fifty pounds</u>.

2. *Interrupters:* Set off incidental words and phrases that require reading pauses in a sentence.

<u>By the way</u>, what time are you going to class today?

I am interested, <u>of course</u>, in getting a good grade and in learning a lot about physics.

<u>Fortunately</u>, I did a lot of scuba diving before diving off the coast of Australia.

My father, <u>as you might know</u>, works with your father at the Lockheed Aircraft plant.

3. *Ending phrases:* To indicate a reading pause, insert a comma before an ending group of words that begins with an *ing*-word or the word *especially* or *particularly.*

Leticia sped through the multiple choice half of her physics test, knowing that the thought problems in the second half would take a lot of time.

Jonathan walked home disappointedly from the Department of Motor Vehicles, wondering if he would ever pass his driving test.

Washington D.C. is beautiful in the spring, especially when the cherry blossoms are in bloom.

Shop at Martin's Boutique for floral arrangements, particularly if you like silk flowers.

Comma Activity 4.13

Place commas in the following sentences according to all the rules you have learned. Some sentences won't require commas. When you finish, proofread your latest draft for correct comma placement.

Example In the early morning hours Mary prowls the house and waits for dawn to break.

Revised In the early morning hours, Mary prowls the house and waits for dawn to break. *(comma after introductory phrase)*

1. John and Henrietta decided to jog to school and back three times a week.

2. John Helen and Henrietta decided to jog to school and they later decided to jog back home as well.

3. Before you try the cornflakes in the cupboard check the packaging date on the box and see how old they are.

4. Samantha really enjoys playing strange characters in plays because the parts are so different from her personality.

5. After Gladys fixed the radiator hose on her Plymouth the fan belt and the smaller radiator hose broke.

6. Working on his stamp collection and watching old "Cisco Kid" reruns on TV are Albert's pastimes and he ignores everything else around him for weeks at a time.

7. For the week-long field trip to Death Valley we'll need picks and shovels tents and cots food and water and heavy jackets.

8. Harvey left third base at the crack of the bat and raced for home plate well ahead of the ball.

9. From the looks of that cut on your head and your bruised knees you'd better see a doctor and do it fast!

10. Louise and Mavis invited Teddie and Rumford to the Lucky Horseshoe Casino and then didn't show up.

11. If I had a dime for every time you had an excuse for being late for work I could retire early and live like a king.

12. Allyson thought about attending Mumsford College and even sent in an application but at the last minute she decided to attend a business college.

13. Rex Garcia who was born in Santa Fe, New Mexico is now the mayor of his hometown.

14. When I returned to my apartment I found Marian Weber an old high school friend waiting for me outside.

15. I wanted to sit in a floor seat at the Tina Turner concert but since all floor seat tickets are sold I'll settle for a balcony seat which costs $15.

16. My uncle by the way knows your family well.

17. I'm not interested in going to the debate especially since it doesn't start until 10:00 p.m.

18. Pao didn't worry about the language entrance exam knowing he could take it again before school started.

19. You'll have no trouble finding the library which is the only round building on campus.

20. Incidentally do you know who our new neighbors are?

CORRECT USAGE

Standard English follows basic rules of grammar that govern the way we write and talk. Such rules make it possible for people to communicate effectively anywhere in the world where English is spoken. Knowledge of these rules and their practical application to writing and speaking is essential to our functioning effectively within the world of educated people.

In this section you are introduced to a new area of grammar—pronoun-antecedent agreement—and you review what you learned about subject-verb agreement in Unit 3. Understanding and applying rules of agreement are fundamental to writing correctly.

Pronoun-Antecedent Agreement

Pronouns replace words that don't need repeating in a sentence or paragraph. To use pronouns most effectively, follow these basic conventions:

1. Replace a word with a pronoun instead of repeating the word unnecessarily.

Awkward   The building lost the building's roof in the tornado.

Better   The building lost its roof in the tornado.

Awkward   Betty was going to be late for class, so Betty called her teacher.

Better   Betty was going to be late for class, so she called her teacher.

2. A pronoun agrees in number and gender with the word it replaces: its *antecedent*. For example, if an antecedent is singular and female (Betty), the pronouns replacing it must be singular and female (she, her, hers). In the following examples, the antecedent is underlined twice; the pronoun replacing it is underlined once.

Examples   A student in dental assisting must take twelve units of science if she wants to get a degree. *(The antecedent* student *is singular, so the pronoun* she *referring to* student *is also singular.)*

One of the boys is missing his watch. *(The antecedent* one *is singular, so the pronoun* his *referring to* one *is also singular.)*

Women should never downgrade their abilities. *(The antecedent* women *is plural, so the pronoun* their *referring to* women *is also plural.)*

Jays are beautiful birds. They are a brilliant blue color in winter. *(The antecedent* jays *is plural, so the pronoun* they *referring to* jays *is also plural, even if it is in a different sentence.)*

3. The following pronoun forms agree with the following antecedents:
    a. singular female antecedent (woman, Barbara): she, her, hers, herself
    b. singular male antecedent (man, Roscoe): he, him, his, himself
    c. singular genderless antecedent (book, desk): it, its, itself
    d. singular male/female antecedent (a person, a student, one): he or she, his or her, himself or herself
    e. plural female antecedent (girls, women): they, them, their, theirs, themselves
    f. plural male antecedent (boys, men): they, them, their, theirs, themselves
    g. plural genderless antecedent (trees, boxes): they, them, their, theirs, themselves
    h. others + yourself (John and I, the class and I): we, our, ours, ourselves
    i. person spoken to ("Mary," "Felix"): you, your, yours, yourself
    j. yourself: I, me, my, mine, myself

The following sentences show a variety of pronoun-antecedent agreement situations (the pronoun is underlined, and an arrow is drawn to the antecedent)

Rita lost her wallet, and she had twelve credit cards in it.

A twenty-dolar bill is lying on the kitchen table, and it had been there for a week.

Jack, Jonathan, and Sylvester all took their SAT tests last Saturday.

Marian and I always take our dirty clothes to the dormitory laundry service.

Clyde doesn't believe that he can maintain his current 3.4 GPA.

Thelma, you look stunning in your pink taffeta dress.

The students all took their compasses with them on the backpacking trip.

A student should always lock his or her car when it's in the parking lot.

Pronoun-Antecedent Activity 4.14

Substitute an appropriate pronoun for each word that is repeated unnecessarily in the following sentences, making sure that the pronoun agrees with its antecedent.

Example   Mary brought Mary's baby brother with Mary to class Monday.

Revised   Mary brought her baby brother with her to class Monday.

1. That building should have been torn down years ago. That building is a terrible fire hazard.

2. Gretchen used to weigh over 190 pounds, but now Gretchen is down to 130.

3. Marian and I used to shop at Macy's, but Marian and I don't shop there anymore.

4. The teachers at the high school are getting old, and the teachers seem bored with the teachers' jobs. A lot of the teachers should retire.

5. That blister on your heel looks sore, and that blister is going to get worse if you don't put medication on that blister.

6. Thelma should do Thelma a favor and get some sleep for a change.

7. John and I don't consider John and me close friends, but John and I do share a lot of interests.

8. My English book got my English book's cover torn off of my English book. Now my English book's pages are starting to come unbound.

9. The new movie playing at the Bijou is frightening. The new movie involves deranged killers on the loose on a college campus, and the college campus looks a lot like Hillcrest Community College.

10. Small earthquakes hit the valley a number of times last month, and although the small earthquakes caused little damage, the small earthquakes kept all of the neighbors on edge. Some of the neighbors are thinking about moving.

Indefinite Pronouns

Indefinite pronouns can cause agreement problems. They are always considered *singular* and therefore always require *singular* pronoun references:

anybody	everybody	nothing
anyone	everyone	one
each	everything	somebody
either	nobody	someone
every	no one	something

The following examples of pronoun-antecedent agreement involve indefinite pronouns. This is the most troublesome agreement situation because the incorrect plural pronoun references don't *sound* wrong to many people. Here are the correct and incorrect forms:

Examples

Incorrect   Everyone should bring <u>their</u> books to the room.

Correct	Everyone should bring <u>his or her</u> books to the room.
Incorrect	Each person should finish <u>their</u> homework before taking a break.
Correct	Each person should finish <u>his or her</u> homework before taking a break.
Incorrect	No one did <u>their</u> best in the marathon because of the oppressive heat.
Correct	No one did <u>his or her</u> best in the marathon because of the oppressive heat.
Incorrect	Somebody must have completed <u>their</u> art project before the contest deadline.
Correct	Somebody must have completed <u>his or her</u> art project before the contest deadline.

Pronoun-Antecedent Activity 4.15

Fill in the blanks in the following sentences with pronouns that agree with their antecedents. Circle the antecedent for each pronoun. When you finish, proofread your latest draft for pronoun-antecedent agreement.

Example   The (mind) can snap if too much stress is placed on _it_ .

1. The opossum hangs upside down beside _____ mate.
2. The man who won the canned hams should bring _____ car to the alley.
3. Each of the women works for _____ room and board.
4. A woman from the Bronx left _____ purse in a Manhattan theatre.
5. One of the trucks lost _____ brakes. _____ careened downhill.
6. Those bags she carries weigh a ton, and _____ are huge.
7. Pronouns should always agree in number with _____ antecedents.
8. A person should never press _____ luck.
9. Every one of the politicians made a promise that _____ couldn't keep.
10. The geraniums are losing _____ flowers very early.
11. John told me that it didn't matter to his instructors if _____ came to class late if _____ homework was completed and _____ maintained an A average on all quizzes.

12. One of the male monkeys in the middle cage kept spitting on _____ sister who shared a swing with _____ .

Writing Review

In the "Writing Review," you apply what you have learned throughout the unit to a second comparison paper. To write your paper, follow the writing process provided, which is a summary of the steps presented in this unit.

WRITING PROCESS

TOPIC SELECTION

1. Write a paper for your classmates comparing two similar subjects: American and Japanese cars, renting or buying a home, leasing or buying an automobile, getting married or living together, attending a four-year or community college, American and foreign students, fast walking or jogging for fitness, dormitory or apartment living, two similar majors (for example, business and business administration), high school and college, high school and college students, two computer programs, college and professional basketball. Answer the following questions to help you decide on your topic:

    a. What topic am I interested in and knowledgeable about?

    b. What topic might be interesting to some of my classmates?

    c. What would my purpose be in writing to them about this topic?

    d. What conclusion might I draw for them based on the comparison?

CRITERIA FOR COMPARISON

2. In what important areas are you going to compare your two subjects? Follow these suggestions:

    a. Come up with four or five areas as your comparative criteria.

    b. Decide in what order you want to compare these areas in your paper.

    c. Evaluate your two subjects in each area before writing.

FIRST DRAFT

3. Write the first draft of your comparison paper following these suggestions:

    a. Include a beginning, middle, and ending to your paper. Introduce your topic in the beginning, make your comparisons in the middle, and draw your conclusion for readers in the ending.

    b. Keep the reading audience—your classmates—in mind as you write, and tell them things that many of them probably don't already know. (In other words, don't just repeat what would be common knowledge for most students.)

    c. Draw a conclusion for readers in the final paragraph(s) based on your comparison.

REVISIONS

4. When you finish your first draft, set it aside for a while before evaluating it. Then read the draft and apply the following revision guidelines. If you want a second opinion, exchange drafts with a classmate. When you are ready, write your second draft, including all revisions for content, organization, and wording improvement.

   a. Evaluate the strength of your opening. Do you introduce your topic in an interesting way? Do readers understand what you are comparing and why? Would they want to read further?

   b. Evaluate the effectiveness of your comparison. Have you compared your subjects in all important areas? Can readers clearly see the differences (and similarities) between subjects? Have you used appropriate details and examples to help readers understand each point of comparison? Have you organized your comparison to help readers follow it clearly?

   c. Evaluate the strength of your conclusion. Does it follow logically from the comparisons you have made? If appropriate, have you given readers the best possible advice for making a decision? Is your conclusion unqualified (same recommendation for everyone) or qualified (optional recommendations based on differences among readers)?

   d. Check your paragraphing to see if readers can move smoothly through your opening, middle, and conclusion. Do you present your points of comparison in different paragraphs? Are your sentences and paragraphs tied together with appropriate transitional wording? Do you have any extremely long paragraphs that need dividing or short paragraphs that need combining or developing further?

   e. Read each sentence carefully to see if you can improve its smoothness, clarity, or conciseness. Also check to see if you have overrelied on certain sentence structures or joining words, and make revisions to improve sentence variety. Finally, check the lengths of sentences and, when appropriate, combine pairs or groups of very short sentences or divide overly long ones.

EDITING

5. When you have completed all revisions, proofread your paper for any remaining errors by following these guidelines:

   a. Make sure you have a period at the end of each sentence. Check your paper carefully for run-on sentences or comma splices that need punctuating or for sentence fragments that need attaching to the sentences they belong with.

   b. Check word endings to make sure you have an *s* on all plural words and an *ed* on regular past tense verbs, and make sure that your present tense verbs agree with their subjects.

   c. Check your spelling carefully, including your use of homonyms such as there/their/they're, know/no, your/you're, threw/through, it's/its, and right/write.

   d. Check internal punctuation. Have you inserted commas in series of words, before coordinate conjunctions in compound sentences, after introductory groups of words, and to set off relative clauses, interrupters, and ending phrases? Have you used apostrophes (') in contractions and possessive words and quotation marks (" ") with direct quotations?

e. Have you used correct subject pronoun forms with compound subjects? (John and I, my mother and I, Rudy and she, the Joneses and they.) Do your pronouns agree in number and gender with their antecedents? (Everyone invited his or her mother to the graduation. The Smiths brought their children with them to the party.)

FINAL DRAFT

6. When you are ready, write or print out the final draft of your comparison paper and share it with classmates and your instructor.

STUDENT TOPIC SELECTION

I think I'll do some kind of comparison with students. I could compare high school and college students, but the differences seem too obvious. I could compare different types of college students on campus—athletes, aggies, student council members, computer whizzes—but I think I'd end up stereotyping groups since I don't know that much about them.

I have met a number of foreign students from Southeast Asia at school and have gotten to know some of them fairly well. They sure have a different perspective on going to college than most American students I know. I could compare foreign students and American students, or more specifically Asian students and American students. I think I'll give it a try.

Since most American students don't mix much with foreign students, and vice versa, I think my best reading audience would be college students in general. I'm not sure what my purpose would be yet. I'll have to think about it some more.

PREWRITING

TOPIC

Asian and American students

CRITERIA FOR COMPARISON

1. attitude toward going to college
2. reasons for attending
3. difficulties faced
4. pressure to succeed

PURPOSE

Help classmates understand their Asian peers on campus better.

American and Asian Students

STUDENT DRAFT

America may be the great "melting pot," but at this college, not much "melting" has taken place yet with the newest wave of foreign students, most typically Southeast Asians. These students are easily distinguished from their American counterparts, both by the way they stick together on campus and by their relative seriousness. They seem to have a determination that is often lacking in American students.

I've gotten to know a few Asian students, not very well, but at least enough to get beyond "How ya doin'?" One thing I've learned is that they don't take college for granted like Americans. In their countries, like Cambodia, Laos, and Vietnam, college was restricted to the well-to-do, so the opportunity for a college education is a great thing for them. While most Americans take college for granted, many foreign students consider it a rare opportunity that shouldn't be wasted.

Many foreign students are attending college for different reasons than American students. They have come to America with hope but little else. Many are living in overcrowded apartments, their parents eking out a living the best they can. These students realize that their passport out of poverty is a college degree, so they are highly motivated to succeed. Many American students come from relatively comfortable backgrounds, and they feel no urgency to change their living conditions or improve their lives. They want to eventually graduate, but in the meantime, life isn't so bad.

Foreign students are also going through tremendous transitions that American students can't relate to. While they are going to school, they are at the same time learning a new language, adjusting to a different culture, and trying to fit into a foreign society. It is little wonder that they stick together on campus and seem to be quiet and shy.

As my friend Latana said (in broken English), "You're never quite sure how Americans feel about you, so you feel uncomfortable a lot. You don't talk much because you feel you talk very poorly and are afraid of sounding stupid." On the other hand, American students have no such transitions to make. As Latana said, "Foreign students have to learn how to walk and run at the same time. American students have been walking all their lives."

A final difference between American and foreign students is the pressure they feel. With Asian students, according to math professor Dr. Lum Cho, there is first the traditional fear of failing in college and "losing face," causing the family disgrace. Second, there is pressure to succeed and help the family, who is counting on you. Third, there is pressure not to "blow" a great opportunity for an education, perhaps the only opportunity you will have. Most American students feel no such pressures, and without the pressures, they are more relaxed and carefree about school.

The more I get to know a few Asian students on campus, the more I like them. They are bright, funny, and very nice. And now that I've gotten beyond "How ya doin'," I can begin to understand their seriousness, their determination, their shyness, and their sense of isolation in a strange land. They don't have a lot in common with the typical American students of today who take education for granted. They probably have a lot in common with the children of Irish, Italian, and German immigrants who, in the 1920s and 1930s, were sent to college with their families' hopes and blessings. In a way I envy them. For foreign students, the American dream is alive and shimmering in the future.

Readings

Why Johnny Can't Read, but Yoshio Can

BY RICHARD LYNN

1   There can be no doubt that American schools compare poorly with Japanese schools. In the latter, there are no serious problems with poor discipline, violence, or truancy; Japanese children take school seriously and work hard. Japanese educational standards are high, and illiteracy is virtually unknown.

2   The evidence of Japan's high educational standards began to appear as long ago as the 1960s. In 1967 there was published the first of a series of studies of educational standards in a dozen or so economically developed nations, based on tests of carefully drawn representative samples of children. The first study was concerned with achievement in math on the part of 13- and 18-year-olds. In both age groups the Japanese children came out well ahead of their coevals in other countries. The American 13-year-olds came out second to last for their age group; the American 18-year-olds, last. In both age groups, European children scored about halfway between the Japanese and the Americans.

3   Since then, further studies have appeared, covering science as well as math. The pattern of results has always been the same: the Japanese have generally scored first, the Americans last or nearly last, and the Europeans have fallen somewhere in between. In early adolescence, when the first tests are taken, Japanese children are two or three years ahead of American children; by age 18, approximately 98 percent of Japanese children surpass their American counterparts.

4   Meanwhile, under the Reagan Administration, the United States at least started to take notice of the problem. In 1983 the President's report, *A Nation at Risk,* described the state of American schools as a national disaster. A follow-up report issued by the then-secretary of education, Mr. William Bennett, earlier this year claims that although some improvements have been made, these have been "disappointingly slow."

5   An examination of Japan's school system suggests that there are three factors responsible for its success, which might be emulated by other countries: a strong national curriculum, stipulated by the government; strong incentives for students; and the stimulating effects of competition between schools.

6   The national curriculum in Japan is drawn up by the Department of Education. It covers Japanese language and literature, math, science, social science, music, moral education, and physical education. From time to time, the Department of Education requests advice on the content of the curriculum from representatives of the teaching profession, industry, and the trade

unions. Syllabi are then drawn up, setting out in detail the subject matter that has to be taught at each grade. These syllabi are issued to school principals, who are responsible for ensuring that the stipulated curriculum is taught in their schools. Inspectors periodically check that this is being done.

7 The Japanese national curriculum ensures such uniformly high standards of teaching that almost all parents are happy to send their children to the local public school. There is no flight into private schools of the kind that has been taking place in America in recent years. Private schools do exist in Japan, but they are attended by less than 1 percent of children in the age range of compulsory schooling (six to 15 years).

8 This tightly stipulated national curriculum provides a striking contrast with the decentralized curriculum of schools in America. Officially, the curriculum in America is the responsibility of school principals with guidelines from state education officials. In practice, even school principals often have little idea of what is actually being taught in the classroom.

9 America and Britain have been unusual in leaving the curriculum so largely in the hands of teachers. Some form of national curriculum is used throughout Continental Europe, although the syllabus is typically not specified in as much detail as in Japan. And now Britain is changing course: legislation currently going through Parliament will introduce a national curriculum for England and Wales, with the principal subjects being English, math, science, technology, a foreign language, history and geography, and art, music, and design. It is envisioned that the new curriculum will take up approximately 70 percent of teaching time, leaving the remainder free for optional subjects such as a second foreign language, or extra science.

10 Under the terms of the new legislation, schoolchildren are going to be given national tests at the ages of 7, 11, 14, and 16 to ensure that the curriculum has been taught and that children have learned it to a satisfactory standard. When the British national curriculum comes into effect, America will be left as the only major economically developed country without one.

11 To achieve high educational standards in schools it is necessary to have motivated students as well as good teachers. A national curriculum acts as a discipline on teachers, causing them to teach efficiently, but it does nothing to provide incentives for students, an area in which American education is particularly weak.

12 One of the key factors in the Japanese education system is that secondary schooling is split into two stages. At the age of 11 or 12, Japanese children enter junior high school. After three years there, they take competitive entrance examinations for senior high schools. In each locality there is a hierarchy of public esteem for these senior high schools, from the two or three that are regarded as the best in the area, through those considered to be good or average, down to those that (at least by Japanese standards) are considered to be poor.

13 The top schools enjoy national reputations, somewhat akin to the famous English schools such as Eton and Harrow. But in England the high fees

exacted by these schools mean that very few parents can afford them. Consequently there are few candidates for entry, and the entrance examinations offer little incentive to work for the great mass of children. By contrast, in Japan the elite senior high schools are open to everyone. While a good number of these schools are private (approximately 30 percent nationwide, though in some major cities the figure is as high as 50 percent), even these schools are enabled, by government subsidies, to keep their fees within the means of a large proportion of parents. The public schools also charge fees, but these are nominal, amounting to only a few hundred dollars a year, and loans are available to cover both fees and living expenses.

14 Thus children have every expectation of being able to attend the best school they can qualify for; and, hence, the hierarchical rankings of senior high schools act as a powerful incentive for children preparing for the entrance examinations. There is no doubt that Japanese children work hard in response to these incentives. Starting as early as age 10, approximately half of them take extra tutoring on weekends, in the evenings, and in the school holidays at supplementary coaching establishments known as *juku,* and even at that early age they do far more homework than American children. At about the age of 12, Japanese children enter the period of their lives known as *examination hell:* during this time, which lasts fully two years, it is said that those who sleep more than five hours a night have no hope of success, either in school or in life. For, in addition to conferring great social and intellectual status on their students, the elite senior high schools provide a first-rate academic education, which, in turn, normally enables the students to get into one of the elite universities and, eventually, to move into a good job in industry or government.

15 Although Japanese children are permitted to leave school at the age of 15, 94 percent of them proceed voluntarily to the senior high schools. Thus virtually all Japanese are exposed in early adolescence to the powerful incentive for academic work represented by the senior-high-school entrance examinations. There is nothing in the school systems of any of the Western countries resembling this powerful incentive.

16 The prestige of the elite senior high schools is sustained by the extensive publicity they receive from the media. Each year the top hundred or so schools in Japan are ranked on the basis of the percentage of their pupils who obtain entry to the University of Tokyo, Japan's most prestigious university. These rankings are widely reported in the print media, and the positions of the top twenty schools are announced on TV news programs, rather like the scores made by leading sports teams in the United States and Europe. At a local level, more detailed media coverage is devoted to the academic achievements of all the schools in the various localities, this time analyzed in terms of their pupils' success in obtaining entry to the lesser, but still highly regarded, local universities.

17 Thus, once Japanese 15-year-olds have been admitted to their senior high schools, they are confronted with a fresh set of incentives in the form of entrance examinations to universities and colleges, which are likewise hier-

archically ordered in public esteem. After the University of Tokyo, which stands at the apex of the status heirarchy, come the University of Kyoto and ten or so other highly prestigious universities, including the former Imperial Universities in the major provincial cities and the technological university of Hitosubashi, whose standing and reputation in Japan resembles that of the Massachusetts Institute of Technology in the United States.

18   Below these top dozen institutions stand some forty or so less prestigious but still well-regarded universities. And after these come numerous smaller universities and colleges of varying degrees of standing and reputation.

19   To some extent the situation in Japan has parallels in the United States and Europe, but there are two factors that make the importance of securing admission to an elite university substantially greater in Japan than in the West. In the first place, the entire Japanese system is geared toward providing lifelong employment, both in the private sector and in the civil service. It is practically unheard of for executives to switch from one corporation to another, or into public service and then back into the private sector, as in the United States and Europe. Employees are recruited directly out of college, and, needless to say, the major corporations and the civil service recruit virtually entirely from the top dozen universities. The smaller Japanese corporations operate along the same lines, although they widen their recruitment net to cover the next forty or so universities in the prestige hierarchy. Thus, obtaining entry to a prestigious university is a far more vital step for a successful career in Japan than it is in the United States or Europe.

20   Secondly, like the elite senior high schools, the elite universities are meritocratic. The great majority of universities are public institutions, receiving substantial government subsidies. Again, as with the senior high schools, fees are quite low, and loans are available to defray expenses. In principle and to a considerable extent in practice, any young Japanese can get into the University of Tokyo, or one of the other elite universities, provided only that he or she is talented enough and is prepared to do the work necessary to pass the entrance examinations. Knowing this, the public believes that *all* the most talented young Japanese go to one of these universities—and, conversely, that anyone who fails to get into one of these schools is necessarily less bright. Avoiding this stigma is, of course, a further incentive for the student to work hard to get in.

21   The third significant factor responsible for the high educational standards in Japan is competition among schools. This operates principally among the senior high schools, and what they are competing for is academic reputation. The most prestigious senior high school in Japan is Kansei in Tokyo, and being a teacher at Kansei is something like being a professor at Harvard. The teachers' self-esteem is bound up with the academic reputation of their schools—a powerful motivator for teachers to teach well.

22   In addition to this important factor of self-esteem, there is practical necessity. Since students are free to attend any school they can get into, if a school failed to provide good-quality teaching, it would no longer attract

students. In business terms, its customers would fade away, and it would be forced to close. Thus the essential feature of the competition among the Japanese senior high schools is that it exposes the teachers to the discipline of the free-enterprise system. In the case of the public senior high schools, the system can be regarded as a form of market socialism in which the competing institutions are state-owned but nevertheless compete against each other for their customers. Here the Japanese have been successfully operating the kind of system that Mikhail Gorbachev may be feeling his way toward introducing in the Soviet Union. The Japanese private senior high schools add a further capitalist element to the system insofar as they offer their educational services more or less like firms operating in a conventional market.

23   The problem of how market disciplines can be brought to bear on schools has been widely discussed in America and also in Britain ever since Milton Friedman raised it a quarter of a century or so ago, but solutions such as Friedman's voucher proposal seem as distant today as they did then. Although the proposal has been looked at sympathetically by Republicans in the United States and by Conservatives in Britain, politicians in both countries have fought shy of introducing it. Probably they have concluded that the problems of getting vouchers into the hands of all parents, and dealing with losses, fraud, counterfeits, and so forth, are likely to be too great for the scheme to be feasible.

24   The Japanese have evolved a different method of exposing schools to market forces. Subsidies are paid directly to the schools on a per-capita basis in accordance with the number of students they have. If a school's rolls decline, so do its incomes, both from subsidies and from fees. This applies to both the public and private senior high schools, although the public schools obviously receive a much greater proportion of their income as subsidies and a smaller portion from fees.

25   A similar scheme is being introduced in Britain. The Thatcher government is currently bringing in legislation that will permit public schools to opt out of local-authority control. Those that opt out will receive subsidies from the central government on the basis of the number of students they have. They will then be on their own, to sink or swim.

26   There is little doubt that this is the route that should be followed in America. The exposure of American schools to the invigorating stimulus of competition, combined with the introduction of a national curriculum and the provision of stronger incentives for students, would work wonders. Rather than complaining about Japanese aggressiveness and instituting counterproductive protectionist measures, Americans ought to be looking to the source of Japan's power.

QUESTIONS FOR DISCUSSION

1. What is Lynn comparing in his essay? Why is he making the comparison?

2. What are the main areas of comparison, and how do Japan and the United States differ in each area?

3. What do you think would happen if the Japanese model were applied to the U.S. school system? How well might it work?

4. What, if any, weaknesses do you see in the Japanese system? What negative effects, if any, might it have on Japanese youth?

5. What factors other than the school system might contribute to the poorer testing prformance of American children?

6. What changes, if any, do you feel would improve the U.S. educational system?

VOCABULARY

Stipulated (5), hierarchy (12), subsidies (13)

Through the One-Way Mirror

BY MARGARET ATWOOD

1   The noses of a great many Canadians resemble Porky Pig's. This comes from spending so much time pressing them against the longest undefended one-way mirror in the world. The Canadians looking through this mirror behave the way people on the hidden side of such mirrors usually do: they observe, analyze, ponder, snoop and wonder what all the activity on the other side means in decipherable human terms.

2   The Americans, bless their innocent little hearts, are rarely aware that they are even being watched, much less by the Canadians. They just go on doing body language, playing in the sandbox of the world, bashing one another on the head and planning how to blow things up, same as always. If they think about Canada at all, it's only when things get a bit snowy or the water goes off or the Canadians start fussing over some piddly detail, such as fish. Then they regard them as unpatriotic; for Americans don't really see Canadians as foreigners, not like the Mexicans, unless they do something weird like speak French or beat the New York Yankees at baseball. Really, think the Americans, the Canadians are just like us, or would be if they could.

3   Or we could switch metaphors and call the border the longest undefended backyard fence in the world. The Canadians are the folks in the neat little bungalow, with the tidy little garden and the duck pond. The Americans are the other folks, the ones in the sprawly mansion with the bad-taste statues on the lawn. There's a perpetual party, or something, going on there—loud music, raucous laughter, smoke billowing from the barbeque. Beer bottles and Coke cans land among the peonies. The Canadians have their own beer bottles and barbecue smoke, but they tend to overlook it. Your own mess is always more forgivable than the mess someone else makes on your patio.

4   The Canadians can't exactly call the police—they suspect that the Americans are the police—and part of their distress, which seems permanent, comes from their uncertainty as to whether or not they've been invited. Sometimes they do drop by next door, and find it exciting but scary. Sometimes

the Americans drop by their house and find it clean. This worries the Canadians. They worry a lot. Maybe those Americans will want to buy up their duck pond, with all the money they seem to have, and turn it into a cesspool or a water-skiing emporium.

5   It also worries them that the Americans don't seem to know who the Canadians are, or even where, exactly, they are. Sometimes the Americans call Canada their backyard, sometimes their front yard, both of which imply ownership. Sometimes they say they are the Mounties and the Canadians are Rose Marie. (All these things have, in fact, been said by American politicians.) Then they accuse the Canadians of being paranoid and having an identity crisis. Heck, there is no call for the Canadians to fret about their identity, because everyone knows they're Americans, really. If the Canadians disagree with that, they're told not to be so insecure.

6   One of the problems is that Canadians and Americans are educated backward from one another. The Canadians—except for the Quebecois, one keeps saying—are taught about the rest of the world first and Canada second. The Americans are taught about the United States first, and maybe later about other places, if they're of strategic importance. The Vietnam War draft dodgers got more culture shock in Canada than they did in Sweden. It's not the clothing that is different, it's those mental noises.

7   Of course, none of this holds true when you get close enough, where concepts like "Americans" and "Canadians" dissolve and people are just people, or anyway some of them are, the ones you happen to approve of. I, for instance, have never met any Americans I didn't like, but I only get to meet the nice ones. That's what the businessmen think too, though they have other individuals in mind. But big-scale national mythologies have a way of showing up in things like foreign policy, and at events like international writers' congresses, where the Canadians often find they have more to talk about with the Australians, the West Indians, the New Zealanders and even the once-loathed snooty Brits, now declining into humanity with the dissolution of empire, than they do with the impenetrable and mysterious Yanks.

8   But only sometimes. Because surely the Canadians understand the Yanks. Shoot, don't they see Yank movies, read Yank mags, bobble round to Yank music and watch Yank telly, as well as their own, when there is any?

9   Sometimes the Canadians think it's their job to interpret the Yanks to the rest of the world; explain them, sort of. This is an illusion: they don't understand the Yanks as much as they think they do, and it isn't their job.

10   But, as we say up here among God's frozen people, when Washington catches a cold, Ottawa sneezes. Some Canadians even refer to their capital city as Washington North and wonder why we're paying those guys in Ottawa when a telephone order service would be cheaper. Canadians make jokes about the relationship with Washington which the Americans, in their thin-skinned, bunion-toed way, construe as anti-American (they tend to see any nonworshipful comment coming from that gray, protoplasmic fuzz outside their borders as anti-American). They are no more anti-American than the jokes Canadians make about the weather: it's there, it's big, it's hard to influence, and it affects your life.

11   Of course, in any conflict with the Dreaded Menace, whatever it might be, the Canadians would line up with the Yanks, probably, if they thought it was a real menace, or if the Yanks twisted their arms or other bodily parts enough or threatened a "scorched-earth policy" (another real quote). Note the qualifiers. The Canadian idea of a menace is not the same as the U.S. one. Canada, for instance, never broke off diplomatic relations with Cuba, and it was quick to recognize China. Contemplating the U.S.–Soviet growling match, Canadians are apt to recall a line from Blake: "They became what they beheld." Certainly both superpowers suffer from the imperial diseases once so noteworthy among the Romans, the British and the French: arrogance and myopia. But the bodily-parts threat is real enough, and accounts for the observable wimpiness and flunkiness of some Ottawa politicians. Nobody, except at welcoming-committee time, pretends this is an equal relationship.

12   Americans don't have Porky Pig noses. Instead they have Mr. Magoo eyes, with which they see the rest of the world. That would not be a problem if the United States were not so powerful. But it is, so it is.

QUESTIONS FOR DISCUSSION

1. What are the main points of comparison between Canadians and Americans in the essay? Why do you think Atwood selected these particular points?

2. Based on the points of comparison, how do Canadians and Americans differ, and how are they similar? What evidence does Atwood use to support her contentions?

3. How is the comparison organized? Outline the organization using A and B for Canada and America and 1, 2, 3, 4, and so on, for the points of comparison. How effective is the organization?

4. What audience do you think the essay is intended for? What is Atwood's purpose for writing the essay? How well is the purpose accomplished?

5. How does your viewpoint of Canada and Canadians compare to how Atwood feels Americans view them? How accurately does Atwood capture America's world view (Americans have "Mr. Magoo eyes")?

6. What, if anything, did you learn from the essay?

VOCABULARY

Decipherable (1), raucous (3), construe (10), protoplasmic (10), myopia (11)

American Space, Chinese Place

BY YI-FU TUAN

1   Americans have a sense of space, not of place. Go to an American home in exurbia, and almost the first thing you do is drift toward the picture window. How curious that the first compliment you pay your host inside his house is to say how lovely it is outside his house! He is pleased that you

should admire his vistas. The distant horizon is not merely a line separating the earth from sky, it is a symbol of the future. The American is not rooted in his place, however lovely: his eyes are drawn by the expanding space to a point on the horizon which is his future.

2   By contrast, consider the traditional Chinese home. Blank walls enclose it. Step behind the spirit wall and you are in a courtyard with perhaps a miniature garden around a corner. Once inside his private compound you are wrapped in an ambiance of calm beauty, an ordered world of buildings, pavement, rock, and decorative vegetation. But you have no distant view: nowhere does space open out before you. Raw nature in such a home is experienced only as weather, and the only open space is the sky above. The Chinese is rooted in his place. When he has to leave, it is not for the promised land on the terrestrial horizon, but for another world altogether along the vertical, religious axis of his imagination.

3   The Chinese tie to place is deeply felt. Wanderlust is an alien sentiment. The Taoist classic *Tao Te Ching* captures the ideal of rootedness in place with these words: "Though there may be another country in the neighborhood so close that they are within sight of each other and the crowing of cocks and barking of dogs in one place can be heard in the other, yet there is no traffic between them; and throughout their lives the two peoples have nothing to do with each other." In theory if not in practice, farmers have ranked high in Chinese society. The reason is not only that they are engaged in a "root" industry of producing food but that, unlike pecuniary merchants, they are tied to the land and do not abandon their country when it is in danger.

4   Nostalgia is a recurrent theme in Chinese poetry. An American reader of translated Chinese poems may well be taken aback—even put off—by the frequency, as well as the sentimentality, of the lament for home. To understand the strength of this sentiment, we need to know that the Chinese desire for stability and rootedness in place is prompted by the constant threat of war, exile, and the natural disasters of flood and drought. Forcible removal makes the Chinese keenly aware of their loss. By contrast, Americans move, for the most part, voluntarily. Their nostalgia for home town is really longing for a childhood to which they cannot return: in the meantime the future beckons and the future is "out there," in open space. When we criticize American rootlessness, we tend to forget that it is a result of ideals we admire, namely, social mobility and optimism about the future. When we admire Chinese rootedness, we forget that the word "place" means both a location in space and position in society: to be tied to place is also to be bound to one's station in life, with little hope of betterment. Space symbolizes hope; place, achievement and stability.

QUESTIONS FOR DISCUSSION

1. What is being compared in the essay? Why do you think Tuan is interested in the topic?

2. What are the main points of comparison? How do Americans and Chinese differ on these points?

3. How is the essay organized? Outline the organization using A and B for the subjects being compared and 1, 2, 3, and so on, for the points of comparison. How effective is the organization?

4. What conclusion does Tuan draw based on the comparison? Do you agree with the conclusion? Why?

5. What audience might the essay be intended for? What is Tuan's purpose in writing the essay? How well is the purpose accomplished?

6. Compare your living circumstances with those that Tuan ascribes to the American home. How are they similar or different? Do you agree with his theory on what the American home symbolizes? Why?

VOCABULARY

Ambiance (2), terrestrial (2), wanderlust (3), nostalgia (4), recurrent (4)

Convincing Others

People write for a variety of reasons: to inform, entertain, educate, problem solve, and analyze. Underlying all other reasons, however, is the writer's need to *persuade*. No matter what writers put on paper, they must convince readers of its credibility in order to accomplish their purpose.

Persuasive writing challenges all writers. Since its purpose is to influence people's thoughts and actions, it is often aimed at an audience whose viewpoint ranges from neutral to hostile. Audience awareness is crucial for persuasive writing, for when you write to persuade, you are often dealing with the most skeptical readers.

Persuasive writing calls on all of the skills you have developed through earlier writing experiences. It tests your ability to think logically, support your viewpoint convincingly, and understand your reading audience.

Prewriting

Many people have viewpoints on controversial issues. You may, for example, have an opinion on gun control, capital punishment, pornography, abortion, or gay rights. Supporting your opinion in a way that convinces readers of its validity or good sense is the challenge of persuasive writing.

First, in analyzing your viewpoint, you may discover that it is based more on emotion than on rational thought, or on beliefs you hold but have never questioned or examined. You may even find that the viewpoint isn't yours at all, but rather that of parents or friends whose opinions you've adopted.

Second, it's easy to write for readers who have the same opinion, but they are not the target audience. There's no point in writing persuasively for people who don't need persuading. Instead, you engage readers who disagree or are sitting on the fence. Such an audience may not accept your viewpoint just because you believe in it strongly.

TOPIC SELECTION

The emphasis in this unit is on persuasive writing. When you write persuasively, you are sharing something you believe in with readers whom you want to influence. Persuasive writing holds little value if it doesn't change some minds, move someone to action, or cause people to think.

To select a topic for your paper in this unit, consider the following criteria:

1. Select a controversial topic—one that people hold different viewpoints on. It may be school related or a hot local, state, national, or international issue. It can come from any field—politics, education, business, sports, medicine, music, science, or religion.

2. Select a topic that you are knowledgeable about. Since this is not a research paper, you need to know enough about the issue to write effectively on it. (This does not prevent you from talking with other people to get more details or different points of view.)

3. Select a topic that you are interested in and in which you would like to influence other people's opinions.

4. Select a specific topic to develop in a two-to-three page paper. For example, gun control is a general topic that you might narrow to a specific writing topic such as "Banning Assault Weapons," "Gun Control and the Fifth Amendment," "California's Handgun Control Initiative," or "Guns in the Home: Protection or Liability?"

Topic Selection Activity 5.1

Following the criteria just presented, select a topic for your persuasive paper.

STUDENT TOPIC SELECTION

What's controversial these days? The state legislature voted to double community college tuition beginning next semester. That's sure controversial with students. The city council is debating whether to spend a couple hundred thousand dollars to "beautify" the downtown area, and people are split on the issue. On campus, there's a controversy on whether condom vending machines should be installed in the bathrooms. There are also the continuing complaints over the price of textbooks at the bookstore and the lousy food in the cafeteria.

What to write about? How about the instant replay debate in professional football? What about steroid use? Trouble is, there's not much to debate there. Most people agree that steroids are bad. What about beer being sold in eating places on college campuses? It's happening a lot, and it seems controversial. Then there's the question of whether campus police should be allowed to carry guns. I don't know what I want to write about yet. I'm going to give it a rest and think some more about my options during the day.

After I gave them further thought, none of the topics mentioned really grabbed me. Then I remembered the rumor that the college newspaper would shut down after this year. I checked it out and it's true. The school is planning on discontinuing the paper after next semester. That I don't like, and it's something I think I'd like to write about. It's sure going to be controversial.

PREWRITING CONSIDERATIONS

Before writing first drafts, writers often do prewriting work such as the following to help plan their persuasive papers:

1. Decide on a tentative thesis for the paper: the viewpoint on the topic that you want readers to consider.

Examples

Topic Gun control: Banning assault weapons does not go far enough in curbing violence in America.

Topic College cafeteria: To improve the quality of food and reduce prices, the college cafeteria should be privatized.

Topic Garbage pickup: Reducing garbage pickup in Rockport from twice to once a week would be a big mistake.

Topic Bosnian war: U.S. military intervention in Bosnia could lead to another Vietnam.

2. Decide on the reading audience: the people you want to influence on the topic. Remember, it does little good to write to people who already agree with you.

3. Decide on your writing purpose: what you hope to accomplish with your readers. Do you want to change their minds? change their behavior? persuade them to vote a particular way on an issue? take a particular action?

4. Generate four to six supporting points for the thesis: reasons why you believe the way you do. These reasons provide the "ammunition" for persuading readers to accept your viewpoint.

5. Generate one or two *opposing* arguments: reasons why some readers might disagree with you. How might you refute (tear down, disprove, prove illogical) those arguments in your paper?

6. Besides what you already know about your topic, what else should you know before writing your paper? Talk with people who can provide you with good information.

Prewriting Activity 5.2

Follow the prewriting suggestions just presented to generate material and provide direction for your paper.

STUDENT PREWRITING

TOPIC

The school newspaper

THESIS

The school newspaper is too important to students to be cut from the college budget.

PRIMARY READING AUDIENCE

The school board, who is considering eliminating the paper

PURPOSE

Convince the school board to save the paper.

SUPPORTIVE POINTS FOR THESIS

- student enjoyment in reading paper
- only source of outside news for most students
- main source of information for college activities
- important source of debates and discussion
- valued tradition of the college

OPPOSING POINTS TO REFUTE

- budget problems at the college
- having trouble staffing paper with students

REFUTATION

1. newspaper is a tiny part of school budget—no big savings
2. newspaper could generate more income through aggressive sales of advertising space
3. most small colleges have some trouble with staffing, but they don't get rid of their papers
4. recruit journalism students in the same way the college recruits athletes and scholars

NEED TO FIND OUT

1. Talk with some students on newspaper staff to see if they have any good ideas for saving paper.
2. Talk with faculty advisor to get exact budget figures for the newspaper and for total school budget.

First Drafts

Now that you have selected a topic for your persuasive paper and done some prewriting planning, you are ready to write the first draft. The following suggestions will help you get started:

1. Open the paper by introducing your topic and presenting your thesis. Do so in a way that will inspire readers to read further.

2. In the middle paragraphs, present and develop your supporting points, and present and refute one or two opposing arguments. (To persuade people, you often must shake the foundation for their beliefs to open their minds to your own.)

3. In the conclusion, make your purpose clear to readers. Why did you write to them? What do you want from them?

Drafting Activity 5.3

Write the first draft of your persuasive paper following the guidelines just presented. You may first want to read the following student draft to get some ideas on openings, middle paragraph development, and conclusions.

*STUDENT FIRST DRAFT
(written to school board
members)*

It is hard to believe the school board is thinking about dropping the newspaper. It's been around since the school began. It's as much a part of the school as the football team, the band, or anything else.

I know a lot of students who read the school paper. In fact, that is the only paper they ever read, so they would be losing their one newspaper source. I know the paper isn't exactly the <u>New York Times,</u> but it serves a purpose. It keeps students interested in what's going on around school. We don't have much involvement in activities and government as it is. Without a newspaper keeping us in touch with sports, activities, meetings, and rallies, there would be even less involvement.

The newspaper also brings in some news of the outside world—things that are happening in education, some world events, things that are happening in state politics. As I said, it's not like major news coverage, but for me and other students, it is the only news we read regularly.

The paper also gives students a chance to put in their two-bits. I like reading letters to the editor and student editorials, and sometimes students do get involved in issues and take sides—for example, when they were considering changing the name of the college. There was some real student involvement, and a lot of it came out of the coverage the paper gave the issue. Students don't get involved in many issues at the college. Without the paper, they wouldn't know any issues to get involved in.

The paper also gives some people a chance for a little attention. It's fun getting your name or picture in the paper. I don't know any student who doesn't like that. A lot of students get their pictures and opinions in when they ask a weekly question like "How do you feel about the new early se-mester calendar?" That's one of my favorite weekly regulars in the paper, and a lot of others too.

The paper also provides some journalism training for a lot of students. Without a paper, where would the journalism majors go? That would wipe out a program.

Finally, the paper can't be a big expense. It doesn't look as though it's expensively done up. What's the big cost to justify dropping the program? Why don't you look for other things to cut that are less important? Why don't you look for ways to save the paper? I'd really miss the paper. It's important to the school. What's a school without a newspaper? Even my old junior high still runs a weekly newspaper. And this college can't?

Revisions

You should always revise with your readers in mind, but it is particularly important to consider your readers' responses to a persuasive paper. For example, you may write a draft that people who agree with you would love but that your reading audience would find offensive or filled with bias. If such a draft isn't skillfully revised, it will surely miss its target.

REVISION GUIDELINES

When evaluating your first draft, consider these suggestions:

1. Evaluate the opening of your paper. Does it introduce your topic clearly and present your thesis so readers know where you stand? Is it interesting enough to keep readers going?

2. Evaluate your middle paragraphs. Do you present some strong suppor-tive points and develop each point effectively? (See the upcoming section "Paragraph Development.") Do you present and refute one or two op-posing arguments?

3. Evaluate your conclusion. Is it a strong part of your paper that leaves readers with something to think about? Does it reveal your purpose so readers know why you have written to them?

4. Evaluate your paragraphing. Does it help readers move smoothly through the opening, middle, and ending of your paper? Have you used transitions (first, second, then, however, therefore, as you can see, for example) to tie sentences and paragraphs together?

5. Read each sentence carefully to see if you can improve its clarity, smooth-ness, or conciseness. In addition, make revisions to improve sentence variety, replace overused joining words, and combine pairs of short sen-tences. (See the section "Sentence Revision" later in the unit.)

6. Read the draft from your readers' perspective. Does it sound as if it was written by a fair and reasonable person who respects his or her readers although they may disagree? Was it written by a thoughtful person whose viewpoint comes from a deep understanding of the issue?

Revision Activity 5.4

With a partner, evaluate the following student draft by applying the revision guidelines just presented. Note suggestions for revision along with things that the writer does well. When you finish, evaluate your own draft similarly. (Your instructor may first have you go over the upcoming sections on paragraph development and sentence revision.) If you desire a second opinion, share drafts with a classmate. When you are ready, write your second draft.

Down with the Greeks

STUDENT FIRST DRAFT

Early Sunday morning, the whole place looked like a disaster area. Windows were broken out, bottles were strewn all over the floors, bodies were lying around, and a goat was on a sofa munching pretzels. The effects of an earthquake? A Chicago gangland massacre? A scene from a bombed-out Italian village in a World War II movie? None of the above. Just another Saturday night bash at the Sigma Nu frat house.

Over the years, fraternities have completely lost sight of why they were created, if there were any good reasons in the first place. Today's fraternities represent a lot of the worst things about our society. They should be disbanded once and for all.

First of all, fraternities are elitist outfits, each one catering to its own kind. For example, while I was at Landsford State, the Theta Chi's wanted nothing but doctors and lawyers-to-be, the Sigmas wanted nothing but jocks, the SAE's nothing but rich party boys, and the Lambda Nu nothing but young Republicans. Each group hung around campus in a big clique, either ignoring or looking down their noses at outsiders. Fraternities aren't for everyone, as they would have you believe.

And once in a fraternity, previously nice guys turned into egotistical snobs, including Tom Anderson from my old high school. Tom, a year ahead of me in school, had always been a friendly, decent guy. When I went to Landsford State as a freshman, I passed by Tom in his AGR sweatshirt with some of his frat friends, and he looked right through me, like I didn't exist. Later I asked a couple of other friends about good old Tom, and they said that he'd "gone frat" and was now a total jerk. So much for the myth that fraternities build character.

Aside from the elitism, fraternities have become a place where bad behavior is valued. For example, the Sigmas have their annual March 31st belching contest, where the guy with the loudest, longest belch wins a case of beer. At the Theta house, there is the legend of Josh the Vomiter, the legendary Theta who came into a frat meeting totally bombed, walked to the front of the room, and regurgitated a half gallon of wine all over the visiting Grand Deacon from Klamath Falls.

Then there's the cheating. I have seen the SAE "testing file" in their basement: a filing cabinet full of hundreds of stolen tests from every department on campus. The new pledge class each year shows their courage by stealing as many tests as possible, a great start on their fraternity careers. And the campus police have their records: over 80 percent of the vandalism reports in the college apartment area west of campus are traced back to fraternity houses, according to campus Police Chief George Shrum.

A lot of the fraternities' problems occur because of all the drinking. Fraternities are basically boozing clubs, and by the fraternities' own admission in the school newspaper, over 200 kegs of beer are consumed in fall pledge week activities alone. Most of the social fraternities have at least three parties a week: a mid-weeker to kill the boredom, a TGIF, of course, and an elaborate drunk on Saturday nights.

With all the emphasis on partying and drinking, it's not surprising that the overall GPA for frat members at Landsford State, according to the school registrar, is a 2.15, just high enough to stay in school. And the school president, Dr. Kirtch, had this to offer after the latest police raid on a frat party: "If some fraternities put half as much effort into encouraging studying as into encouraging drinking, they could do their members some good."

Finally, fraternities are sexist, racist organizations, and the facts speak for themselves. First, women cannot belong to fraternities, but each fraternity has a "little sisters' auxiliary," which is used, according to an ex-little sister, to clean up after parties, to get members dates, to console them when they're depressed, and to be their hostesses at parties. They are college geisha girls, in other words. As to racism, at Landsford College, 96 percent of the frat members are white, 2 percent are oriental, and 2 percent are black. And that is with a school population that is 70 percent white, 20 percent black, and 8 percent oriental. It is no wonder that the Black Student Union on campus has petitioned the college to start a new fraternity; they know the present fraternities aren't for them.

I know what happens to many fraternity types when they get older. We have a number of service clubs in town and one club called the Order of the Eagles. They aren't civic minded; they just like to party: an open bar at every meeting, plus casino nights, stag nights, and trips to Las Vegas. And they don't care about their public image. In fact, they're proud of it. So fraternity types never die; they just join the Order of the Eagles somewhere and continue their self-centered, purposeless ways. If Landsford abolished all fraternities tomorrow, I wonder what negative effects that might have on students or the college. After two hours, I'm still thinking.

PARAGRAPH DEVELOPMENT

Paragraph development in a persuasive paper is important to accomplishing your purpose. Think of it as answering skeptical readers' questions such as,

How do you know that? How can you prove that? Why is that the case? or Why does that matter?

Providing Evidence

A big part of paragraph development in persuasive writing is providing evidence that what you are saying is true or sensible. Here are examples of statements that need "backing up" for readers to judge them fairly.

Examples   Handgun control laws are working well in New Hampshire. (Give examples of how they are working well.)

Most people on welfare could be working. (Provide evidence. How do you know that is the case?)

The college bookstore is overcharging students for textbooks. (How can you prove that? Give examples.)

Yosemite Falls is a scenic wonderland. (Provide convincing details.)

Melissa and Jaime tend to fight over nothing. (Give an example or two.)

The college newspaper budget is a fraction of the total school budget. (Give the figures that show the ratio.)

To convince readers that you are making credible statements, follow these guidelines:

1. Provide evidence for all supporting points of your thesis.

Example

Thesis   Community College transfer students are better risks for success at four-year schools than incoming freshmen.

Supporting Points

a. Transfer students are more mature. (How are they "more mature"? How does being "more mature" help with success?)

b. Transfer students have already made the transition to college. (What does that mean? How does it affect success?)

c. Transfer students have already proven that they can handle college work. (How have they proven that? Give examples.)

d. Transfer students are by and large more serious about college. (How can that be proved? What evidence is there to support that claim?)

2. Provide evidence for any statement that readers wouldn't necessarily accept as true.

Examples   America is an ethnically diverse country. (No evidence needed. A true statement that readers would concur with.)

Today's immigrants create problems that earlier immigrants didn't. (**Evidence needed to support statement. What kind of problems? What proof do you have? What examples can you give?**)

America would be better off if it closed its borders to immigrants. (**Evidence needed to support statement. Why should we close our borders? How would we be better off? What proof do you have? What examples can you give?**)

3. For a particular statement, provide the most effective kinds of evidence: facts, examples, details, statistics, explanations, or reasons.

Examples   Meredith Quiring is guilty of extorting money from her ailing grandmother. (**Provide facts that support the claim.**)

America's trade relationship with Japan is deteriorating. (**Provide examples to support the claim.**)

A standard car leasing agreement is rather complicated. (**Provide details that reveal its complicated nature.**)

Our school district has a problem with unfunded equity. (**Explain what "unfunded equity" means, and then explain the problem.**)

Children of divorced parents are more likely to divorce as adults than children whose parents stay together. (**Provide statistics to prove the statement.**)

Claton would make a better governor than McWilliams. (**Provide the reasons why Claton would be superior.**)

Revision Activity 5.5

Read the following draft and underline statements that the writer needs to provide evidence for in the next draft. In addition, decide what kind(s) of evidence should be provided.

Next, read your latest draft for statements that readers may not accept without some evidence. Underline the statements and provide evidence in the next draft that will make the statements credible to readers.

Welfare Fraud

If you see someone driving around in a Cadillac, he may be a hard-working American who's made his money honestly. On the other hand, he may be a welfare recipient who receives taxpayers' money for doing nothing. Working Americans are getting ripped off by welfare chiselers, and it's time to dismantle the system.

Most able-bodied men and women are on welfare because they are too lazy to work. The government literally pays them for being lazy. Most of these people are making more money sitting home doing nothing than they would make if they had a job. Something is wrong with a system that rewards laziness more than hard work.

What's more, they are producing another generation of welfare addicts: their children. They learn from their parents how to play the welfare game, and then they teach their own children through example. The vicious cycle goes on and on.

The system is greased by government officials who get kickbacks from the welfare industry. By continuing to pass welfare legislation, they get a little welfare of their own from the welfare bureaucrats whose jobs are dependent on the system's survival. It's no wonder that few people on Capitol Hill question the tremendous abuses that pervade the welfare system.

I'm calling on all Americans to write their congressperson and demand that legislation be initiated to dismantle our present welfare system. For every person it helps legitimately, there are ten people who take advantage of it. Get these welfare chiselers off their sofas and into jobs. Then we'd also see many related problems solved: violent crime, illegitimate births, and the breakdown of the American family. It all begins with the welfare system.

SENTENCE REVISION

All writers share the task of revising first draft sentences. The goal of such revision is to create sentences that flow smoothly and express your thoughts clearly. Like most writers, you will continue to improve your revision skills as long as you write.

Wording Problems Review

The first step in revising first draft sentences is learning to spot sentences that need some work. Basically, you are looking for sentences that seem vague, awkward, or wordy. If a sentence doesn't seem right to you, it will probably cause readers problems.

When you locate a problem sentence, experiment with different wording options until you find the best combination. Here is an example:

First Draft Sentence	With sentence revision, you are working with both improving the clarity of a sentence's content and the wording through which to express that content best.
Revised	With sentence revision, you are improving both your clarity of thought and the wording through which that thought is expressed.
Revised	Through sentence revision, you are both clarifying your thoughts and improving the way in which they are expressed.

Final Draft   Through sentence revision, you are both clarifying your thoughts and improving the way they are worded.

To see the value in such experimentation, compare the first and final drafts of the sentence. The first sentence struggles to get the writer's thoughts on paper; the final draft expresses them clearly, smoothly, and concisely.

Sentence Revision Activity 5.6

For revision practice, rewrite the following paragraph to make the sentences clearer, smoother, or less wordy.

At first, I felt sorry for my roommate because she was lonely. I did things with her, tried to cheer her up when she was depressed, and my clothes she could borrow anytime. Nothing seemed to help out the situation for long though because I'd come back to the dorm after class and there she'd be just staring at the ceiling or just crying for no reason on the bed. I couldn't be with her all the time. One night a dance was put on by the college and I met a guy who seemed really nice. We started going out, and my roommate was made very angry by that. She wouldn't talk to me or say anything to me when I came back from dates. It was like as if she was being betrayed by me for having a boyfriend. On top of that, my clothes were now borrowed by her without asking, and she was even getting into my make-up. Finally, I'd had enough. Anxious to get out of that room, I asked the dorm adviser when another dorm room would become vacant. I moved out of that room and into a single room, and even though I had to pay more for it, having to pay the extra money was worth the freedom that I received from my old roommate. I hope some psychological counseling can be gotten by her both for her own good and before she drives another roommate crazy.

Sentence Variety Review

In the "Sentence Variety" sections, you practice using different sentence structures to learn new ways to express yourself effectively. Like many writers, you may sometimes overrely on favored structures and joining words, which can lead to monotonous writing and limited expression. Working with different structures makes you more aware of your options and more comfortable in using them.

Sentence Revision Activity 5.7

Revise the following paragraph by combining sentences to form more effective and informative ones. Your revised paragraph should include a variety of simple, compound, and complex sentences, including some with relative (who, which, that) clauses.

The drinking water in town is tasting awful. The city is chlorinating it. They are doing this to kill bacteria. The bacteria count is higher than the allowable level. The level is established by the county health department. The water now has a strong aftertaste. It is safe. It is practically undrinkable. Most people are opting for bottled water. They can buy it in any supermarket. It costs about a quarter a gallon. There is another option. Some people are installing water-treatment units. These units have carbon filters. The filters take out all of the chlorine. The water tastes normal. It tastes just like bottled water. Both options are better than drinking chlorinated water. I prefer the water-treatment unit. It's more convenient. It still allows me to drink tap water. It's sad that the untreated city water isn't safe enough to drink. This is the result of underground contaminants polluting the water system. The contaminants come from agricultural pesticide spraying.

Other Structural Problems

Three specific sentence problems are covered in the "Sentence Revision" section of the appendix: nonparallel construction, dangling modifiers, and misplaced modifiers. Your instructor may refer you to those sections if you have problems with them in your writing.

Final Editing

The last step in the writing process is to give your draft a final proofreading for errors. Rather than looking for grammatical, spelling, and punctuation errors all at once, concentrate on one area at a time. That way you are least likely to overlook a particular kind of error.

PROOFREADING GUIDELINES

When proofreading your draft, make sure to cover the following areas:

1. *Sentence endings:* Make sure you have a period at the end of each sentence, and correct any run-on sentences, comma splices, or sentence fragments. (If you have a particular problem with run-on sentences or fragments, see the upcoming review section.)

2. *Word endings:* Check to make sure plural words end in *s,* regular past tense verbs end in *ed,* and present tense verbs agree with their subjects. Also check for *er* and *est* endings on comparative and superlative adjectives. (See the upcoming section on comparative and superlative adjectives under "Correct Usage.")

3. *Spelling:* Check your spelling carefully, and look up any words you are uncertain of. Also check your use of homonyms such as there/their/they're, your/you're, no/know, through/threw, and its/it's.

4. *Internal punctuation:* Check your use of commas with words in series, before conjunctions in compound sentences, after introductory groups of words, and to set off relative clauses, interrupters, and ending phrases beginning with *especially, particularly,* and *ing*-words. (See the section on comma usage review later in the unit.) Check for apostrophes in contractions and possessives, and for quotation marks around direct quotations. Finally, check your use of semicolons and colons (covered later under "Punctuation").

5. *Pronoun usage:* Check your subject pronoun usage (Marianne and I, my brother and he, we and they), and make sure that all pronouns agree with their antecedents. (See the upcoming review section on pronoun-antecedent agreement.)

Editing Activity 5.8

Proofread your latest draft for errors following the guidelines just presented. Concentrate in particular on your personal error tendencies. (Your instructor may have you cover the upcoming punctuation and grammar sections before proofreading.) When you have corrected all errors, write or print out the final draft of your paper to share with readers.

SENTENCE PROBLEMS

The following activity is for students who continue to have problems with run-on sentences and fragments. If you have such problems, do the activity before proofreading your draft.

Run-on and Fragment Review Activity 5.9

The following passage contains run-on sentences and fragments. Rewrite the passage and correct errors by changing or adding punctuation, or by adding joining words to combine sentences.

Example   The service at the restaurant was terrible. Because there was one waitress for ten tables. People got frustrated, they left without ordering.

Revised   The service at the restaurant was terrible because there was one waitress for ten tables. People got frustrated, and they left without ordering.

This was the last semester that Charlotte would car pool. Because she had too many bad experiences. She had gotten in a car pool at the beginning of the semester, with three other girls who lived nearby. When Elvira drove, she was always five to ten minutes late, she always had elaborate excuses. Minerva, on the other hand, was always ten minutes early, tooting her horn and waking up the neighborhood. The third girl was totally unpredictable, she relied on her brother to pick her up. One day she was on time, the next day early, the next day late, sometimes she wouldn't come at all. Since Charlotte was the only one with first-period classes, the others weren't concerned about the time. Next semester Charlotte will take the bus to school. Even though the bus stop is a mile from her house.

CORRECT USAGE

The following section introduces a new grammatical area that causes some writers problems: comparative and superlative adjectives. In addition, pronoun-antecedent agreement is reviewed from the last unit.

Comparative and Superlative Adjectives

Writers frequently use adjectives to compare things: people, cars, colleges, movies, jobs, cities, or religions. They may use adjectives to compare the size of four brothers, the speed of two sports cars, the cost of tuition at a number of colleges, the endings of Alfred Hitchcock movies, the difficulty of different jobs, the crime rate in different cities, or the creation myths in different religions. Adjectives that are used in comparisons take special forms, which are covered in this section.

An adjective may be used to describe a single thing, to compare two things, or to compare one thing to many others. Here are examples of these three uses for adjectives and the three forms the adjectives take:

Descriptive Sally is short. (Short *describes Sally.*)

Comparative Sally is shorter than Sue. (Shorter *compares the height of Sally to that of Sue.*)

Superlative Sally is the shortest person in her family. (Shortest *compares the height of Sally to that of the rest of her family.*)

Notice that with the one-syllable adjective *short,* the *er* ending is added for comparing two things, and the *est* ending is added for comparing *more than two things*. Here are three more examples of the uses for adjectives with a longer descriptive word:

Descriptive Sally is considerate. (Considerate *describes Sally.*)

Comparative Sally is more considerate than Sue. (More considerate *compares Sally to Sue.*)

Superlative Sally is the most considerate person in the class. (Most considerate *compares Sally to all of her classmates.*)

Notice that with longer adjectives (two syllables or more), a *more* is added before the adjective for comparing two things, and a *most* is added before the adjective for comparing more than two things.

Now that you have a general idea of the forms that adjectives take, the following basic rules for making comparisons with adjectives should help you use them correctly in your writing.

Comparative Form (Comparing *Two* Things)

1. Add *er* to *one-syllable adjectives.*

I am <u>shorter</u> than you are.
Sam is <u>smarter</u> than Phil.
Mercury lights are <u>brighter</u> than flourescent lights.

2. Add *more* in front of adjectives with *two or more syllables.*

I am <u>more depressed</u> than you are.
Sam is <u>more graceful</u> than Phil.
Mercury lights are <u>more effective</u> than flourescent lights.

3. Add *er* to two-syllable words ending in *y* or *ow* (drop the *y* and add *ier*).

I am <u>lonelier</u> than you are.
Sam is <u>sillier</u> than Phil.
Mercury lights are <u>prettier</u> than fluorescent lights.
The river is <u>shallower</u> today than last week.

4. The word *than* often comes after the adjective in sentences comparing two things. (See all of the examples from items 1, 2, and 3.)

5. Never use both *more* and an *er* ending with an adjective.

Wrong	You are <u>more smarter</u> than I am.
Right	You are <u>smarter</u> than I am.
Wrong	You are <u>more beautifuler</u> than ever.
Right	You are <u>more beautiful</u> than ever.

Superlative Form (Comparing *Three or More* Things)

1. Add *est* to *one-syllable adjectives.*

I am the <u>shortest</u> person in my family.
Sam is the <u>smartest</u> elephant in the zoo.
Mercury lights are the <u>brightest</u> lights for tennis courts.

2. Add *most* in front of adjectives with *two or more syllables.*

I am the <u>most dependable</u> person in the family.
Sam is the <u>most curious</u> elephant in the zoo.
Mercury lights are the <u>most expensive</u> lights on the market.

3. Add *est* to two-syllable words ending in *y* or *ow* (drop the *y* and add *iest*).

I am the <u>rowdiest</u> person in my family.

Sam is the <u>heaviest</u> elephant in the zoo.
Mercury lights give off the <u>loveliest</u> glow of any outdoor lights.
That is the <u>shallowest</u> that I've ever seen Lake Placid.

4. The word *the* often comes before the adjective in sentences comparing three or more things. (See all of the examples in items 1, 2, and 3.)

5. Never use both *most* and an *est* ending with an adjective.

Wrong	You are the <u>most smartest</u> person I know.
Right	You are the <u>smartest</u> person I know.
Wrong	Francine is the <u>most remarkablest</u> artist in the school.
Right	Francine is the <u>most remarkable</u> artist in the school.

Adjective Activity 5.10

Each of the following sentences compares two things. Fill in the correct *comparative* form of each adjective in parentheses. Count the number of syllables the adjective has; add *er* to one-syllable adjectives and two-syllable adjectives ending in *y* or *ow,* and add *more* in front of other adjectives of two syllables or more.

Examples   (quick)   You are a *quicker* runner this year than last.

(beautiful)   The nearby hills are *more beautiful* in the spring than in the summer.

1. (interesting)   The first day of school was _____
than I thought it would be.

2. (friendly)   The teachers were _____
than I imagined.

3. (fascinating)   The lectures were _____
than my high school lectures.

4. (short)   The classes were also _____
than usual, since it was the first day.

5. (fast)   The whole day went by _____
than I expected.

6. (tedious)   I thought college would be _____
than it was.

7. (enthusiastic)   Now I am _____ than
ever about coming back tomorrow.

8. (long)   However, tomorrow's classes will be much _____
_____ than today's.

9. (difficult)   The homework will definitely be _____
_____ than today's.

10. (typical)   Tomorrow will be _____ of
a regular college day than today was.

Adjective Activity 5.11

Each of the following sentences compares three or more things. Fill in the correct *superlative* form of each adjective in parentheses. Count the number of syllables the adjective has; add *est* to one-syllable adjectives and two-syllable adjectives ending in *y* or *ow,* and add *most* in front of other adjectives with two syllables or more.

Examples   (quick)   I felt the *quickest* today in track in track practice that I've ever felt.

(unusual)   The antique knife display in the library is the *most unusual* display of the year.

1. (interesting)   The first day of school was the _____
of the week.

2. (friendly)   I met some of the _____
teachers I have ever met.

3. (fascinating)   The lectures were the _____ I
have ever taken.

4. (short)   The classes were also the _____
I have ever attended.

5. (fast)   It was the _____ day of
school I've been through.

6. (tedious)   I thought college would be the _____
part of my education.

7. (enthusiastic)   Now I am the _____ I've
ever been about going to school.

8. (long)   Although the classes tomorrow will be the _____
_____ I've had, I should still
enjoy them.

9. (difficult)   Although the homework will be the _____
_____ I've done, I don't think
I'll mind it.

10. (typical)   Students say that the second week of college is the _____
_____ week to judge school
by, so I hope it goes as well as the first.

Pronoun-Antecedent Agreement Review

As you recall from the previous unit, pronouns must agree in number and gender with their antecedents:

John visited <u>his</u> grandparents in Florida by <u>himself</u>.

Melissa and I took <u>our</u> final a day early because <u>we</u> had to work the next day.

The boat tore <u>its</u> hull on some rocks, and <u>it</u> began sinking rapidly.

Writers sometimes have problems when an *indefinite pronoun* is the antecedent: each, one, everyone, someone, no one, somebody, everybody. Indefinite pronouns are singular and require singular pronoun references:

Everyone brought <u>his or her</u> blue book to the history final.

One of the boys lost <u>his</u> wallet at the baseball game.

Each of the mothers took <u>her</u> turn working at the school bake sale.

Nobody wants <u>his or her</u> name slandered by gossip.

Pronoun-Antecedent Activity 5.12

For more practice with pronoun-antecedent agreement, fill in the blanks in the following sentences with pronouns that agree in number with their antecedents. Circle the antecedent for each pronoun.

Example   (People) can usually be trusted if *they* are given responsibility.

1. The old shack lost _____ tin roof in the hurricane.
2. Each of the girls has a room to _____ in the bungalow.
3. Two men from New Zealand left _____ passports at the airport.
4. A student needs to set _____ priorities straight before _____ can do well in college.
5. Every one of the geraniums got _____ bloom at the same time.
6. Hawaii is a favorite vacation spot for Japanese tourists. _____ is _____ island home away from home, and _____ flock there by the thousands.
7. Humans are _____ own worst enemy in destroying _____ environment. _____ must reverse the destructive process _____ have initiated.

8. Maria did _____ math totally by _____
   for the first time in _____ life, and _____
   was very proud.

9. A person in need of financial help should consult an expert, and
   _____ should stay away from well-meaning friends no better
   off than _____ is.

10. Each cadet was instructed to do _____ own locker inspection,
    and no one was to leave the barracks before _____
    had finished _____ chores.

11. The watches that I bought from the catalog have all lost _____
    plastic covers because _____ weren't properly attached to the
    faces.

12. Skateboards are being seen on college campuses again. _____
    lost _____ appeal to students in the late seventies, but now
    _____ are back in vogue as a means of transportation.

13. Either Sarah or Brunhilda left _____ beaker in the chemistry
    lab.

14. The presents that you bought me for my birthday lost _____
    charm when I heard you paid for _____ with my credit card.

15. The women who got the best bargains at the garage sale did _____
    shopping before 7:00 a.m., and the rest of us were left with what
    _____ had picked over.

PUNCTUATION

This section introduces two new punctuation marks that writers find useful:
semicolons and colons. It also includes a review of comma usage.

Semicolons and Colons

The semicolon (;) and colon (:) allow writers to vary their sentence structure
and add flexibility to their writing. Semicolons and colons are used in the
following ways.

1. *Semicolon:* joins two complete sentences that are related in meaning and
   that are reasonably short (used as an alternative to separating sentences
   with a period or joining sentences with a conjunction).

   Examples   Marion should be at the checkout any minute; her ten-minute
               break is almost over.

               Hank's health is his number one concern; nothing else seems
               important right now.

Melissa should never have tried to run a hard mile without warming up; she knows better.

2. *Colon:* (a) used after a *complete thought* to indicate that a series of items follows.

Examples   We need the following utensils for the picnic: knives, forks, spoons, spatulas, and a cheese grater.

Sandra has the characteristics of an outstanding athlete: intelligence, dedication, coachability, goal orientation, and confidence.

3. *Colon:* (b) used after a *complete thought* to highlight a single item that follows.

Examples   There's one virtue that Peter definitely lacks: patience.

The answer to Maria's financial problem is obvious: find a better job.

As a camp counselor, you've made one thing apparent: your concern for troubled children.

I've got something that you need: the keys to the house.

Punctuation Activity 5.13

Add semicolons and colons to the following sentences where they are needed. Put a C in front of each correctly punctuated sentence.

Example   You show a real aptitude for computer programming; you have a promising future.

1. ___ There's one class in college I've had trouble passing physiology.

2. ___ I know how to get from our dormitory to the downtown library I went there several times last semester.

3. ___ Everyone fails occasionally don't get discouraged.

4. ___ Freda replaced her computer's floppy disk system with a hard disk drive the new system is much faster and stores more information.

5. ___ Millicent has been taking aerobic dance four times a week for four years she started when she was forty-five years old.

6. ___ One attribute comes to mind when considering golfer Jack Nicklaus's years of unparalleled success mental toughness.

7. ___ The chain saw equipment in the garage should include two 16-inch Weber chain saws, a bag of extra chains, a gallon of gasoline, three cleaning rags, and four pints of chain saw oil.

8. ____ My aunt's cat Tiger is a fearless fighter her other cat Chubby prefers hiding behind the washing machine.

Punctuation Activity 5.14

For practice, write five of your own sentences that need semicolons and five more that need colons, and punctuate them correctly. (Use the words *however* and *therefore* after the semicolons in at least two sentences, and write some sentences in which the colon is followed by a single word and others in which it is followed by a series.) When you finish, check your latest draft to see where you might use semicolons or colons.

Comma Usage Review

The following review activity is for students who are still a little uncertain about where to insert commas in their sentences.

Comma Review Activity 5.15

Following the comma usage rules presented in the text, insert commas where they are needed in the following essay.

My freshman year I really enjoyed the freedom that came with college. After having been in "prison" for four years of high school it felt great not having classes every hour of the day and even greater being able to miss a class now and then.

The problem was the "now and then" became more frequent as the semester went on. I mostly had large lecture classes and the teachers didn't take roll or worry about who was there and who wasn't. Therefore I started sleeping in more and more often and I often relied on the notes that friends would take in class.

My grades started slipping more and more but I was determined to make up for it all by doing well on my finals. The trouble was I had missed so much class and gotten so far behind that I tried to do about a month's studying in a few nights. I vowed to stay up all night studying before each final but it never worked out. I was hopelessly behind and I did terrible on my finals.

For the first semester I ended up with one C and the rest D's and F's. I was so ashamed that I lied to my parents and my friends. Basically I blew my first semester of college and I learned that the freedom of college was deceptive. In college they give you enough rope to hang yourself so that's what I did.

If you don't learn to take the responsibility to go to class and put your free time to good use you'll end up in a hole. This semester I'm having to dig myself out including taking two classes over again. I'll also have to go to summer school if I want to end up with thirty units for the year. I'm going to class regularly, taking my own notes, and keeping up on my reading better. So far I'm doing okay but there's still twelve weeks to go. I hope I've learned my lesson especially since my parents are paying my tuition.

Writing Review

In the "Writing Review," you apply what you have learned throughout the unit to a second persuasive paper. Follow the writing process provided, which summarizes the steps presented throughout the unit.

WRITING PROCESS

TOPIC SELECTION

1. Write a paper to a particular person persuading him or her to do something: give up a bad habit (smoking, drinking, taking drugs for example); help you with something (financing a car, paying tuition, sharing an apartment, hiring you for a job); or change a negative situation (something particular at work, at home, at school, in the community). Follow these suggestions:

   a. Pick a topic that is important to you—something that you would definitely like to see happen.

   b. Decide on your thesis for the paper: the main point you want to express to the person.

   c. Decide on your purpose for the paper: exactly what you would like the person to do.

   d. Write your paper in the form of a letter.

PREWRITING

2. To help plan your paper, do the following prewriting work:

   a. List a few supporting points for your thesis: reasons the person should do what you are asking of him or her. Then decide what kind of evidence (facts, examples, details, explanations, reasons) you might use to substantiate each point.

   b. List one or two opposing arguments—reasons the person might disagree with you—and decide how you might refute those arguments in your paper.

FIRST DRAFT

3. When you complete your prewriting, write the first draft of your paper following these suggestions:

   a. In the opening, introduce your topic and thesis in a way that will engage your reader's interest or concern.

   b. In the middle paragraphs, develop your supporting points, and present and refute one or two opposing arguments.

c. In the conclusion, make your purpose clear and provide whatever wrap-up you feel would best accomplish your purpose.

d. Keep your reader in mind, and write in a way that you feel will produce the best response.

REVISIONS

4. Set your draft aside for a while, and then evaluate it for possible revisions. Follow these guidelines:

a. Evaluate the strength of your opening. Are your topic and thesis clearly presented? Does your reader have a good idea why you are writing?

b. Evaluate your middle paragraphs. Do you have some strong supportive points for your thesis? Do you provide evidence to substantiate each point? Have you effectively refuted an opposing argument or two that your reader may have?

c. Evaluate the strength of your conclusion. Will the reader clearly understand your purpose? Do you conclude in a way that will elicit a positive response from him or her?

d. Revise sentences to make them clearer, smoother, and more concise, and to vary sentence structures and joining words.

e. Read the draft from your reader's perspective, and make any final changes that you feel will make the person more responsive to your message.

EDITING

5. Proofread your latest draft for errors following these guidelines:

a. Make sure each sentence ends with a period, and that you correct any run-on sentences, comma splices, or fragments.

b. Check word endings to make sure that plural words end in *s,* regular past tense verbs end in *ed,* present tense verbs agree with their subjects, and comparative and superlative adjectives have appropriate *er* and *est* endings.

c. Check your spelling carefully, including your use of homonyms such as there/their/they're, your/you're, know/no, its/it's, and through/threw.

d. Check your internal punctuation: comma usage, apostrophes in contractions and possessives, quotation marks around direct quotations, and semicolon and colon usage, if any.

e. Check your pronoun usage: correct subject pronouns in compound subjects (Joan and I, my mom and she, we and they) and pronouns that agree with their antecedents (A person should do *his or her* best in life. Mal and I did *our* projects by *ourselves.*)

FINAL DRAFT

6. Write the final draft of your letter and share it with the person it is written to.

STUDENT WRITING PROCESS

TOPIC SELECTION

Something that I think needs changing is the college's practice of overscheduling courses each semester and then canceling course sections that get lower enrollments. I've had three or four classes canceled, which really messed up my schedule a couple of semesters.

TOPIC	The college's overscheduling of courses.
THESIS	When the college overschedules and then cancels courses, students get hurt.
PURPOSE	Convince the school to stop the practice and offer only those classes that have a good chance of making enrollment.
READER	I'll write my letter to the Dean of Instruction, who is ultimately responsible for class scheduling.

PREWRITING

SUPPORTING POINTS FOR THESIS

- My own experience with canceled courses. (Provide example from last semester.)
- Students believe their schedules are set. (Explain why.)
- Students have to change their entire schedules. (Give examples.)
- Students often can't get into other classes. (Explain why.)
- Classes often aren't canceled until second or third week. (Explain effects on students in canceled classes.)
- Practice can jeopardize students' full-time status. (Explain negative effects.)

OPPOSING ARGUMENTS TO REFUTE

- Cost effective for school to maintain only high enrollment classes. (Refute: What's good for school is bad for students in this case. Offer fewer courses to begin with and put them in prime times for maximum enrollment.)
- Can schedule faculty most effectively this way. (Refute: College is here for the students, not for the convenience of instructors.)

Scheduling Woes

STUDENT FIRST DRAFT

Last semester I was lucky enough to enroll in all five classes that I needed for general education requirements. All the course sections I had in my schedule were still open when I registered. I didn't have to worry about back-up classes since I figured my schedule was set.

By the end of the second week of the semester, three of my five classes had been canceled, due to a lack of the "necessary" enrollment. Then I was forced, along with many other students, to scrounge around for other classes, which was frustrating and difficult. I ended up getting into only two other courses, neither of which I would have taken by choice. Clearly, there's something wrong with the scheduling practice at the college, and students are suffering.

For the second semester now, the college has scheduled significantly more sections of general ed courses than have been "made." It appears the school, or deans, or whoever makes the enrollment decisions waits to see which sections reach the magic minimum of twenty enrollees, and then cancels all those with fewer than twenty. Students caught in the smaller classes are then compelled to seek out other sections or courses, with no guarantees that they'll be allowed in.

To make matters worse, sometimes smaller sections are "carried" through the second week in hopes of late enrollments, leaving students desperately seeking classes in the third week of the semester. Some instructors have a policy of not accepting any students after the second week of the semester, and the students are often treated as if they have no business trying to get into classes late!

The effects of sections being canceled are obvious. First, students are lulled into believing that their schedules are set for the semester, so they don't worry about "double enrolling" in additional courses to cover themselves, a practice the college frowns on. Second, they are left, often for two weeks into the semester, with the uncertainty and anxiety of not knowing which of their classes will "make" and which will be canceled. Third, once classes are canceled, students are left with the responsibility of finding other classes to fill their schedules, and the college guarantees them nothing. Finally, and most damaging, they often end up taking classes they didn't want or need, and taking fewer classes than they had planned, which could jeopardize their grant eligibility and lengthen their stay at the college.

I'm sure the college has its reasons for overscheduling sections of courses. It can see which sections fill and then cancel the smaller sections that are more costly. It can also list the instructors for most sections as "staff" and then place teachers in sections where there are the best enrollments. And the college knows that with many small sections being canceled, the enrollment in the sections that "make" will only get better. In short, the administrators are doing what's best financially for the college at the expense of the students.

The college's current practice of overscheduling sections of courses is very unfair to students. The number of sections offered any semester should reflect the number of classes that realistically should fill with at least twenty students. That number can be pretty well determined by checking the number of sections of a course that "made" the same semester of the previous year. A two- or three-year study, taking college enrollment fluctuations into account, might provide an even more accurate indicator. The excuse that the college can't really predict how many sections to offer in any given semester just doesn't wash.

Last semester, according to the college admission's office, twenty-four sections of general ed pattern courses were canceled due to small enrollment. That is a scandalously high number. I think anyone could understand four or five sections needing to be canceled or added, based on enrollment fluctuations, but twenty-four canceled sections indicates a clearly intended practice of overscheduling and canceling classes, strictly for the financial benefit and convenience of the school and at the expense of the students.

This practice needs to be stopped immediately, and I am asking the administration to meet with a student committee before next semester's schedule is published. We want to ensure that all of the classes scheduled, based on current overall enrollment, have a realistic chance of reaching minimum enrollment figures. When that occurs, students' registration schedules will accurately reflect their load for the semester, students won't be forced to scrounge for classes after the semester begins, and students will have a better chance of getting the classes and the units they need. After all, the college is here for the students, and not the other way around.

Readings

The Euphemism of Lethal Injection

BY DAVID BOROFKA

1   The use of lethal injection as the preferred form of execution is the latest effort to make capital punishment socially—not to mention legally—palatable. This development says some interesting things about our collective psyche as well as our social attitudes regarding capital punishment itself.

2   First, it would seem to indicate that although we have no qualms about a punishment that allows no redress in the event of error, we do have some misgivings about the form that that punishment takes. We would like to believe that we are somehow more evolved socially by distancing ourselves from our recent history and what is perceived as more torturous, not to mention atavistic, forms of execution: the electric chair, the gas chamber, the firing squad, the hangman's noose. We no longer draw and quarter the criminal, nor do we burn the accused at the stake. We shudder at the suggestion of the guillotine or the cross.

3   On the other hand, the use of lethal injection replaces the grim reality of Death Row with the relatively benign figure of the hospital. Our most extreme form of punishment is no longer "cruel and unusual" because it is performed under a doctor's care. But this is where the problem lies—when allegory is turned on its head. Instead of the figure informing the reality, our reality is supplanted and masked by the metaphor: the inmate is turned into a patient; the executioner becomes a doctor; and the execution order is nothing more than a prescription for treatment. Death itself is transformed into sleep, maybe the greatest euphemism of all. We can now wash our hands of a felon's sociopathology as well as the felon's life, without feeling guilty about causing further pain and suffering.

4   However, this desire to separate death from cruelty and pain demands that we rethink our position with respect to capital punishment entirely. We are caught in the middle of a whole complex of beliefs about ourselves, feelings that are as intense as they are paradoxical. We would like to believe that our communities are formed in the majority by people who are good, and that good people do not kill one another. And yet according to poll after poll we believe that those who violate the most fundamental aspects of the social contract deserve to be punished—not only by removing that person from the community but by removing that person from life itself. As though we could eliminate those hidden impulses within us all by killing the person who has expressed them. We choose to inflict death—the toll of punishment and revenge—even as our choice of lethal injection allows us to distance ourselves from our own complicity in the death of a fellow human being. We yearn for catharsis—relief not only from our fears of the outside threat but the anxiety of our own inner demons—although we would like to feel nothing.

5   And therein lies the danger: of forgetting that a community is an organism in which the circumstances of one life affect all lives. When we kill—whether as an act of the irrational individual or the rational collective—we kill a part of everyone in the community. And when we kill via lethal injection we are emotionally deadening ourselves, masking our true motives in the counterfeit of sensitivity. For when we put one of ourselves to death in the name of justice and call it humane, we put our collective self to sleep in the misapplication of mercy.

QUESTIONS FOR DISCUSSION

1. What is the essay's thesis?

2. How does Borofka view lethal injection as a "metaphor." How does this metaphor influence people's thinking and feeling?

3. Discuss lethal injection as a "humane" form of execution. How do you feel about its use?

4. Does the essay speak in favor or against the death penalty, or is it only concerned with the form of execution? Do you agree with the author's viewpoint?

5. What audience may the essay be intended for? What may the author's purpose be in writing it?

VOCABULARY

Euphemism, palatable (1), benign (3), allegory (3), metaphor (3), paradoxical (4), catharsis (4).

Limiting Handguns

BY ROBERT deGRAZIA

1   We buried Donald Brown in May. He was murdered by three men who wanted to rob the supermarket manager he was protecting. Patrolman Brown was 61 years old, six months from retirement. He and his wife intended to retire to Florida at the end of the year. Now there will be no retirement in the sun, and she is alone.

2   Donald Brown was the second police officer to die since I became commissioner here on Nov. 15, 1972.

3   The first was John Schroeder, a detective shot in a pawnshop robbery last November. John Schroeder was the brother of Walter Schroeder, who was killed in a bank robbery in 1970. Their names are together on the honor roll in the lobby of Police Headquarters.

4   John Murphy didn't die. He was shot in the head last February as he chased a robbery suspect into the Washington Street subway station. He lived, but he will be brain-damaged for the rest of his life, unable to walk or talk.

5   At least two of these police officers were shot by a handgun, the kind one can buy nearly everywhere for a few dollars. Those who don't want to buy one can steal one, and half a million are stolen each year. There are forty million handguns circulating in this country; two and a half million are sold each year.

6   Anybody can get a gun. Ownership of handguns has become so widespread that the gun is no longer merely the instrument of crime; it is now a cause of violent crime. Of the eleven Boston police officers killed since 1962, seven were killed with handguns; of the seventeen wounded by guns since 1962, sixteen were shot with handguns.

7   Police officers, of course, are not the only people who die. Ten thousand other Americans are dead at the price of our promiscuous right to bear arms. Gun advocates are fond of saying that guns don't kill, people do. But guns do kill.

8   Half of the people who commit suicide do so with handguns. Fifty-four percent of the murders committed in 1972 were committed with handguns. Killing with handguns simply is a good deal easier than killing with other weapons.

9   Rifles and shotguns are difficult to conceal. People can run away from knife-wielding assailants. People do die each year by drownings, bludgeonings and strangulation. But assaults with handguns are five times more likely to kill.

10   No one can convince me, after returning from Patrolman Brown's funeral, after standing in the rain with hundreds of others from this department and others, that we should allow people to own handguns.

11   I know that many people feel deeply and honestly about their right to own and enjoy guns. I realize that gun ownership and self-protection are deeply held American values. I am asking that people give them up.

12   I am committed to doing what I can to take guns away from the people. In my view, private ownership of handguns must be banished from this country. I am not asking for registration or licensing or outlawing cheap guns. I am saying that no private citizen, whatever his claim, should possess a handgun. Only police officers should.

QUESTIONS FOR DISCUSSION

1. What is the topic of this essay? What is deGrazia's thesis? Where is the thesis specifically stated? Where is it implied?

2. What is presented in the first five paragraphs? What impact do these paragraphs have on the reader? Why do you think deGrazia opened his essay this way?

3. What are deGrazia's main arguments against handguns? Where do these arguments appear in the essay? Are they convincing?

4. Discuss the organization of the essay: the opening five paragraphs, the middle paragraphs, and the final three paragraphs. What is accomplished in each part? Is the organization effective? How might the essay be organized differently?

5. What audience do you think deGrazia is trying to reach in the essay? What might his purpose be in writing it? Do you agree with his viewpoint on handguns?

VOCABULARY

Promiscuous (7), wielding (9), assailants (9), bludgeonings (9), banished (12)

Let's Tell the Story of All America's Cultures

BY JI-YEON MARY YUHFILL

1   I grew up hearing, seeing and almost believing that America was white—albeit with a little black tinged here and there—and that white was best.

2   The white people were everywhere in my 1970s Chicago childhood: Founding Fathers, Lewis and Clark, Lincoln, Daniel Boone, Carnegie,* presidents, explorers and industrialists galore. The only black people were slaves. The only Indians were scalpers.

3   I never heard one word about how Benjamin Franklin was so impressed by the Iroquois federation of nations that he adapted that model into our system of state and federal government. Or that the Indian tribes were systematically betrayed and massacred by a greedy young nation that stole their land and called it the United States.

4   I never heard one word about how Asian immigrants were among the first to turn California's desert into fields of plenty. Or about Chinese immigrant Ah Bing, who bred the cherry now on sale in groceries across the nation. Or that plantation owners in Hawaii imported labor from China, Japan, Korea and the Philippines to work the sugar cane fields. I never learned that Asian immigrants were the only immigrants denied U.S. citizenship, even though they served honorably in World War I. All the immigrants in my textbook were white.

5   I never learned about Frederick Douglass, the runaway slave who became a leading abolitionist and statesman, or about black scholar W. E. B. Du Bois. I never learned that black people rose up in arms against slavery. Nat Turner wasn't one of the heroes in my childhood history class.

6   I never learned that the American Southwest and California were already settled by Mexicans when they were annexed after the Mexican-American War. I never learned that Mexico once had a problem keeping land-hungry white men on the U.S. side of the border.

7   So when other children called me a slant-eyed chink and told me to go back where I came from, I was ready to believe that I wasn't really an American because I wasn't white.

---

* Eds. Note—Andrew Carnegie (1835–1919), American industrialist and philanthropist.

8   America's bittersweet legacy of struggling and failing and getting another step closer to democratic ideals of liberty and equality and justice for all wasn't for the likes of me, an immigrant child from Korea. The history books said so.

9   Well, the history books were wrong.

10 Educators around the country are finally realizing what I realized as a teenager in the library, looking up the history I wasn't getting in school. America is a multicultural nation, composed of many people with varying histories and varying traditions who have little in common except their humanity, a belief in democracy and a desire for freedom.

11 America changed them, but they changed America too.

12 A committee of scholars and teachers gathered by the New York State Department of Education recognizes this in their recent report, "One Nation, Many Peoples: A Declaration of Cultural Interdependence."

13 They recommend that public schools provide a "multicultural education, anchored to the shared principles of a liberal democracy."

14 What that means, according to the report, is recognizing that America was shaped and continues to be shaped by people of diverse backgrounds. It calls for students to be taught that history is an ongoing process of discovery and interpretation of the past, and that there is more than one way of viewing the world.

15 Thus, the westward migration of white Americans is not just a heroic settling of an untamed wild, but also the conquest of indigenous peoples. Immigrants were not just white, but Asian as well. Blacks were not merely passive slaves freed by northern whites, but active fighters for their own liberation.

16 In particular, according to the report, the curriculum should help children "to access critically the reasons for the inconsistencies between the ideals of the U.S. and social realities. It should provide information and intellectual tools that can permit them to contribute to bringing reality closer to the ideals."

17 In other words, show children the good with the bad, and give them the skills to help improve their country. What could be more patriotic?

18 Several dissenting members of the New York committee publicly worry that America will splinter into ethnic fragments if this multicultural curriculum is adopted. They argue that the committee's report puts the focus on ethnicity at the expense of national unity.

19 But downplaying ethnicity will not bolster national unity. The history of America is the story of how and why people from all over the world came to the United States, and how in struggling to make a better life for themselves, they changed each other, they changed the country, and they all came to call themselves Americans.

20 *E pluribus unum*. Out of many, one.

21 This is why I, with my Korean background, and my childhood tormentors, with their lost-in-the-mist-of-time-European backgrounds, are all Americans.

22   It is the unique beauty of this country. It is high time we let all our children gaze upon it.

QUESTIONS FOR DISCUSSION

1. What is the thesis of the essay, which Yuhfill came to realize as a young woman? How does she support her thesis?

2. What is the purpose of the seven-paragraph opening? Why does Yuhfill choose to fill the first half of her essay with examples?

3. How do traditional textbooks paint a distorted picture of America's development? In what ways does this picture affect non-white American students?

4. What is a multicultural approach to education? How would it change children's perceptions of themselves and their country?

5. What arguments are posed against multicultural education? How would you respond to those arguments?

VOCABULARY

Systematically (3), abolitionist (5), bittersweet (8), legacy (8), multicultural (10), ethnicity (18)

Exploring New Territory

In the first five units, you wrote papers by drawing on your knowledge and experience. Writing is also a voyage of discovery in which you explore new topics and share what you learn with readers.

As a writer, you usually begin with what you know and how you feel about something. However, what you know and feel doesn't help you write about everything that may interest you. For example, you may be curious about whether life exists on other planets, but your interest may exceed your knowledge. Sometimes you need to become better informed before writing.

Prewriting

Much of the writing you do in college and beyond will require some topic exploration. Although you may know something about the topic, you will need to investigate it further in order to write knowledgeably for your readers. In this unit, such prewriting investigation is crucial to writing an effective paper.

TOPIC SELECTION

One purpose of investigative writing is to expand your knowledge in a particular area of interest. To get the most out of your writing for this unit, select a topic that goes beyond your current knowledge and experience. Your goal is to learn as much from this assignment as your readers.

Topic Selection Activity 6.1

To select an investigative writing topic, follow these guidelines:

1. Your topic will answer the question: What is it like _____ ? For example, what is it like being a foreign student in an American college? being an older returning student? being a college instructor? working full time and going to school? being a single parent? being raised by a single parent? being gay in a straight world? working as an attorney, accountant, forest ranger, probation officer, or computer programmer? living with a particular disability? being of a particular ethnic minority? being an athlete on scholarship? growing up in a very large family?

    Pick a topic that you know little about but that interests you.

2. Your investigative work is to talk with people who belong to the group that your topic is about (for example, foreign students, single mothers or fathers, accountants, college athletes). Select a topic for which you can find knowledgeable people to interview.

STUDENT TOPIC SELECTION

Let's see, there are lots of things I'm interested in, but they are things I know something about. What do I know little about that interests me? I wonder what it's like to be a really famous model or movie star. That's out since I don't know any to interview. That big rubber plant I drive by going to school always has foul-smelling smoke coming out of its stacks. I've always thought that would be a lousy place to work, but I really have no idea. That sort of interests me.

What's it like to be mayor of Glenburg? Naw, I don't really care. A lot of my friends' folks are divorced, probably more so than not. I've never really asked them what it's like to go through all that. I've just felt lucky my parents are together. I do have some curiosity about that, and it sure affects a lot of people. Maybe I'll write on what it's like for children to deal with their parents' divorce. I think I'd write this to a rather general audience although I'll make that decision after I talk to some of my friends.

INVESTIGATING YOUR TOPIC

There are different ways to learn more about a particular topic: through reading, experiencing, or talking with knowledgeable people. Before writing your investigative paper, you will be talking with people who are experiencing (or have experienced) the situation you are writing about.

Interview Process

The best way to talk to people is individually so that they can be most candid and won't be influenced by what others say. Here are some suggestions for conducting your informal interviews:

1. Let the interviewees know your purpose for interviewing them, and assure them that their names will be kept confidential. Make them feel comfortable.

2. Generate a list of questions that cover the most important (and interesting) aspects of the topic. Have six to eight questions ready, and begin by asking the easiest questions to get the person talking.

3. Don't expect each interviewee to provide detailed responses. Be prepared to ask follow-up questions to get the examples and details you'll need to write an interesting paper. Ask questions like, "Why do you feel that way about . . . ?" "Can you give me an example of what you consider . . . ?" "How would you define . . . ?" "What details do you remember about the incident?" "How did that experience affect you?"

   Interviewees will often speak in generalities, and your follow-up questions will help you get interesting information.

4. Allow an interview to go in unexpected directions. Since the interviewee knows more about the topic than you do, he or she may get into areas you haven't considered.

5. Interview five or six people, and take detailed notes. Don't rely on your memory to recall the specific examples and details that will be important when you write the paper.

Prewriting Activity 6.2

Come up with six to eight questions to ask each interviewee about the topic you have selected. End each interview with the question, "What haven't I covered that people should know about _____ ?" Then find people who are knowledgeable about your topic and willing to talk. Conduct five or six interviews to get different perspectives on the subject.

Take notes as your interviewees answer questions, and ask them to give examples whenever possible to support and clarify their statements. Your notes will provide the basis for your paper.

STUDENT INTERVIEW
QUESTIONS

Children of Divorce

1. What was it like when your parents first got divorced? What thoughts and feelings did you have?

2. Who did you live with after the divorce, and how did you feel about each of your parents?

3. In what different ways did the divorce affect your life?

4. What have been the hardest things to deal with? What, if any, positive things have come from the experience?

5. Now that you are an adult, how do you view the situation? What is your family life like now?

6. What advice would you give to children who, like yourself, have to go through their parents' divorce?

7. In what ways, if at all, has the experience affected your attitude toward marriage and family?

The following excerpts are from an interview based on the preceding questions.

INTERVIEW #1
(in interviewer's words)

The divorce was awful. She couldn't believe it was happening, had never thought of the possibility. She remembers crying for days and being embarrassed to tell anyone. She felt a great loss when her dad left the house because they were close. Their relationship has never really been the same. She hoped for a long time that her parents would get back together.

Everything was harder after the divorce. She was alone more and didn't get as much attention. Her mother had to work more and wasn't home as much. She only saw her dad on weekends. She and her brother grew closer as a result and she had someone to talk to about everything.

She could find nothing positive about the divorce. It still affects her now, some eight years later, because she and her dad have grown further apart and she is not close to her stepfather. She doesn't blame her mom for remarrying, but she doesn't feel as comfortable in her home anymore. Holidays are no longer a time of joy, because they bring back memories of a happy family life that no longer is there. She has real doubts about marriage and would hate to put children of her own through what she's been through.

First Drafts

At this point in the writing process, you have a topic and a set of notes from your interviews. Your next step is to consider how to use your interview material in your paper.

FROM NOTES TO DRAFT

As you read over your notes and consider your first draft, keep the following in mind:

1. What similarities run through the interviews? Are there aspects of the topic that most interviewees agree with or have in common?

2. What important differences run through the interviews? What do the differences signify?

3. In what general categories might you group your notes to help organize the draft?

4. What specific examples can you use from the interviews to support the main points that interviewees made?

5. What potential thesis does the interview material support: the main point that you want to share with your readers?

Planning Activity 6.3

Review your interview notes and apply the preceding questions to help you plan your draft. Make a list of general categories that you might use to organize your draft. Then write a thesis statement that the interview material supports.

STUDENT LIST OF CATEGORIES (Topic: Effects of divorce)

1. initial reactions to divorce
2. effects on children's lives
3. perspective as an adult
4. effects on attitude toward marriage and family

POSSIBLE THESIS STATEMENT

Divorce can be devastating to children and have lasting effects.

WRITER'S PRESENCE

As you write your draft, you are doing more than recording the thoughts and opinions of the people you have interviewed. The following suggestions will help put you in control of your paper:

1. Create your opening without using material from the interviews. Engage your readers' interest in the topic, reveal your own interest in some way, and present your thesis.

2. Rather than just presenting the interview material, use it to make certain points. For example, if foreign students all spoke of their language difficulties when interviewed, you could make the point, "most foreign students face a language barrier," and then give examples from the interviews.

3. Integrate the interview material in your paper. By presenting the material through different categories (initial reactions to divorce, effects on one's life, perspective as an adult, effects on attitude toward marriage and family), you integrate material from all of the interviews throughout the paper. The other less effective option—to present each interview separately—diminishes the writer's role and may lead to a less insightful paper.

4. Have a clear purpose for writing the paper. If you are writing about the effects of divorce on children, your purpose may be to make readers more aware of and sensitive to the things that such children go through, even into their adult years. As you write the paper, do your best to make your readers understand that.

Drafting Activity 6.4

Write your first draft following the suggestions just presented. Write this paper for your classmates as well as for other readers who may be interested in your topic.

STUDENT FIRST DRAFT

The parents of many of my friends are divorced, and have been for some time. We've never talked much about it. It's so common that it's not something I've ever given much thought to. However, once I decided to find out more about how divorce has affected my friends' lives, and undoubtedly the lives of thousands of others, I began to realize how different things have been for them than for me.

Divorce is very traumatic on children. All my friends agreed that it changed their lives forever. Their emotions at the time of divorce run the gamut: sadness, anger, fear, regret, embarrassment. Some blamed themselves in some way for their parents' divorce, while others blamed the parent that left the house, invariably the father. Their family lives as they had always known them were torn apart, and for the most part with little forewarning. Their all-emcompassing thought was, "What's going to happen to me now?" Insecurity invaded their lives and sometimes stayed with them for years.

Divorce changes a child's life in hard ways. Generally, they see much less of their fathers, and those who were close to them feel abandoned and sometimes unloved. "If he really loved me, he would never have left" was a common thought. Mothers often have to work more out of the home after a divorce to make ends meet, so children are on their own more. Loneliness sets in, and siblings often grow closer, looking to each other for support. It's not surprising that children frequently hold out hope that their parents will get back together: "For years, I held the illusion that things would go back as they used to be. It was hard to give up that dream."

As the years go on after the divorce, a sense of order is usually established in the children's lives, but often at a price. Some children are raised by their mothers and establish good relations with their fathers. Some have stepfathers, and stepmothers as well, and feelings for stepparents run from love to indifference to hatred. Some also have stepbrothers or stepsisters they live with. Children of divorce are forced to cope with many things, including adjusting to living with new people and working out relationships with step-relatives. Said one girl, "In some ways it's like a foster situation. You can be moved to a different home and live with different people, except for your mom being there. The new situation can be bad or it can be alright, but it's never like it was."

My friends had little positive to say about divorce, except in situations where the family life was bad before the divorce. In instances where mothers and fathers argued constantly or where the father was distant or even abusive to the children, divorce improved the situation. Said one friend, "I was a lot happier when my dad left. He was mean to mom and mean to us kids, and it was better when he wasn't around." However, even in marriages that were rocky, most children would still have preferred the family to stay together. "Sure, things were far from perfect, but at least we were a family, and families are supposed to stay together," said one guy.

Adulthood does not make everything okay for former children of divorces. Most of my friends still have fond memories of their family that will be with them forever. Some think that if their parents hadn't divorced, their lives would have been better than they were. Some still think about being children of divorced parents, like a stigma they carry with them. They somehow feel less worthy or less complete than their friends who have families intact. "I've always felt some embarrassment about my folks being divorced, and it's made me less secure about myself," said one friend. Said another, "Even today events that are supposed to be happy, like birthdays and Christmas and Thanksgiving and family weddings, are often sad. You can't be with both your father and mother, and you feel that sense of loss the most on special days."

Finally, children of divorce are often uncertain about their own marital futures. They've seen the effects of divorce, and some wonder if marriage is worth it. Others are determined that if they get married, they'll never do to their children what was done to them. Some don't see marriage as a permanent situation anymore. Said one friend, "I'm not going to have children because who knows how long the marriage will last. Why take the chance?"

After talking to my friends, I realize how much most of them lost through their parents' divorce: stability, security, confidence, innocence, and a part of their former lives. They don't want anyone feeling sorry for them, and they don't care much for sitting around and talking about their situations. But they do carry with them a certain burden that children whose parents remain together don't have. They've had it tougher as kids, and they have it tougher as young adults. Things that I take for granted every day with my family they only have distant memories of. Divorce is a real American tragedy, and children of divorce often hurt the worst and the longest.

Revisions

When you finish your first draft, set it aside before reviewing it. Although you can't distance yourself completely from its authorship, the more objectively you can look at a draft, the better you can recognize both its strengths and weaknesses.

REVISION GUIDELINES

When evaluating your draft, consider the following revision guidelines:

1. What does the opening offer the reader in the way of interest and content? Is the topic clearly introduced? Is the thesis (or a thesis-related question) for the paper included? What is there to the opening that would attract the reader's attention?

2. What supporting points for the thesis are included in the middle paragraphs? Are examples provided from the interview material to clarify and develop each point? Is the interview material effectively incorporated?

3. Is the draft paragraphed so that readers can follow the writer's thoughts easily? In each paragraph, do all the sentences relate to a main idea? Do *transitions* tie sentences and paragraphs together?

4. Is the draft organized effectively? Does the reader get a sense of moving from opening to middle to conclusion? Is there a better way to organize any part of the paper?

5. Are there any wordy, awkward, or unclear sentences that need rewording? Are sentences sufficiently varied in structure?

6. What will readers learn from the paper that you learned from your interviews? Have you left out anything important?

Revision Activity 6.5

Read the following first draft, and with a partner, evaluate it by applying the questions for revision. Then evaluate your own draft similarly, making changes that you feel will improve it. When you are ready, write the next draft of your paper, and continue the drafting and evaluation process until you are satisfied with your final draft.

Back to College

STUDENT DRAFT

When I went to my first college night class last semester, I was surprised to find I was one of the younger students in the class. At least a dozen of the students were women ranging from thirty to fifty years of age. The last thing I pictured myself doing at their age was being in college, so I wondered why so many older women were there.

As the semester progressed, I got to know several of the women, and I really enjoyed being in class with them. I also found out more about their background and their reasons for being in school. Judging from their comments, the experience of being back in school is different for each of them.

Women come back to school for a lot of reasons. Some are filling a void in their lives created when their children grew up and left home. Some are picking up on career ambitions that were put aside when they got married. Many are back out of necessity: some are divorced and need training for a good-paying job; others need to contribute to new house payments.

Some women are returning just to prove something to themselves. They may have a low self-image from earlier school years that they want to improve, or they may want to know if they have what it takes to graduate. Some just enjoy the challenge; they want to test their wits against the younger generation or see how much they can learn about all kinds of subjects.

Women's first impressions on returning to school also varied. Some were relieved to see so many people their age in school, and they felt comfortable right away. Some were depressed by the amount of reading and studying they would have to do, and they wondered how they'd find time. Many were apprehensive about their ability to succeed, and they were intimidated by the younger students' abilities.

One woman's experience was seconded by some of the others. She was in a biology class with mainly younger students who asked lots of questions in class and appeared much abler than she was. She studied like mad for the first test, hoping just to pass and not score lowest in the class. She ended up with the third highest grade on the test, which surprised and thrilled her. She began to realize that college students hadn't changed much—most of them just do enough to get by—and she knew then that she could succeed.

Most of the women had positive things to say about being in school. One woman enjoyed making friends with other students her own age. Another loved being around the younger students, some of whom called her "Mom." Another woman found she had a real aptitude for computer work, and she couldn't wait to take more computer classes. Still another felt good about how kind her teachers were to her. Many of them said it felt good to have a goal to be shooting for, and one woman in her fifties said, "This is the first time I've really used my brain for twenty years!"

All was not rosy, however, for these women. They had their share of problems, too.

One of the biggest complaints was the lack of time. Women who had jobs or who had children at home never felt they had enough time to get everything done. Many had to stay up late studying every weeknight, and some had to drop classes that required too much homework. One woman said she felt exhausted all week long, and all she did was sleep on weekends to recuperate.

Some women had trouble at home; their husbands complained that dinner was never ready and they were neglected. The women whose husbands didn't really support their being in school suffered the most. Then there were the problems with failed tests and bad grades that all students occasionally face. There were also those who couldn't see the end of it all. One woman said, "If I keep taking my six units a semester, I won't graduate for eight years. I'll never last that long." Finally a few women didn't really know what they were doing in school or what direction they were heading. One said, "I'm not really accomplishing much, but maybe if I just hang on another semester, I'll get my act together."

From what I observed from the older women in my night class, some will graduate and go on to universities, some will complete two-year programs and get jobs, some will get a few basic skills and be a little better for it, some will keep taking classes just because they enjoy it, some will drop out in frustration, and some will be dropped because they can't make it. There are probably as many ways for these women to exit college as there were reasons for them to enter.

However, succeed or fail, few women have regrets about being back in school. As one woman put it, "If I don't learn anything else, I'll have learned some things about myself that I wanted to know." And as another said, "This is my one last chance to give school a try. It's now or never."

PARAGRAPHING REVIEW

By this time in the course, you should have a good understanding of basic paragraphing and its importance in helping you organize your ideas and convey them effectively to readers. This final review activity is for students who could benefit from some additional practice in paragraphing papers and using transitional wording.

Paragraphing Activity 6.6

Divide the following essay into paragraphs by placing the paragraph symbol (¶) in front of each new paragraph. Change paragraphs each time the writer moves to a different aspect of her topic.

Next, insert transitional wording into sentences to tie paragraphs together. Look in particular at the first sentences of paragraphs to see what transition(s) would help readers move smoothly into the paragraph. Commonly used transitions include *first, second, next, then, also, in addition, therefore, however, for example, on the other hand, as you can see, finally,* and *in conclusion.*

Franklin Arena was packed with people. There were so many bodies I wondered if there was enough air to breathe. It was hot and stuffy and I got a feeling of claustrophobia. Queen came out and a roar went up around the arena. It was really loud. The group went into one of their latest hits and everyone went crazy. The sound of the guitars was unbelievably loud. I'd never heard anything as loud as those amplifiers. The sound bounced off the walls and filled my head. Once I got used to it, it seemed like it had taken over my body. The crowd was good. You hear all this stuff about the crazies everywhere, but I didn't see many. There was a lot of pot going around and you could smell it and see this cloud hanging over the arena, and there were some drunk people, but everyone was having a good time and not bothering people. A lot of girls were on top of boys' shoulders, and some people were dancing. Most were just clapping their hands over their heads and screaming wildly after each song. The time went very fast. I didn't once think about how long I'd been there. Time didn't seem to matter at all. It just began and then it was over. Queen was great. They played with great energy, and they really came to entertain. You could tell they were here to give everyone their money's worth. Their energy carried to the audience and kept it on a high. They never stopped playing long enough to break the trance. It was the closest thing to hysteria I'd been around, but it wasn't a bad hysteria. It was happy and wild and joyful. I loved the experience. The light show was great. It added to the magic, to the fantasy of the experience; it put you in another world. It helped create the experience—the flashing strobes, the lightning bolts of reds and greens and blues, the fiery explosions. It was the Fourth of July on Mars. It took me a long time to come down from the emotion after the concert. I had really been pumped up and excited by everything. Maybe it was partly because it was my first concert. Maybe it seemed routine to some people. But the way everyone was responding, I'll bet it's the same wild time whenever a great group comes to town.

SENTENCE REVISION REVIEW

This final review section gives you more practice revising first draft sentences to improve their wording and structural variety. Sentence revision is a critical part of the writing process, and your revising skills will continue to grow as long as you write.

Wording Problems

To help you improve first draft sentences, here is a summary of the different kinds of sentence problems that writers often revise.

1. *Wordiness:* Sentences often contain more words than necessary to express a writer's thoughts. These sentences contain repeated words and phrases or unnecessarily complicated wording to make simple statements. To revise wordy sentences, eliminate unnecessary words and replace complicated phrases with simpler ones.

Wordy sentence	We were out in the rays of the sun for six hours of daylight, but we didn't burn due to the fact that we wore a sunscreen that kept us from burning.

Revised   We were out in the sun for six hours, but we didn't burn because we wore a sunscreen.

2. *Awkward phrasing:* First draft sentences often contain awkward wording that occurs when a writer first tries out his or her thoughts on paper. If a sentence sounds odd to a writer, it will probably give a reader problems. To correct awkward wording, find a better way to express the thought. Changing a word or two may make the difference, or you may have to revise the entire sentence.

Awkward sentence   There is a square cement floor with trees and bushes that are around the cement.

Revised   Oak trees and a few bushes surround the cement patio.

3. *Poor word choices:* First draft sentences sometimes contain words that don't say quite what the writer wants. You can often tell when you've used a word in a first draft that doesn't sound right, but you can't think of a better choice. On returning to a draft after a few hours or days, the poorer word choices stand out even more, and often, better choices will come to you. To correct poor word choices, replace them with more appropriate words.

Poor word choice   The clown made the boy full of fear instead of enjoying him.

Revised   The clown frightened the boy instead of entertaining him.

4. *Concrete language:* Vague, general wording should be replaced by concrete language that *shows* the reader what the writer sees, hears, and feels.

Vague wording   The boy works one part of the year.

Revised   My ten-year-old neighbor, Jim Jones, works all summer at his father's feed store.

Sentence Revision Activity 6.7

The following paragraph needs revising for sentence improvement. Rewrite the paragraph making each sentence as clear and smooth as possible.

It was a hot day for a parade. The band of the school had a five-mile walk through the middle of the town. Before the parade began, the band members standing at attention for an hour. Most band members were wet with sweat before they had walked one step. One tuba player he passed out from the heat and is taken to the hospital. Finally, the band began marching and starts playing "When the Saints Go Marching In." Every one of the members of that band was sick of that song "When the Saints Go Marching

In" before they got even halfway through the parade route they were marching along. By the time the band reached the judges' stand, their lips were too parched to suck, their march was a stagger, and their white uniforms are colored by sweat. The band finally went to the park and on the lawn collapsed. They stripped off their hats, coats, and shoes that they wore for the parade. They drank gallons of lemonade and compare blisters on their feet and compare scuffed up shoes.

Sentence Variety

Here is a summary of what you have learned about sentence variety in your writing:

1. Some writers have a tendency to overuse certain sentence structures and joining words, which can lead to monotonous prose.

2. Check your first draft sentences to see whether you have overrelied on a particular structure, for example, simple sentences (one subject, one verb) or compound sentences joined primarily by *and, but,* or *so.*

3. Vary sentence structures to include a combination of simple, compound, and complex sentences, and vary joining words by using many of the following: and, but, so, for, yet, or, when, before, after, while, as, until, since, although, unless, if, because, who, whose, which, that.

4. Some writers have a tendency to string pairs or groups of short sentences together, or to write overly long, involved sentences.

5. Check your first drafts to find short sentences that could be effectively combined or overly long sentences that could be divided by inserting periods and eliminating some joining words.

Sentence Variety Activity 6.8

Revise the following first draft sentences in different ways: combine sentences with joining words and eliminate unnecessary words; group similar words; and divide overly long sentences by inserting periods and deleting joining words. Vary your sentence structures and joining words, and don't try to squeeze too many sentences uncomfortably into a single sentence.

Example   Melba likes to listen to her stereo. Thad likes to listen to his. They both enjoy using their headphones. They are brother and sister.

Combined   Melba and Thad, who are brother and sister, enjoy listening to their stereos and using their headphones.

1. Sheri is an interesting girl. She is a freshman in college. She is a practicing minister. She is an assistant manager of a shoe store.

2. The spaniel ran all over the hills. He was delighted to be in the open. He is owned by Mr. Jacobs. Mr. Jacobs turned him loose for an afternoon.

3. The old Keystone Building, which is on 52nd Street, is going to be demolished, and it will be replaced by a high rise, which will be built by the end of summer and have thirty stories.

4. Some children in town will be bused to school. They live on the northeast side of town. This will only be for one semester. Their school is being refurbished. It was damaged in an earthquake.

5. Clyde rushed to school. He opened his locker. He removed his notebook. He ran to his biology lab. He was late.

6. We found thousands of cockroaches in the old house, and we found them behind the refrigerator, and we found them this summer, but they were dead, for they had starved to death.

7. Greta is young. She is naive. She is impressionable. She is quick to learn.

8. The house is for sale. It's a dark brown. It's on the east corner of 5th Street. It's listed for $55,000. That is a real steal.

9. Jonathan, who is a nineteen-year-old fireman, is going bald, but he couldn't care less about going bald because he is not vain, and his fiancee loves him the way he is.

10. Ann rooms with Helen. Marie rooms with both of them. They are sophomores from Natchez. They live in off-campus housing. They live there during the semester. They move home in the summer.

11. Freda is friendly. She acts this way with everyone. She has no close friends. She moves often with her job.

12. Harley contemplates his future. He sits in his room. He forgets his past. It is troubled.

13. Mary likes to win. She isn't afraid of losing. She is the captain of the lawn bowling team. The team is from Friar Hill.

14. Teddy is my brother. He is younger than I am. He is bigger than I am. He doesn't weigh as much.

15. Harold has trouble with allergies, so he carries a box of tissues in his car, and he goes through the box in a day, and he does this in the springtime, for this is when his allergies are the worst.

16. Mattie found her first grade class picture. She found it in the attic. It was among boxes of old albums. She was rummaging around for an old sweater.

17. Think of a way to get out of health science today. Come up with something new. Make it ingenious. I'm not prepared for the test. Neither are you.

18. Alexandra had to make a choice. She had to choose between beauty college and art school. She had to decide in the next week. Both schools enrolled students on Monday.

Final Editing

By this time in the course, you may need little guidance in proofreading your drafts and correcting errors. You may have even worked out your own error detection process. Undoubtedly, you are aware of your personal error tendencies and conscientiously scrutinize your drafts in those areas.

For those of you who rely on the proofreading guidelines in the text, a final summary is provided. In the future, you need to internalize these guidelines to use them for any writing you may do.

PROOFREADING GUIDELINES

1. Check to make sure you have a period at the end of each sentence, and correct any run-on sentences, comma splices, or sentence fragments.

2. Check your word endings to make sure that plural words end in *s*, regular past tense verbs end in *ed*, one-syllable comparative and superlative adjectives end in *er* and *est*, respectively, and present tense verbs with singular subjects end in *s*.

3. Check your spelling carefully, looking up any words you are uncertain of. Also check your use of homonyms such as there/their/they're, know/no, its/it's, your/you're, and threw/through.

4. Check your comma usage in words in series and compound sentences, after introductory groups of words, and to set off relative clauses, interrupters, and ending phrases beginning with *especially, particularly,* and *ing*-words. Also check your use of apostrophes, quotation marks, semicolons, and colons.

5. Check pronoun usage to make sure you are using the correct subject pronouns in compound subjects and that all pronouns agree in number and gender with their antecedents.

Editing Activity 6.9

Proofread your latest draft following the guidelines presented. (Your instructor may have you do the upcoming editing review activities before proofreading your draft.) Correct any remaining errors, and then write or print out your final draft and share it with your classmates and instructor.

SENTENCE PROBLEMS REVIEW

The following review activity is for students who still have some problems with run-on sentences, comma splices, or fragments. Punctuating sentences correctly is fundamental to effective writing, so if run-ons or fragments still nag your writing, keep working on the problem whenever you write.

Proofreading Activity 6.10

Proofread the following paragraphs for run-on sentences, comma splices, and sentence fragments. Separate run-ons and comma splices with periods or join the sentences to form compound or complex sentences. Attach fragments to the sentences they belong with or add words to form complete sentences.

Community colleges have both advantages and disadvantages compared to four-year schools. One advantage of community colleges is their cost. Throughout the country, community college tuition is less expensive than for four-year colleges, ranging from $300 to $600 per year. Most community college students also live at home, saving on the cost of room and board. Four-year colleges, on the other hand, range in tuition from $1,500 a year for some state-operated colleges to $15,000–$25,000 a year for private schools on top of that, most four-year college students live away from home. Spending $5,000–$8,000 per year on room and board. It is not surprising that many students choose to spend two years at a community college. Before transferring to a more expensive four-year school.

On the whole, community colleges are not as difficult as four-year colleges. Studies show that GPAs for community college transfer students drop in their third year while those of four-year college students do not. Surveys also indicate that most community college transfer students find their four-year college courses more difficult and time-consuming than community college courses. Therefore, it appears that community colleges may not prepare students as well as four-year colleges do, some community students may find themselves at a disadvantage when they transfer.

Community colleges also don't have the activities that four-year colleges do. Since community colleges are by and large "commuter" schools. With students living at home, participation in campus activities is much lower than at four-year schools with their live-in dormitory populations. Participation in school government and on-campus clubs is limited student attendance at football and basketball games often numbers a hundred or fewer. Community college students on the whole miss out on the excitement and social involvement that can be an important part of the college experience.

CORRECT USAGE REVIEW

The first five units covered grammar usage situations in which writers sometimes make mistakes: past tense verbs, subject-verb agreement, subject pronoun usage, pronoun-antecedent agreement, and comparative and superlative adjectives. This section provides a final proofreading activity to help you recognize and correct such errors in your writing.

Proofreading Activity 6.11

Proofread the following paragraphs for grammar errors involving subject-verb agreement, subject pronouns, pronoun-antecedent agreement, or superlative and comparative adjectives. Make the necessary corrections.

STUDENT FIRST DRAFT

The thing I like least about the apartments I live in are the topless dumpsters sitting in front of the west bank of apartments. First, it creates a bad smell. In the summer when it is full of garbage and used diapers, a putrid odor sweeps across the apartments when the afternoon breeze come up. Second, it is too small to accommodate a week's supply of trash. The garbage that gets piled up on top fall out, and dogs and the wind scatter them all over the driveway and lawn. By Friday before pickup time, the place is a littered mess.

The most worst problem are the flies. The garbage in the open dumpsters attract thousands of flies in warm weather, and they take up residence at the apartments. If you are outside, you constantly have to swat them off your face and body. They also find his or her way indoors, congregating in the kitchen while you eat and attacking your face while you sleep at night. From May to September, you can always hear flies buzzing somewhere in the apartment. They are the terriblest health problem at the apartments.

Obviously, the apartments need new dumpsters, ones that is covered to keep the flies away and the stench in, and ones that is large enough to hold a week's worth of garbage. It should also be moved to the east side of the apartments so that the breeze will carry the odor away from the buildings. If the owner isn't willing to pay a little more for decent covered dumpsters, I think the health department should be called. Some of the neighbors and me are prepared to do just that.

PUNCTUATION REVIEW

This final section provides a proofreading activity covering everything you have learned about using commas, apostrophes, quotation marks, semicolons, and colons in your writing.

Proofreading Activity 6.12

Proofread the following paragraphs for punctuation omissions, and insert commas, apostrophes, quotation marks, semicolons, and colons where they are needed.

The Inequity of College Grants

When I walk through the business services office at school I often notice a line of students getting their grant checks for the month. I don't begrudge them their checks because I know they need the money but when I see them Im reminded that I applied for every local and state grant I could and I didn't qualify for anything.

Because I get no financial aid I have to work at least thirty hours a week to help pay for my college and living expenses. I work at least four hours a day during the week and ten hours on weekends. With the colleges expenses so high, something needs to be done for lower-middle-income students like myself who are caught in between too "well off" for aid but too poor to survive without working long hours. I often ask myself why are people in my situation not given help?

As an example my mother and fathers combined income is $25,000. That may sound pretty good, but when there are four kids in the family house payments and the usual bills theres not much left for college expenses. My parents can't come close to paying for my tuition books fees and living expenses yet because of their salary bracket I didn't qualify for any grants. To stay in school I have to make at least $500 a month.

Having to work long hours I'm at a real disadvantage. Most students on grants don't work a lot and many students from middle- and upper-income families don't work at all. While I'm working thirty hours a week they can be putting those hours into studying. I never feel there's enough hours in the day to get my reading and studying done.

Another problem is I usually end up taking only the 12-unit minimum per semester to maintain a full-time students status I don't have time for more classes. This means I'll have to put in an extra semester or year of college to graduate or go to summer school every summer which is even more expensive than regular semesters. I also have to cram all of my classes into the morning hours so I can be at work by one o'clock on weekdays limiting my choice of courses and instructors.

The most aggravating thing is I know I could do so much better in school. When I was at home and going to high school my grades were good because I only worked a few hours a week. Now I feel like I have two full-time jobs and I don't have the time or energy to do my best in school. I end up settling for C's when I know I could be getting A's and B's. If I decide one day to apply for graduate school my grades are going to be a problem.

However I know I'm not in this alone. There are a lot of students caught in the same dilemma who tell me I have the same problems that you have. It just doesn't seem fair that going to college has to be made so much more difficult for some students than for others. In America everyone has the right to a college education but having the right and being given a fair opportunity to succeed are two different things. With some financial aid and a reduced work load I know I could succeed.

In the future I don't realistically see college expenses going down. Therefore I feel that for students like myself the salary limit for grant qualification should be raised. Im not saying I should have the full grant status that poorer students have but I feel that I should be entitled to at least a partial grant. Why couldnt someone in my position receive a half or quarter grant rather than being shut out completely? And why has the salary qualification level remained the same the last four years when the cost of college has gone up tremendously? One thing should be raised automatically with increased college expenses: the ceiling on grants.

Writing Review

A second way to investigate a topic is to observe something for yourself. For your final paper, you will observe a group of people and share what you learn with your classmates.

WRITING PROCESS

TOPIC SELECTION

1. Select a specific group of people that you would like to write about: shoppers at a particular store, a particular group of students in the cafeteria, school board members at a monthly meeting, children at a day-care center, teenagers at a concert, gang members at a local hangout, workers at McDonald's, spectators at a competition, and so on. Select a group that will be easy for you to observe.

PREWRITING OBSERVATION

2. Spend an hour or so observing the group you choose, and follow these suggestions:

   a. Use all of your observational senses. Be aware of what you see, hear, and smell, and how you feel about everything.

   b. Make note of group similarities—ways in which the people are alike—and differences—behavior, looks, and attitudes that distinguish individuals.

   c. Pay attention to detail, which you will use to help develop your paper.

   d. Make tentative judgments. Based on what you observe, what general conclusion(s) can you draw about your group?

PREWRITING PLAN

3. After you have observed your group, do the following:

   a. Decide on your thesis for the paper: the main point that you want to make about this group of people based on your observations.

   b. Make a list of supporting points you want to include in the paper, and consider what details and examples you might use from your observation to develop each point.

   c. Decide on a purpose for your paper: the reason you are writing to your classmates.

FIRST DRAFT

4. Write the first draft of your paper, keeping the following in mind:

   a. Include an opening, middle, and ending to your paper.

   b. Bring the group to life for readers. Help readers see, hear, and feel as you did when you were observing.

c. Keep your thesis in mind as you write: the main point you are developing.

5. When you finish your first draft, set it aside for a while before rereading it. When you are ready, evaluate the draft by applying the following revision guidelines, and then write your second draft.

   a. Evaluate your opening. Have you introduced your topic in an interesting way and presented your thesis? What might you do to engage your readers' interest even more?

   b. Evaluate your middle paragraphs. Have you presented some interesting points about the group that will help readers characterize them accurately? Have you used details and examples that bring the group to life?

   c. Evaluate your ending. Have you drawn conclusions about the group that will help readers understand them? Are readers left with a clear idea of how you feel about the group?

   d. Evaluate individual sentences, and revise them to improve their clarity, smoothness, conciseness, and variety.

   e. Read the draft through your readers' (classmates') eyes, and consider what you might add to make the paper more interesting or insightful for them.

6. Proofread your latest draft for errors and make the necessary corrections. Cover all the areas you covered in earlier papers: punctuation, spelling, word endings, and grammar usage (subject-verb agreement, subject pronouns, pronoun-antecedent agreement, comparative and superlative pronouns).

7. Write or print out your final error-free draft, and share it with classmates and your instructor.

Since I'm going to a rock concert this weekend, I think I'll write about it. I can't think of anything else that might be more interesting. Besides, this is my first rock concert, so it should be interesting. I don't know what to expect.

I'm not sure who my audience will be for the paper or what my thesis might be. I'll figure all that out after I do the observation. I'll watch the concert and then free write on it the next morning.

I want to write to people my age who have never gone to a concert.

I want them to see what they're missing.

Attenting a rock concert can be a powerful emotional experience.

1. first impressions
2. the crowd

3. the rock group
4. the music
5. the total experience

Rock Concert

STUDENT FIRST DRAFT

Here I was twenty-one years old and carrying a terrible secret around. You see, I figured I was the only twenty-one-year-old in the country who had never been to a rock concert. In high school I didn't live close enough to a big city to attend a concert, and three years of army duty in South Korea presented no opportunities. Now I was back in the States, back in school, and anxious to lose my concert "virginity."

After waiting in line for over an hour to get into the arena where Huey Lewis and the News were playing, I passed my bottle-frisking by a security guard and went in. My first impression on being inside was frightening. There were so many people packed into the dimly lit arena that I began to panic. What if a fire broke out? What if these thousands of people sucked up what breathable air was left in the smoke-filled room? I took air in large gulps and felt my body getting hot and clammy.

As my eyes adjusted to the light, I began to relax a bit. As the blur of bodies took on form, I realized that there was enough space between people standing on the floor for survival. Looking around the arena, I saw thousands of people in the rows of seats rising toward the ceiling on all sides. And there was plenty of air to breathe in the spacious, high-ceiling arena. I was also struck by how quiet 20,000 rock fans could be, only a low hum of expectation rising and falling. This could be a Billy Graham crusade crowd, I began thinking, until a strong whiff of marijuana smoke dispelled that notion.

All of a sudden, the arena got pitch dark, a dozen spotlights danced wildly around the room, and a throaty roar went up from the crowd, followed by 20,000 voices chanting in unison, "Huey, Huey, Huey, Huey, Huey." It was impossible not to get caught up in the excitement, and I was chanting as loudly as anyone.

I heard Huey and his group before I saw them. A guitar blast shot from the massive honeycomb of speakers and filled every inch of the arena. The heavy beat of the drummer accentuated by the bass guitar hit people like an electrode, throwing thousands of arms and legs involuntarily into rhythmic motion, including my own. Then the stage lit up to reveal Huey and the News jumping enthusiastically into "Hip to Be Square," a rocker for all ages. The sound was unbelievably loud and the pounding beat literally shook the floor. The music joyfully invaded every pore of my body like a fantastic drug. Nothing had ever carried me away as delightfully as this high-amp rock 'n' roll.

And the entire audience was responding as one. Here were all ages of people, from teenyboppers to couples in their thirties, and all types, from punks to preppies, molded into one enthusiastic body. Differences were forgotten, and everyone was enjoying everyone else having a great time. We sang, clapped, our arms stretched above our heads, and danced to the beat for a solid two hours. Huey's music was the common denominator; we were all rock lovers caught up in a great performance, forgetting everything but the music and the sheer joy it brought with it.

Huey Lewis was terrific in concert. He and his band played with great enthusiasm, and they seemed to enjoy playing as much as we enjoyed listening. His style was no-frills, straight-at-you rock 'n' roll, and he gave us every minute of the two hours: no breaks, no small talk, no cute stuff. Yet, when he finally left stage, a strange hush fell over the arena in place of a wild ovation.

Then, suddenly, the darkness glowed with thousands of fireflies, actually matches and cigarette lighters, silently calling Huey back to stage in an eerily religious gesture. Then an explosion came from the audience; Huey was back on stage for one last rocker, a quick, "Thanks folks, it was great," and a final roar of appreciation to which I added what was left of my vocal chords. I slowly filed out with the crowd, sweat drenched, emotionally wired, and very happy. "Man, that was great," said one dude with spiked hair and a safety pin in his ear. "Yeah, man," I said. "That was great."

Readings

Winners, Losers, or Just Kids?

BY DAN WIGHTMAN

1   If I envied anyone in high school, it was the winners. You know who I mean. The ones who earned straight A's and scored high on their Scholastic Aptitude Tests. The attractive ones who smiled coyly, drove their own sports cars and flaunted those hard, smooth bodies that they kept tan the year round.

2   By contrast, my high-school friends were mostly losers. We spent a lot of time tuning cars and drinking beer. Our girlfriends were pale and frumpy, and we had more D's than B's on our report cards. After graduation, many of us went into the Army instead of to a university; two of us came back from Vietnam in coffins, three more on stretchers. On weekends, when we drank Colt 45 together in my father's battered Ford, we'd laughingly refer to ourselves as the "out crowd." But, unless we were thoroughly blotto, we never laughed hard when we said it. And I, for one, rarely got blotto when I was 16.

3   The reason I mention this is that last month 183 winners and losers from my Northern California high-school graduating class got together at a swank country club for a revealing 15-year reunion.

4   Predictably, only happy and successful people attended. The strange thing, though, was that the people I once pegged as losers outnumbered the winners at this reunion by a visible margin. And, during a long session at the bar with my informative friend Paula, I got an earful about the messy lives of people I'd once envied, and the remarkable metamorphoses of people I'd once pitied.

5   Paula reported that Len, a former class officer, was now a lost soul in Colorado, hopelessly estranged from his charming wife. Tim, one of the sorriest students I'd ever known, was a successful sportswriter, at ease with himself.

6   Estelle, who was modestly attractive in her teens, was now a part-time stripper in the Midwest, working to support her young son. Connie, a former car-club "kitten," had become a sophisticated international flight attendant.

7   Paula told me that Gary, a college scholarship winner, was overweight, underemployed and morose. Ron, who had shown little flair for music, had become a symphony violinist.

8   Sipping a piña colada, I thought to myself how terribly mistaken my senior counselor had been when she told me that high-school performance indicates how one will fare later.

9   I looked at Paula, a high-school troublemaker with a naughty smile, whose outgoing personality and rebellious spirit had endeared her to me so long ago. Together, we once stole a teacher's grade book, changed some of

our low marks, then dropped the book in the lost-and-found box. The savvy teacher never said a word about the incident, but at the end of the year, when report cards were issued, gave us the D's we deserved.

10   Now Paula was a housewife, a volunteer worker and the mother of two sons. She wore a marriage-encounter pin on her modest dress, and sat at the bar tippling Perrier on ice.

11   She shook her head when I reminded her of the grade-book escapade, and the sheepish look on her face reminded me how presumptuous it is to anticipate the lives of others.

12   It also got me thinking about my own life since high school—how I'd gradually shaken my loser's image, gotten through college, found a decent job, married wisely, and finally realized a speck of my potential.

13   I thought about numerous situations where I could have despaired, regressed, given up—and how I hadn't, though others had—and I wondered why I was different, and had more luck, less guilt.

14   "The past is fiction," wrote William Burroughs. And, although I don't subscribe to that philosophy entirely, the people I admire most today are those who overcome their mistakes, seize second chances and fight to pull themselves together, day after day.

15   Often they're the sort of people who leave high school with blotchy complexions, crummy work habits, fingernails bitten down to the quick. And of course they're bitterly unsure of themselves and slow to make friends.

16   But they're also the ones who show up transformed at 15-year reunions, and the inference I draw is that the distinction between winners and losers is often slight and seldom crucial—and frequently overrated.

17   In high school, especially, many people are slow getting started. But, finding their stride, they quickly catch up, and in their prime often return to surprise and delight us—their lives so much richer than we'd ever imagined.

QUESTIONS FOR DISCUSSION

1. What groups of people are being compared by Wightman? What group does he identify with?

2. How does Wightman investigate his subject? Was this a good way to make a comparison? How else could he have studied his groups?

3. What conclusion does Wightman make about his former classmates? What is his thesis on winners and losers? Do you agree?

4. How does Wightman support his thesis in the essay? Find examples of such support. Is it convincing? Are there enough examples?

5. Discuss the essay's organization: the opening, middle, and concluding paragraphs. Where does each section begin and end? What is accomplished in each section? How effective is this organization?

6. What kind of an audience is this essay intended for? How does Wightman try to relate to this audience in the essay? Who else might benefit from this essay? Why?

VOCABULARY

Flaunted (1), frumpy (2), metamorphoses (4), morose (7), savvy (9), presumptuous (11)

The Eye of the Beholder

BY THOMAS F. CASH AND LOUIS H. JANDA

1   Ask most people to list what makes them like someone on first meeting and they'll tell you personality, intelligence, sense of humor. But they're probably deceiving themselves. The characteristic that impresses people the most, when meeting anyone from a job applicant to a blind date, is appearance. And unfair and unenlightened as it may seem, attractive people are frequently preferred over their less attractive peers.

2   Research begun in the early 1970s has shown that not only do good looks influence such things as choice of friends, lovers, and mates, but that they can also affect school grades, selection for jobs, and even the outcome of a trial. Psychologist Ellen Berscheid of the University of Minnesota and psychologist Elaine Walster, then at the University of Wisconsin, were among the first researchers to deal with the topic of attractiveness. Their seminal 1974 paper on the subject showed that the more attractive a person, the more desirable characteristics others will attribute to him or her. Attractive people are viewed as being happier, more sensitive, more interesting, warmer, more poised, more sociable, and as having better character than their less attractive counterparts. Psychologist Karen Dion of the University of Toronto has dubbed this stereotypical view as: "What is beautiful is good."

3   Our current work at Old Dominion University in Norfolk, Virginia, with colleagues and students, focuses on the role that appearance plays in judgments made about people. Our studies have been done in a variety of settings: basic research laboratories, beauty and cosmetics industry labs, plastic and reconstructive surgery practices, psychiatric hospitals, and psychotherapeutic consulting rooms.

4   One topic that has led to many avenues of research is how attractiveness influences sex-typing—the tendency of people to attribute certain stereotypical qualities to each sex. Besides being perceived as sensitive, kind, interesting, and generally happy, attractive people tend to fit easily into sexual stereotypes, according to a study done by Barry Gillen, a social psychologist in our department.

5   Gillen speculated that attractive people possess two types of "goodness," one related to and the other unrelated to their sex. To test this hypothesis he showed a group of students photographs of both men and women of high, moderate, and low attractiveness, as determined by the previous rankings of students according to a seven-point scale (contrary to popular belief, researchers usually don't use the Bo Derek scale of 10). The judges were asked to rate the subjects according to the masculinity, femininity, and social

desirability scales of the Bem Sex Role Inventory. Gillen's study found that attractive women were perceived as being more feminine, and that attractive men were viewed as being more masculine than their less attractive counterparts. This suggests a second stereotype: "What is beautiful is sex-typed."

6   One implication of Gillen's work that we wanted to test was whether good looks are a disadvantage for some people, especially women, in work situations that conflict with sexual stereotypes. By the late 1970s, there was already a sizable body of literature documenting the problems women face because of sex-role stereotypes. We speculated that attractive women might be at a real disadvantage when they aspire to occupations in which stereotypically masculine traits—such as being strong, independent, and decisive—are thought to be required for success.

7   To test that possibility we did a study with Gillen and Steve Burns, a student in our department, in which professional personnel consultants were hired to rate a "job applicant's" suitability for six positions. We matched the positions for the skill required, the prestige offered, and the degree of supervisory independence allowed. Two jobs were stereotypically masculine (automobile salesperson and wholesale hardware shipping and receiving clerk), two feminine (telephone operator and office receptionist), and two were sex-neutral (motel desk clerk and photographic darkroom assistant).

8   Each of the seventy-two personnel consultants who participated received a résumé package for an individual that contained the typical kinds of information that a job applicant might submit: academic standing, a list of hobbies and interests, specific skills and recommendations from teachers and counselors. All of the résumés were identical with the exception of the name ("John" vs. "Janet" Williams) and the inclusion of a photograph of the applicant. Photographs showed either an extremely attractive appliant or an unattractive one, previously judged on an attractiveness scale.

9   The results documented the existence of both sexism and "beautyism." On the sexism front, men were given stronger endorsements by the personnel consultants for the traditionally masculine jobs, while women were rated higher for the traditionally feminine jobs. Men were also judged to have just as much chance of success on the neutral jobs as on the masculine ones, while women were perceived to be less likely to succeed on the neutral jobs than on the feminine ones.

10   "Beautyism" had several facets: attractive men were favored over their less attractive male competitors for all three types of jobs. Similarly, attractiveness gave women a competitive edge against other women, but only for traditionally female or neutral jobs. When it came to jobs inappropriate to society's traditional sex roles, the attractive women were rated lower than their less attractive female competitors.

11   These findings gain support from a subsequent study by Madeline Heilman and Lois Saruwatari, psychologists at Yale University. They examined the effects of appearance and gender on selection for both managerial and nonmanagerial jobs. Male and female students in a business administration class received résumé packages for equally qualified candidates. Each résumé

included a photograph of either an attractive or unattractive man or woman. Being attractive was always an advantage for men. Attractive men received stronger recommendations for hiring, were judged to have better qualifications, and were given higher suggested starting salaries than unattractive men for both the managerial and the nonmanagerial positions.

12   Among women, however, those who were less attractive actually had a significant edge over their more attractive peers when seeking a place in management, a traditionally masculine occupation. Good looks were an advantage only when women were applying for the nonmanagerial positions. Attractiveness resulted in lower salary recommendations when the women were viewed as stepping into an out-of-sex-role position.

13   Heilman says that her findings "imply that women should strive to appear as unattractive and masculine as possible if they are to succeed in advancing their careers by moving into powerful organizational positions."

14   So, beauty—at least in a woman—doesn't always pay in the work place, nor does it guarantee higher marks in the classroom. Recently, we tested the notion that attractiveness can work against women attempting to cross sex-role boundaries in academic as well as work settings. We constructed a series of essays, purportedly written by college freshmen, that were equivalent in quality, but which varied in the "masculinity" or "femininity" of the topic. The essays were accompanied by photographs of attractive and unattractive "authors."

15   The masculine topics were "How to Hunt Safely" and "How to Buy a Used Motorcycle," and the feminine topics were "How to Make a Quilt" and "How to Give a Manicure." The essays were read and judged by 216 female college students.

16   Once again, attractiveness proved to be an advantage for the men, regardless of the sex-typing of the essay topic. For the women, however, beauty was an advantage only when they stuck to a feminine topic. When they were presented as authors of the masculine essays, the attractive women were given a lower score relative to their less attractive peers.

17   It is clear that beauty can be a double-edged sword for women. Attractive women are viewed as having a host of desirable personality characteristics, except the ones needed to step out of prescribed sex roles.

18   What are the specific cues for gender role stereotyping? Grooming—the way people dress, use cosmetics, and style their hair—appears to be a factor. The differing ideal physiques—thin for women, more muscular for men—also influence gender stereotyping, according to recent experiments by Purdue psychologists Kay Deaux and Laurie Lewis. People who are tall, strong, sturdy, and broad-shouldered—regardless of gender—are viewed as more likely to have masculine personality traits, to fit the assertive, breadwinner role, and to hold a traditionally masculine occupation. Meanwhile, people who are dainty, graceful, and soft in voice and appearance are expected to have typically feminine traits, roles, and occupations.

19   How does grooming affect sex-typing of attractive women, especially as it relates to their employability? This question was partially answered by a

series of studies in which we asked male and female corporate personnel consultants to judge how qualified various attractive women, shown in photographs, were for jobs in corporate management. In the first study, we showed sixteen personnel managers photographs of women wearing various types of clothing, jewelry, hair styles, and cosmetics. The results showed that the more sex-typed, or "feminized," the grooming styles, the less likely were personnel consultants to judge the women to be potential managers.

20   In a second study, personnel consultants judged businesswomen photographed under two different grooming conditions: one very feminine and made up, the other plainer and less sex-typed. The more feminine style included longer hair or hair styles that concealed the face; soft sweaters, low necklines, or ruffled blouses; dangling jewelry; and heavy makeup. In the other condition "candidates" wore tailored clothes with a jacket, subtle makeup, and either short hair or hair swept away from the face. These criteria were chosen on the basis of descriptions given by judges in the previous study.

21   Once again the corporate personnel consultants made choices suggesting that the less feminine the appearance, the more competent the woman, even though the candidates had been perceived by the consultants as equally attractive under both conditions. Specifically, candidates groomed in a more feminine style were perceived to be less managerial; less intrinsically interested in work; less likely to be taken seriously by others; more illogical and overemotional in critical decision making; less financially responsible; more helpless and dependent on the influences of others; sexier and more flirtatious in social relations; and less assertive, independent, and self-confident than those groomed in a less sex-typed style.

22   In the third phase of this project, male and female executives and managers from more than two hundred corporations in major cities nationwide were shown applications containing photographs of attractive businesswomen in various grooming styles and asked how they thought they would fare in the corporate world. Once again, candidates groomed in a less sex-typed style were expected to have a better chance at reaching the management levels of the corporate structure, to be offered higher salaries, and to be afforded greater social acceptance and credibility on the job than when they were groomed in a more traditionally feminine manner. These effects were especially prominent when the judges were men, often the gatekeepers of corporate management.

23   These studies, taken together, suggest that grooming style has a definite effect on whether women are sex-typed, and thus whether they are viewed as having good management potential. To some extent, our research has confirmed what many people always suspected: if a woman wants to succeed in a man's world, she had better not look too feminine. Several "dress for success" books have made it to the best-seller list by advising women to get ahead in business by wearing their hair short, using cosmetics sparingly, and wearing conservative suits. Our research suggests, sadly, that the advice is sound.

24   It is interesting how deeply ingrained these attitudes are. Many people, both men and women, who are seriously concerned and offended by the sexism in our society never question this dress-for-success formula, which has different standards for men than it does for women. Men must follow certain clothing norms in the office in regard to neatness and formality, but not masculinity. No one would suggest to a man that he try not to look too masculine when he shows up at the office or expect him to comb his hair one way for the office and another way when he goes out to dinner. It is doubtful that any man has ever been advised not to look too good if he wants to be taken seriously at the next board meeting. But rules of dress for women are far more complex.

25   Prejudices are slow to fade away. It will be interesting to see if grooming styles for women become more flexible as they move up the corporate ladder in greater numbers and become more powerful.

26   Attractive women can face problems outside the boardroom as well. Everyone wants to be thought of as desirable and attractive, but a woman's beauty can invite unwanted advances and treatment as a sex object. Perhaps, then, it should come as no surprise that social psychologist Harry Reis of the University of Rochester found attractive women to be more distrustful of men than were their plainer counterparts.

27   Our research has also confirmed that a third stereotype exists: "What is beautiful is self-centered." We've found that many people assume that attractive people are vain and egotistical. After all, if what is beautiful is good, then the beautiful people must know how wonderful they are. Further, people of low and average attractiveness are often reluctant to choose extremely attractive mates for fear of losing them. In fact, breakups are more common among couples who are mismatched on attractiveness. So once again, thorns appear on the rose of beauty.

28   We have been discussing how people judge and react to the attractiveness of others. What about people's perceptions of themselves? Currently, in collaboration with Barbara Winstead, a psychologist at Old Dominion, we are examining how body images—the feelings people have about their own appearance—influence their lives. Surprisingly, how people view their own level of attractiveness has almost nothing to do with how others view them. People whom others consider beautiful may not like their looks at all. Conversely, people whom others might judge as downright unattractive or even ugly feel completely comfortable with their appearance.

29   Using our newly developed Winstead-Cash Body Self-Relations Questionnaire, we are beginning to accumulate evidence that body image may have as much impact on one's life as external evaluations of beauty. In a study with Steve Noles, a graduate student in the Virginia Consortium for Professional Psychology, for example, we have found a greater vulnerability to depression among people who place importance on being good-looking yet see themselves as less attractive than they really are.

30   Aristotle once maintained that "beauty is a greater recommendation than any letter of introduction." In many respects he was right. But then again, maybe he should have collected more data.

QUESTIONS FOR DISCUSSION

1. What types of investigation did the authors use to analyze their topic? How valid were the studies they conducted?

2. What conclusions did the authors draw from their studies on the effects of male and female attractiveness? Do you agree with these conclusions?

3. What contradictory findings did the authors present regarding female attractiveness? What causes lie behind this contradiction?

4. According to the authors, how do people's perceptions of themselves often differ from how others view them? What is the significance of this difference?

5. In the final two paragraphs, what do the authors theorize about how self-image affects one's life? Do you agree with them?

6. How do your personal experiences and observations compare with the authors' findings?

VOCABULARY

Counterpart (2), stereotype (4), purportedly (14)

FROM *A Child of Crack*

BY MICHELE L. NORRIS

1   Dooney Waters, a thickset six-year-old missing two front teeth, sat hunched over a notebook, drawing a family portrait.

2   First he sketched a stick-figure woman smoking a pipe twice her size. A coil of smoke rose from the pipe, which held a white square he called a "rock." Above that, he drew a picture of himself, another stick figure with tears falling from its face.

3   "Drugs have wrecked my mother," Dooney said as he doodled. "Drugs have wrecked a lot of mothers and fathers and children and babies. If I don't be careful, drugs are going to wreck me too."

4   His was a graphic rendering of the life of a child growing up in what police and social workers have identified as a crack house, an apartment in Washington Heights, a federally subsidized complex in Landover, Maryland, where people congregated to buy and use drugs. Dooney's life was punctuated by days when he hid behind his bed to eat sandwiches sent by teachers who knew he would get nothing else. Nights when Dooney wet his bed because people were "yelling and doing drugs and stuff." And weeks in which he barely saw his thirty-two-year-old mother, who spent most of her time searching for drugs.

5   Addie Lorraine Waters, who described herself as a "slave to cocaine," said she let drug dealers use her apartment in exchange for the steady support of her habit. The arrangement turned Dooney's home into a modern-day

opium den where pipes, spoons, and needles were in supply like ketchup and mustard at a fast-food restaurant. . . .

6   Addie's apartment was on Capital View Drive, site of more than a dozen slayings last year. Yet, the locks were removed from the front door to allow an unyielding tide of addicts and dealers to flow in and out. Children, particularly toddlers, often peered inside to ask: "Is my mommy here?"

7   While he was living in the crack house, Dooney was burned when a woman tossed boiling water at his mother's face in a drug dispute, and his right palm was singed when his thirteen-year-old half brother handed him a soft drink can that had been used to heat crack cocaine on the stove.

8   Teachers say that Dooney often begged to be taken to their homes, once asking if he could stay overnight in his classroom. "I'll sleep on the floor," Dooney told an instructor in Greenbelt Center Elementary School's after-school counseling and tutorial program. "Please don't make me go home. I don't want to go back there."

9   Dooney was painfully shy or exhaustively outgoing, depending largely on whether he was at home or in school—the one place where he could relax. In class, he played practical jokes on friends and passed out kisses and hugs to teachers. But his mood darkened when he boarded a bus for home.

10   The violence that surrounded Dooney at home was, in most cases, a byproduct of the bustling drug trade. Washington Heights was host to one of the largest open-air drug markets in Prince George's County, Maryland, until a series of police raids last winter drove the problem indoors.

11   On Saturday, April 29, Dooney was sitting in the living room near his mother when a fifteen-year-old drug dealer burst in and tossed a pan of boiling water, a weapon that anybody with a stove could afford. Dooney, his mother, and two neighbors recalled that the dealer then plopped down on a sofa and watched as Dooney's weeping mother soothed the burns on her shoulder and neck. Dooney also was at home when another adolescent enforcer leaned through an open window on Sunday, May 14, and pitched a blend of bleach and boiling water in the face of nineteen-year-old Clifford E. Bernard, a regular in the apartment, for ignoring a $150 debt.

12   "People around here don't play when you owe them money," said Sherry Brown, twenty-five, a friend of Addie Waters who frequented the apartment. Brown said she smokes crack every day and has given birth to two crack-addicted babies in the past three years. "These young boys around here will burn you in a minute if you so much as look at them the wrong way," she said. "I'm telling you sure as I'm sitting here, crack has made people crazy."

13   Almost everyone was welcome at "Addie's place." Her patrons included some unlikely characters, but as one said, "Addie don't turn nobody away." Not the fifteen-year-old who in May burned her furniture and clothing intentionally with a miniature blow torch. Not even the twenty-one-year-old man who "accidentally" shot her thirteen-year-old son, Frank Russell West, five inches above the heart last Dec. 16. Police ascribed the shooting to a "drug deal gone bad."

14   Dooney was sleeping when Russell, shot in the left shoulder, stumbled back into the apartment. Dooney will not talk about the night his half brother was shot except to say, "Russell was shot 'cause of drugs."

15   Waters did not press charges against Edward "June" Powell, the man police charged with shooting Russell. Powell, whose trial has been continued because he did not have an attorney, is out on bail. "He didn't mean to do it," said Waters, who referred to Powell as a close friend of the family. "It was an accident. He meant to kill someone else." . . .

16   Dooney's mother and others who congregated in her apartment were bound by a common desperation for drugs. The majority, in their late twenties or early thirties, described themselves as "recreational" drug users until they tried the highly addictive crack. Many said they had swapped welfare checks, food stamps, furniture, and sexual favors to support their craving for crack. They had lost jobs, spouses, homes, and self-respect. Nearly all were in danger of losing children, too.

17   To help Dooney and others like him, teachers are being called on increasingly to attend to physical and emotional needs that are ignored in the pupils' homes.

18   "You do more parenting than teaching nowadays," says Wendy Geagan, an instructional aide who tutors children with learning problems at Greenbelt Center. "It's all so different now. We have always had to help children with their problems, but these kids want to be held. They want to be mothered. They need affection. They need their emotions soothed." . . .

19   Dooney's teachers began to suspect that his mother had a drug problem shortly after he entered kindergarten.

20   "It was rather sudden," said Janet Pelkey, Dooney's kindergarten teacher. "He wasn't bathed. He became very angry and started striking out. He started gobbling down food whenever he got it, even candy and snacks in the classroom. It was obvious that something was going on at home."

21   School officials said they could not reach Dooney's mother by phone and no one answered the door during several home visits. The school-community link is difficult to maintain for many pupils from Washington Heights because they are bused to the school for desegregation purposes. Many families in Washington Heights do not own cars, making it difficult to visit a school that took three bus transfers to reach. Conversely, teachers say they are afraid to visit Washington Heights, particularly during the winter, when daylight is scarce. So teachers had little or no contact with the parents of pupils with the most turbulent home lives.

22   Concerned about his emotional problems, Dooney's kindergarten teacher placed him in the "transitional first grade," a class for students with academic problems that set them a few steps behind other children their age.

23   Dooney's condition worsened when he entered first grade last September, teachers said. He was given to fits of screaming and crying and came to school wearing torn and filthy clothes. "It was almost like he was shell-

shocked when he came to school . . . ," Field said. "He is such a sad little boy. He walks around with his head down and he's always sucking his little thumb."

24   "When I discovered what he was going through at home, I thought, 'My goodness, it's amazing that he even gets to school.'" Field said.

25   His mood swung like a pendulum. "Sometimes he comes in and he is just starving for affection," said Susan Bennett, an instructional assistant. "He clings to his teacher like he is afraid to let go. . . . Or sometimes when he comes to school he is angry. You brush by him and he is ready to attack."

26   Dooney entered first grade lacking several basic skills children normally master before leaving kindergarten. Teachers say he had a difficult time distinguishing among colors and could not count past ten. But Dooney's academic skills improved in classes that provided special equipment and individual tutoring. By the end of the year, his test scores put him in line with others his age, though he still had trouble tying his shoes and telling time.

27   Acting on the advice of teachers, the Prince George's County Department of Child Protective Services investigated Dooney's mother in April 1988.

28   "Based on the provided investigative information, the allegations of neglect have been indicated," child protective services worker Conchita A. Woods wrote in a letter to Waters dated April 24, 1989, a year after the investigation began. But a caseworker said that it would be "months, maybe even years" before they could seek to remove Dooney from his mother's custody.

29   Russell Brown, the investigator, said he had about twenty cases on his desk just like Waters's.

30   "We have a lot of cases that are much worse than that," Brown said. "There's probably not a whole lot I can do" for Dooney. Brown said that he does not have time to go through the arduous process of taking a child from a parent unless there is imminent danger.

31   "It's up to you guys to help this little boy because we just don't have the manpower to do it," Brown told Dooney's teachers over lunch on April 27. . . .

32   At the principal's urging, Prince George's school and government officials created a pilot after-school program that offers tutoring, counseling, and drug education for students at Greenbelt Center. Equally important, it shields them from neighborhood violence for a few extra hours. Although its primary function is to help children with drug-related trauma, the program also provides academic enrichment and free day care for other students. From 3:00 to 6:30 P.M., children get help with homework, counseling, playtime, and a snack—the last meal of the day for many of them.

33   School officials around the country say such programs may be the vanguard of school reform as more children enter schools with a crush of physical and emotional problems that detract from standard academic work.

34   "It's become apparent that schools cannot do all that they are supposed to be doing in a six-hour day," says Nancy Kochuk, a spokeswoman for the National Education Association. "The schools are basically set up as an

industrial model. It's like a factory line. That doesn't seem to serve our society very well anymore when we are dealing with children with such intense and overwhelming problems." . . .

35   Last spring Dooney said he hated drugs and what they have done to his life. Yet he seemed to view the drug trade as an inevitable calling in the way that some children look at the steel mills and coal mines in which their forebears worked.

36   Asked if he would sell or use drugs when he grows up, Dooney shook his head violently and wrinkled his nose in disgust. But the expression faded, and Dooney looked at the floor: "I don't want to sell drugs, but I will probably have to."

QUESTIONS FOR DISCUSSION

1. How did Norris investigate the circumstances of Dooney Waters's life? Why did she choose the types of sources that she used?

2. What examples of the daily horrors of Dooney's life stand out to you? Is his situation exceptional or typical for many children?

3. How are schools forced to change their traditional role in order to help children like Dooney? Is this the best answer to the problems of such children?

4. Are drugs the cause of the terrible problems presented in the essay or a symptom of deeper societal ills in the inner city? What can be done to improve the situation?

5. What future do you envision for the Dooneys of our country? What can be done to bring hope to them?

6. What personal experiences or observations can you share to shed light on the lives of "at risk" children?

VOCABULARY

Desegregation (21), conversely (21), allegations (28), vanguard (33)

Appendix

This appendix contains a number of writing activities
that individual students may find useful. As your instructor becomes familiar with your writing needs, he
or she may assign specific activities from the appendix on a diagnostic basis. For example, if you struggle
with irregular verb tenses, dangling modifiers, or
punctuation of possessive words, you will find help
in the appendix.

The appendix is intended to be used as an ongoing
supplement to the rest of the text. The material has
not been relegated to the appendix because it is less
important, but because all students will not use it
similarly. For example, one student may find the
"Spelling" section valuable while another may have
no need for it. Putting such writing elements in the
appendix makes them available to students without
cluttering the units and distracting students from the
writing process.

Sentence Revision

Sentence revision is a task shared by all writers. This section will help you write and revise sentences more effectively by broadening your sentence repertoire and making you aware of common structural problems.

COMBINING SENTENCES

The best way to get rid of short, monotonous sentences in a draft is to combine pairs or groups of sentences to form more informative and interesting ones. Here are ways to combine short sentences:

1. Eliminate unnecessary words that are duplicated in the sentences.
2. Move descriptive words in front of the word they describe.
3. Join similar sentence parts with an *and, or,* or *but.*

Here are examples of groups of short sentences that have been combined in the revised versions following the methods just described.

Examples

Draft	Joanie is a student. She is a very good one.
Revised	Joanie is a very good student.
Draft	Fernando bought a shirt. It was red. It was long sleeved.
Revised	Fernando bought a red, long-sleeved shirt.
Draft	Alan went to the barbecue. Felicia went with him.
Revised	Alan and Felicia went to the barbecue together.

Combining Activity 1

Each pair or group of short sentences below can be combined to form one improved sentence. Combine the sentences into single sentences by eliminating and moving words around and by joining similar words or groups of words with *and, or,* or *but.*

Example	Gwen went to school. Maria went to school. They went with Bob.
Revised	Gwen and Maria went to school with Bob.

1. The frog leaped onto the log. He plopped into the water. He disappeared.
2. Harry was tired. He was thirsty. He wasn't hungry.
3. Ellie got a B on her term paper. She got the same grade on her algebra test. She flunked her pop quiz in German.

4. Your X rays could be in the drawer. They could be on the shelf. They could be almost anywhere in the house.

5. The kitten was fat. It was fluffy. It was playing with a grasshopper. The grasshopper was badly injured.

6. Marge finally got a letter. It was from her parole officer. She was relieved.

7. The week was long. It was boring. It was almost over. Julian was very happy.

8. Susan's clothes were plain. They were cheap. They were also stylish. They were also in good taste.

9. The car spun toward the wall. It crashed. It burst into flames. The driver wasn't injured. He was lucky.

10. That puppy is very cute. It is black and white. It has droopy ears. It is in the pet store window. It isn't for sale.

A second way to combine shorter sentences is to join two complete sentences with *coordinate conjunctions* to form *compound sentences*. These are the most commonly used coordinate conjunctions:

and   or   but   so   yet   for

The following are examples of two first draft sentences joined by coordinate conjunctions to form single compound sentences. Notice that different conjunctions show different relationships between the two sentences they join. The conjunctions are underlined.

Example   The Rolling Stones were popular in the 1960s. They are still popular today.

Revised   The Rolling Stones were popular in the 1960s, <u>and</u> they are still popular today. (**And** *joins the information together.*)

Example   Divorce statistics are rising. Couples are marrying in record numbers.

Revised   Divorce statistics are rising, <u>but</u> couples are marrying in record numbers. (**But** *shows a contrast; something happened despite something else.*)

Example   Rita may go to a movie tonight. She may stay home and read a mystery novel.

Revised   Rita may go to a movie tonight, <u>or</u> she may stay home and read a mystery novel. (**Or** *shows a choice; alternatives are available.*)

Example   James makes his own shirts. He enjoys sewing.

Revised   James makes his own shirts, <u>for</u> he enjoys sewing. (**For** *means* because; *something occurs because of something else.*)

Example	Working and going to school is difficult. Many students do both.
Revised	Working and going to school is difficult, <u>yet</u> many students do both. (**Yet** *is similar to* but; *it shows a contrast.*)
Example	The air is moist and cold. We'd better bundle up for the parade.
Revised	The air is moist and cold, <u>so</u> we'd better bundle up for the parade. (**So** *is like* therefore; *one thing leads to another.*)

As you can see, different conjunctions serve different purposes. Being able to use a variety of conjunctions at appropriate times makes your writing more effective.

Combining Activity 2

Combine the following pairs of shorter sentences with *conjunctions* to form compound sentences. Use the conjunction that best joins each sentence pair: *and, or, but, so, yet, for.* Put a *comma* before the conjunction.

Example	The weather is miserable today. It should be better tomorrow.
Revised	The weather is miserable today, but it should be better tomorrow.

1. Jogging is a popular exercise. Some doctors don't recommend it.
2. You can take typing this semester. You can take it next semester.
3. Ms. Avery is an unpopular teacher. She lectures too fast.
4. Jodie didn't like the foreign movie. It was praised by the critics.
5. The smells from the cafeteria were wonderful. The food was disappointing.
6. Rain collected in jars on the back porch. We used the water to test for acid rain.
7. Freddie may be at the Pizza Palace. He may be at the roller derby with Lucinda.
8. Lupe joined the swim team. She wanted the exercise and the units.
9. Sam tried to return the defective smoke alarm. The store was closed.
10. Alicia couldn't study for the essay test. She got a good night's sleep instead.

A third way to combine sentences is to join two complete sentences with words called *subordinate conjunctions* to form *complex sentences.* Subordinate conjunctions may be placed between the two sentences or at the beginning of the first sentence. The following subordinate conjunctions are most commonly used in complex sentences.

after	if	whenever
although	since	where
as	unless	whereas
because	until	wherever
before	when	while

The following examples show two first draft sentences joined by subordinate conjunctions to form complex sentences. Notice the different relationships that the subordinate conjunctions show and their use at the beginning or in the middle of the complex sentence. The subordinate conjunctions are underlined.

Example You are going to be late for biology class. You should contact your teacher.

Revised Since you are going to be late for biology class, you should contact your teacher.

Example Fred's friends took him home. They went out for pizza.

Revised After Fred's friends took him home, they went out for pizza.

Example I'm cleaning up your mess. You are watching television!

Revised I'm cleaning up your mess while you are watching television!

Example You have worked very hard. You have gained everyone's respect.

Revised Because you have worked very hard, you have gained everyone's respect.

Example George wants to pass the geography test. He will have to identify six mountain ranges.

Revised If George wants to pass the geography test, he will have to identify six mountain ranges.

Example Joanna refuses to exercise. She would like to be in shape.

Revised Joanna refuses to exercise although she would like to be in shape.

As you can see, subordinate conjunctions can show different relationships: time (*when, as, after, while*), cause and effect (*since, because, if, unless*), place (*where, wherever*), or contrast (*although, even though, whereas*). You may use them at the beginning or in the middle of a complex sentence depending on what you want to emphasize. Using complex sentences adds variety to your writing and helps you express a wide range of relationships between ideas.

Combining Activity 3

Join the following pairs of shorter sentences with appropriate subordinate conjunctions to form *complex sentences.* You will begin some sentences with subordinate conjunctions and use others between sentences. *When you begin a sentence with a subordinate conjunction, put a comma between the two sentences you are combining.* (Some sentence pairs won't go together well until they are combined with a subordinate conjunction.)

Example   The party was over. Ruby drove around until dawn.

Revised   After the party was over, Ruby drove around until dawn.

Example   The dog limped along the road. It had a thorn in its paw.

Revised   The dog limped along the road because it had a thorn in its paw.

1. You leave for school tomorrow. Please pick me up at the corner.
2. Jim dropped his gymnastics class. He had a time conflict.
3. The economy improves greatly. The unemployment rate will climb.
4. Gina spent a lot of time reading romances. She still did well in school.
5. You believe everything Harley says. You are very naive.
6. I told you before. I'll be glad to water your ferns this weekend.
7. Ms. Howard is a fascinating teacher. She uses slides, movies, and field trips in her anthropology class.
8. The electricity is off in the apartments. Everyone is buying candles.
9. The shower door was broken. Manuel moved into the dormitory.
10. You've had experience with electrical work. Don't try to change that outlet.

Combining Activity 4

Rewrite the following passage. Combine sentences by adding joining words, moving words and phrases around, and eliminating unnecessary words. Combine the fourteen sample sentences into a few well-crafted ones.

Example   Nona moved into her apartment today. She paid her rent a week ago. She was living alone. She was looking for a roommate to share expenses.

Revised   Nona moved into her apartment today, <u>but</u> she paid her rent a week ago. <u>Although</u> she was living alone, she was looking for a roommate to share expenses.

Corrine collects records from the fifties and sixties. She has over one thousand 45 rpm discs. Her brother is a disc jockey. She buys duplicate records from his station cheaply. She enjoys the music of the eighties. She prefers the sound of early rock 'n' roll. She has every record Buddy Holly ever recorded. He was her favorite singer. She'll invite her friends over. They'll listen to old songs for hours. She's heard them hundreds of times. She never gets tired of them. She never considers her collection complete. She'll spend the weekend looking for records by Bo Diddley and Danny and the Juniors.

Combining Activity 5

Combine the following sentences to form single sentences using the combining methods you have learned.

Example   The bed is below the picture. It has a walnut headboard. It is a single bed.

Revised   The single bed with the walnut headboard is below the picture.

Example   Jane got to the museum early. She still had to wait in line for an hour.

Revised   Jane got to the museum early, but she still had to wait in line for an hour.

Example   Sam had a good time at the drag races. He thought they would be boring.

Revised   Sam had a good time at the drag races, although he thought they would be boring.

1. The gymnast was short. She was slender. She was strong for her size. She was determined.
2. The seats were slashed. They were in the back of the theatre. A gang of girls did it. They did it maliciously.
3. I met a man on the train. He was very friendly. He was very tall. He was going to Memphis. He was from Cleveland.
4. Marge was having trouble breathing. She went to the infirmary. The doctor kept her there overnight. He wanted to observe her.
5. We are planning on taking a ferry to Falcon Island. Our plans for Saturday could change. They could stay the same.

6. Jacques often missed class. It was history. His instructor seldom noticed. Jacques sat in the back of the room. He was very quiet.

7. Marsha was tired of wearing her shirt. It was an old sweat shirt. She bought a new one. It was just like her old one.

8. The large sailboat battled the wind for hours. It was off the coast of North Carolina. It finally capsized. No one was hurt.

9. Gilda was awakened by thunder. She couldn't go back to sleep. She tossed and turned. She did this until morning.

10. Max was a great clown. Holly was a great clown too. Ralph was a lousy clown. Marvin was a lousy clown. They all had fun.

Combining Activity 6

Combine the following sentences to form single sentences using the combining methods you have learned. Here is an example of each method:

Draft   The desk is in the corner. It is walnut. It is for studying. It is twelve years old.

Revised   The walnut study desk in the corner is twelve years old. (*repeated words eliminated, modifying words moved in front of word they describe*)

Draft   I never had problems with my hearing. Lately I don't hear the television well.

Revised   I never had problems with my hearing, but lately I don't hear the television well. (*compound sentence formed by using coordinate conjunction* but *to join sentences*)

Draft   She is really tired of school. She'll stick it out for her last semester.

Revised   Although she is really tired of school, she'll stick it out for her last semester. (*complex sentence formed by adding subordinate conjunction* although *to join sentence*)

Draft   Josephine finally went to an acupuncturist. She was bothered by nagging headaches.

Revised   Bothered by nagging headaches, Josephine finally went to an acupuncturist. (*introductory phrase used in place of second sentence and unnecessary words eliminated*)

1. The lake is full of golden trout. It lies at the foot of Mt. Cirano. They will rise to any bait.

2. I don't think anyone was injured in the accident. I could tell from the looks of the cars involved. I couldn't say for certain.

3. Maria is tired of working. She is looking forward to school. Helena feels the same way as Maria. Joleen is enjoying working. She isn't looking forward to school.

4. The debate team swept through every match. They did it easily. They were from Des Moines. They competed against some of the best teams in the state.

5. You can take English 6 this semester. You can wait for summer school. It's easier in the summer. You don't learn as much.

6. Hilda is very friendly. She is generous with her time. She is generous with her money. She doesn't like to be used.

7. My German shepherd is six months old. It is being trained as a Seeing Eye dog. The Nunnley School for the Blind is training it. They will place it with a blind person. They will do this when the training is completed.

8. Freddie got a C− on his biology report. He worked very hard on the report.

9. The liquidambar is a tree. It is a good source of shade. It grows well in most climates. It fares best in warm weather. It fares worst in cold weather.

10. Please get ten more boxes of gingersnaps. Get the same brand. Do it this morning. Do it before I leave for work.

11. Mary has a terrible toothache. It's keeping her from eating. She should see a dentist. It could get even worse.

12. That man is mysterious looking. He has a patch over his left eye. He keeps looking at you. He seems to know you.

SENTENCE PROBLEMS

Three structural problems that may occasionally creep into your sentences are *nonparallel constructions, dangling modifiers,* and *misplaced modifiers.* This section will help you identify and eliminate such problems in your writing.

Parallel Construction

One sentence problem that leads to awkward and confusing wording involves *parallel construction.* It is not uncommon for a writer to join two or more groups of words together in a sentence. For the sentence to be clear, these groups of words need to be very similar, or *parallel,* in structure. Here is an example of a sentence with parallel construction. The groups of words joined together are underlined.

Example   Last night we <u>ate outside</u>, <u>sat by the river</u>, and <u>listened to the frogs</u>.

The underlined groups of words are parallel because they follow the same structure: past tense verb followed by modifying words. Now read the same sentence with some problems with parallelism.

Example   Last night we <u>ate outside</u>, <u>by the river sat</u>, and <u>listening to the frogs</u>.

This sentence is very awkward. In the second group of words, the order of the past tense verb and the modifying words is changed, and in the last group, the verb has the wrong ending. The resulting sentence would bother any reader.

Here are other examples of sentences with nonparallel constructions followed by revised corrected versions.

Example   Joleen is <u>tall</u>, <u>slender</u>, and <u>brown hair</u>. (**Brown hair** *isn't parallel with* **tall** *and* **slender**.)

Revised   Joleen is tall and slender and has brown hair.

Example   I <u>leaped across the creek</u>, <u>landed on the bank</u>, and <u>back in the water did slip</u>. (**Back in the water did slip** *is not parallel with the first two parts*.)

Revised   I leaped across the creek, landed on the bank, and slipped back into the water.

Example   <u>Swimming</u>, <u>jogging</u>, and <u>a tennis game</u> are good forms of exercise. (**A tennis game** *is not parallel with* **swimming** *and* **jogging**.)

Revised   Swimming, jogging, and tennis are good forms of exercise.

Example   The MG <u>is metallic blue</u>, <u>has four speeds</u>, and <u>racy</u>. (**Racy** *isn't parallel with the other parts*.)

Revised   The MG is metallic blue, has four speeds, and is racy.

Revision Activity 7

The following sentences have problems with parallel construction. Rewrite each sentence and improve the wording by correcting the nonparallel part of the sentence.

Example   John looked out the window, scanned in all directions, and no one.

Revised   John looked out the window, scanned in all directions, and saw no one.

1. I enjoy skating, reading, to swim, and the sport of hockey.

2. Claude is short, stout, intelligent, brown eyes, and generosity.

3. We walked through the field, finding hundreds of acorns, and bring them home in baskets.

4. You may check out the periodical or in the library you may read it.

5. Doing dishes, cleaning her room, homework, to baby-sit her brother, and the flossing of her teeth were chores Eileen avoided.

6. Mildred walked into the class, does one hundred push-ups, and out the door.

7. You can chew gum in Kaser's class, but gum chewing in Bowie's class you can't do, and no gum in Borafka's class.

8. Not only is college harder than high school but also greater is the cost and more is the difficulty.

9. The news about the earthquake was terrible, the reports being shockingly graphic, the death count is tragically high, and more bodies being uncovered still.

10. Georgia is willing to organize activities for her sorority but no more tutoring pledges for their finals, and not willing to chair the pledge meetings.

Misplaced and Dangling Modifiers

Two common wording problems that can confuse readers involve *misplaced* and *dangling modifiers*. While the misplaced modifying phrase is located in an awkward position in a sentence, a dangling modifying phrase has nothing in the sentence to modify.

Follow these suggestions for identifying and correcting problems with misplaced and dangling modifiers:

1. A misplaced modifying phrase is usually some distance from the word it modifies, creating confusion about what the modified word is supposed to be.

   Examples (modifying phrases underlined)

   The man applied for a job in Chicago <u>from Toledo</u>.

   The students can't hear the lecture <u>sitting in the back of the room</u>.

   The house is for sale for fifty thousand dollars <u>across the street</u>.

   The girl chased the elephant through the house <u>in pigtails</u>.

   The young man was brought into the emergency room <u>bitten by a snake</u>.

2. To correct most misplaced modifiers, place the phrase directly after the word it modifies. Occasionally the phrase will fit more smoothly directly before the modified word.

Examples   The man <u>from Toledo</u> applied for a job in Chicago.

The students <u>sitting in the back of the room</u> can't hear the lecture.

The house <u>across the street</u> is for sale for fifty thousand dollars.

The girl <u>in pigtails</u> chased the elephant through the house.

The young man <u>bitten by a snake</u> was brought into the emergency room.

3. Dangling modifiers usually begin sentences, often start with words with *ing* and *ed* endings, and are followed by a subject they don't modify. The modifiers are "dangling" because they clearly don't modify the subject.

Examples   (dangling phrase underlined)

<u>Driving to work yesterday</u>, the road was very slippery. (*The subject,* road, *can't drive.*)

<u>Worried about her daughter's whereabouts</u>, the police were called immediately. (*The subject,* police, *weren't "worried about her daughter's whereabouts."*)

<u>Grounded for three weeks for bad grades</u>, John's sister got to use his car. (*The subject,* sister, *wasn't the one who was grounded.*)

<u>Running through the park</u>, the cool breeze felt great on our faces. (*The subject,* breeze, *can't run through the park.*)

4. To correct a dangling modifier, either (a) change the subject of the sentence so that it goes with the modifying phrase or (b) add a subordinating conjunction and subject to the modifying phrase to form a complex sentence.

Examples   Driving to work today, I noticed how slippery the road was.

or

While I was driving to work today, the road was very slippery.

Worried about her daughter's whereabouts, Gretchen called the police immediately.

or

Because Gretchen was worried about her daughter's whereabouts, the police were called immediately.

Grounded for three weeks for bad grades, John couldn't drive his car so his sister got to.

or

Because John was grounded for three weeks for bad grades, his sister got to use his car.

Running through the park, we felt the cool breeze on our faces.

or

As we were running through the park, the cool breeze felt great on our faces.

Revision Activity 8

Each of the following sentences has a misplaced modifier. Rewrite each sentence and put the misplaced modifier in a more appropriate location. The result will be clearer, smoother sentences.

Example   The girl showed up in a trench coat from the dorms.

Revised   The girl from the dorms showed up in a trench coat.

1. The movie is very dull showing at the drive-in.

2. I was born in New Mexico of about one hundred families in a small town.

3. He didn't know that well how to drive a stick shift.

4. The cigarette that you finished smoking for your health is very bad.

5. He is a man used by God of many talents, for he is a pastor.

6. The girl was very wet from perspiring from Texas after the race.

7. The van was stolen from the front of the gym belonging to the school.

8. The jelly is from your knife in the peanut butter.

9. The candy bars have melted with nuts in the heat.

10. The patient has great courage in room 301.

Revision Activity 9

Each of the following sentences begins with a dangling modifier. Rewrite the sentence to correct the problem either by changing the subject so that it goes with the modifying phrase or by adding a subordinating conjunction and subject to the dangling phrase to form a complex sentence. In each case, use the correction method that generates the smoothest, clearest sentence.

Example	Working in the backyard all morning, my clothes got very dirty.
Revised	While I was working in the backyard all morning, my clothes got very dirty.
Example	Thrilled by his semester grades, everyone John knew got a phone call.
Revised	Thrilled by his semester grades, John phoned everyone he knew.

1. Sitting on the sofa in the living room, my feet got very cold.

2. Bothered by a sore throat, Mary's doctor suggested that she stay home.

3. Angered over an unfair speeding ticket, the judge got a lecture from Ned.

4. Driving down Manning Avenue, the grape vineyards are beautiful in the spring.

5. Locked out of the house, the only way for John to enter was through a window.

6. Waiting for a taxi on "G" Street, four taxis drove right by me.

7. Bored by the movie on TV, the channel was changed by Gladys.

8. Trying for a school record in the high jump, the bar was raised for Marie to 5 feet 10 inches.

Correct Usage

This section is for students who have problems with past tense verbs: omitting the *ed* ending or using incorrect irregular verb forms.

PAST TENSE VERBS

Not all of your writing is done in the present tense. You use *past tense* verbs when writing about an event that has already occurred, whether it happened a minute or a decade ago. The most common errors involving past tense verbs include leaving off the *ed* ending on *regular* past tense verbs and using incorrect *irregular* verb forms.

Regular Past Tense Verbs

Most verbs form their past tense by adding *ed* to the regular verb. Here are examples of regular past tense verbs:

Verb	Past Tense Form	Verb	Past Tense Form
answer	answered	instruct	instructed
ask	asked	kick	kicked

borrow	borrowed	learn	learned
climb	climbed	part	parted
count	counted	question	questioned
detail	detailed	rush	rushed
edit	edited	sail	sailed
fish	fished	scale	scaled
flood	flooded	talk	talked
head	headed	walk	walked

Regular verbs that end in certain letters offer slight variations to the basic *ed* verb ending.

1. Verbs already ending in *e* just add the *d*

Verb	Past Tense Form
believe	believed
create	created
hate	hated
invite	invited
love	loved
receive	received

2. Verbs ending in *y* preceded by a *consonant* change the *y* to *i* and add *ed*.

Verb	Past Tense Form
bury	buried
carry	carried
marry	married
rely	relied
reply	replied
tarry	tarried

3. Verbs ending in *y* preceded by a *vowel* merely add *ed*.

Verb	Past Tense Form
annoy	annoyed
betray	betrayed
delay	delayed
destroy	destroyed
relay	relayed

4. A number of short regular verbs ending in consonants preceded by vowels with a *short vowel* sound (*plăn, bŭg, fĭt*) *double* their last letter before adding *ed*.

Verb	Past Tense Form	Verb	Past Tense Form
acquit	acquitted	knit	knitted
admit	admitted	mar	marred
bat	batted	plan	planned
bug	bugged	ram	rammed
can	canned	scan	scanned
cram	crammed	slug	slugged
fit	fitted	tar	tarred

Verb Activity 10

Write the past tense form for the following regular verbs. Some verbs will add *ed*, some will change *y* to *i* and add *ed*, and some will double the final letter and add *ed*.

Examples   slice *sliced*   cry *cried*   plan *planned*

1. betray _____   **13.** bury _____

2. flood _____   **14.** believe _____

3. cite _____   **15.** instruct _____

4. learn _____   **16.** reply _____

5. plan _____   **17.** fund _____

6. deny _____   **18.** inflate _____

7. marry _____   **19.** cheat _____

8. announce _____   **20.** hurry _____

9. save _____   **21.** bellow _____

10. annoy _____   **22.** admit _____

11. time _____   **23.** cap _____

12. dam _____   **24.** decide _____

Verb Activity 11

The following passage is written in the present tense. Rewrite the passage changing the verbs to the past tense. Make sure to add *ed* endings to all regular past tense verbs.

Example   Gertrude likes mustard on her rice.

Past tense   Gertrude liked mustard on her rice.

Tonight the moon looks strange. Wispy clouds cover its surface, and a huge halo that looks perfectly round encircles it. Moisture drips from the air, and the moon glistens behind the veil of clouds. It appears eerie and beautiful. I watch the moon from my window and then drift to sleep. I enjoy enchanted dreams about hidden moon caves and moonmaids that lure sleepers into their caverns.

Irregular Verbs

Many verbs do not form their past tense with the regular *ed* verb ending. Instead, they form their past tense in different, *irregular* ways that involve changes within the verb instead of the addition of an ending. Although certain groups of irregular verbs form their past tense in similar ways, there are no rules to follow like the *ed* rule for regular verbs; therefore, you must memorize *irregular verb* forms to have them at your command.

The following is a list of frequently used irregular verbs whose forms are often confused. The verbs with similar forms are grouped as much as possible. The third column, "Past Participle," contains the irregular verb forms used with *helping verbs* such as *has, have, had, was,* and *were.* Here are examples of sentences containing the past tense and past participle verb forms:

Examples
John <u>flew</u> cross-country in a single-prop Cessna. (*past tense, action completed*)

John <u>has flown</u> cross-country many times. (*past participle + helping verb* has; *action continuing into the present*)

Lillie <u>sang</u> beautifully at the graduation ceremony. (*past tense, action completed*)

Lillie <u>has sung</u> at many graduation ceremonies. (*past participle + helping verb* has; *action continuing in present*)

Lillie <u>had sung</u> at many graduation ceremonies. (*past participle + helping verb* had; *action completed*)

Present Tense	Past Tense	Past Participle
become	became	become
come	came	come
run	ran	run
begin	began	begun
drink	drank	drunk
ring	rang	rung
sing	sang	sung
swim	swam	swum

fly	flew	flown
grow	grew	grown
know	knew	known
throw	threw	thrown
burst	burst	burst
cut	cut	cut
quit	quit	quit
set	set	set
choose	chose	chosen
drive	drove	driven
eat	ate	eaten
get	got	got, gotten
give	gave	given
rise	rose	risen
speak	spoke	spoken
take	took	taken
write	wrote	written
bring	brought	brought
build	built	built
catch	caught	caught
has	had	had
lead	led	led
sit	sat	sat
do	did	done
go	went	gone
see	saw	seen
lay	laid	laid *(to place or set something down)*
lie	lay	lain *(to recline or rest)*

Verb Activity 12

Fill in the blanks with the correct past tense and past participle forms of the irregular verbs in parentheses. Use the past participle form when a helping verb (such as *has, have, was, were*) comes before it.

Examples   (get) She has _gotten_ good grades on her math quizzes.

(run) George _ran_ into a brick wall.

1. (write) Ted has _____ more this semester than ever before.
2. (lead) The winding path _____ to a gazebo among the pines.
3. (drive) You have _____ me wild with your accusations.
4. (sit) Grace _____ on a stump contemplating her future.
5. (eat) Have you _____ the stuffed peppers in the cafeteria?
6. (build) Ted has _____ model planes since he was in grade school.
7. (begin) It has _____ to drizzle outside.
8. (throw) Mia _____ her back out in aerobic dance class.
9. (know) Hal has _____ some very strange people.
10. (set) Judy _____ her collection of figurines on the mantel.
11. (fly) We've _____ with six different airlines.
12. (drink) You have _____ enough coffee to last you a month.
13. (see) No one _____ or heard from Ezekiel for over two months.
14. (choose) You have _____ the most expensive brand of panty hose.
15. (come) By the time Ames had _____ home, everyone was asleep.
16. (become) You have _____ very proficient at archery.
17. (go) Mattie has _____ to collect dry firewood by the lake.
18. (bring) Grover _____ swamp mud in on his shoes.
19. (give) Reading has _____ Louise great pleasure for years.
20. (swim) Have you _____ across the lake by yourself yet?
21. (lie) Yesterday I _____ down at noon and awakened at 6:00 p.m.
22. (lay) Where have you _____ your pipe?
23. (lie) Have you ever _____ in a hammock?
24. (lay) The construction crew _____ five miles of asphalt in a day.
25. (see) Has anyone _____ my red pajamas?

Verb Activity 13

Here is more practice using irregular verbs. Write sentences using the following irregular verbs in the tenses indicated.

Examples   run (past)   Last night John ran past my house at
                                        3:00 a.m.

               eat (past participle)   You have eaten all of the cherries I was
                                        saving for the picnic.

1. fly (past participle)

2. burst (past)

3. choose (past)

4. fly (past participle)

5. drink (past participle)

6. write (past participle)

7. set (past)

8. rise (past)

9. take (past)

10. see (past)

11. lie (past participle)

12. swim (past participle)

13. drive (past participle)

14. become (past participle)

15. ring (past participle)

16. bring (past)

17. lead (past)

18. lay (past)

19. throw (past participle)

20. drive (past participle)

Verb Activity 14

Fill in your own choices of past tense and past participle verb forms to complete the following sentences. Spell correctly.

1. Freda _____ angry last night when her roommate _____
_____ her bed.

2. The Gomez family has _____ all the way from Florida for their son's graduation.

3. It seems that we have _____ out of things to argue about.

4. It _____ raining early this morning.

5. Have you ever _____ as much cider as you _____ last night?

6. Jacqueline _____ across the lake and back in three hours.

7. That fifty-pound pumpkin was _____ with a special fertilizer.

8. Have you _____ the table for lunch yet?

9. I have _____ all along that you were a special person.

10. The balloon _____ high in the air and then _____ on a tree limb.

11. You have _____ to be very obnoxious with your Al Capone impressions.

12. Fran _____ her new car around town and _____ up boys.

13. Your father has _____, and that is the end of that!

14. Have you _____ good care of your health this semester?

15. The criminal was finally _____ to justice after years of evading the law.

16. Have you _____ all of your math homework?

17. Sammy _____ to the movies last night and _____ Attack of the Killer Tomatoes.

18. Have you ever _____ on a sharp tack that someone _____ _____ on your seat?

19. You have _____ everyone with your time and patience.

20. The new Chevies aren't _____ to last like the older ones.

21. You _____ your history test easily, but you _____ your P.E. physical.

22. They _____ the missing painting and _____ it to its owner.

23. Ms. Hornsby _____ your story about little green men, but I _____ .

24. Have you _____ your dear mother lately, or have you _____ her?

25. Henrietta _____ a mean saxophone at the party, and everyone _____ .

26. I _____ to invite you to tea, but I _____ .

27. Trudy has _____ twenty-three units of pottery classes and has _____ six of them.

28. The roses have _____ their flowers because you haven't _____ them.

29. Sam _____ the tree, _____ from a branch, and _____ his tongue out at a sparrow.

30. I have _____ to help you but you haven't _____ , so I've _____ up hope that you'll ever become a sword swallower.

Verb Activity 15

The following passage is written in the present tense. Rewrite the passage in the past tense by adding *ed* to regular past tense verbs and by using the correct past tense and past participle forms for the irregular verbs.

Example   Clyde buys his shoes at Zody's and wears them for years.

Revised   Clyde bought his shoes at Zody's and wore them for years.

    The campus goes berserk at Halloween. Boys sneak into girls' dormitories, hide in the closets, and scare them when they return from the cafeteria. Students bombard motorists' cars with water balloons, and there isn't a person asleep anywhere on campus. An army of dorm students attacks its rivals across campus. The students capture the dorm president and spray his body with green paint. They steal the dorm banner and hide it in a car trunk. Students from off campus begin a shaving cream war with on-campus students. They quit when the campus police finally intervene at 3:00 a.m. Then everyone is quiet for about a half hour, but the wildness begins again when the police leave.

Spelling

This final section is for students who struggle with their spelling. It covers contractions and possessive words, commonly misspelled words, and homonyms that cause writers problems.

POSSESSIVES

One of the most frequently omitted punctuation marks is the apostrophe that is needed in possessive words. A *possessive* word is usually followed directly by something *belonging to it*. Here are some sentences with the possessive words correctly punctuated with apostrophes. The possessive words are underlined.

Examples   My <u>mother's</u> brother owns a fruit stand in the country.

Today's weather looks menacing with those dark clouds in the east.

I am going to Celia's surprise party tomorrow night.

The men's room at the Forum is flooded.

My three brothers' cars are all 1974 Plymouths.

The ladies' club holds its meetings at the Howbarth Tavern.

As you can see, the word directly following the possessive word belongs to it: mother's *brother,* today's *weather,* Celia's *surprise party,* men's *room,* brothers' *cars,* and ladies' *club.* Notice that sometimes the apostrophe comes before the *s* and sometimes it comes after the *s.* Here are the rules for showing possession:

1. *Singular possessive word:* Add apostrophe and *s* to the word:

a boy's dog, the tree's bark, May's hair.

2. *Plural possessive word:* Add the apostrophe *after* the *s:*

three boys' dogs, all the trees' bark, many girls' hair.

There are two exceptions to the possessive rules:

1. Plural words that form their possessive without adding *s* (man/men, woman/women, child/children, goose/geese) are punctuated as *singular* possessives (*'s*): men's hats, women's shoes, children's lessons, geese's feathers.

2. Possessive pronouns such as *yours, theirs, his, ours,* and *hers* do *not* require apostrophes since the form of the pronoun itself indicates possession.

Possessive Activity 16

Put apostrophes in the following possessive words to show singular and plural possessive forms.

Examples   a dog's life

the boys' club

1. the banks vault

2. a childs prayer

3. my uncles wife

4. six countries treaties

5. thirty books covers

6. the geeses feathers

7. a mans opinion

8. omens strength

9. twenty schools fight songs

10. four doctors nurses

11. Tuesdays child

12. the wars effect

Possessive Activity 17

Write your own sentences showing the possessive relationship that is given for each sentence. Follow the rules for adding 's or s'. Make sure the possessive word is followed by the thing belonging to it.

Example	a dog belonging to Mark
Revised	Mark's dog is a cocker spaniel.
Example	the bones of all the dogs in the neighborhood
Revised	All of the dogs' bones are hidden in the lot behind my house.

1. the hamster belonging to Mary
2. the snow of this morning
3. the lockers belonging to the men
4. the right to an education belonging to a student
5. the socks belonging to your grandmother
6. the station wagons belonging to six families
7. the great force of the ocean waves
8. the diagnosis of a doctor

CONTRACTIONS

A *contraction* is a word formed by combining two words and inserting an apostrophe to replace omitted letters. The most common contractions combine pronouns with verbs (I'm, he's, you've, we're) and verbs with the word *not* (isn't, wasn't, don't, won't, aren't).

Here are examples of common contractions and the word pairs from which they are formed:

Contraction	Word Pair	Contraction	Word Pair
I'm	I am	aren't	are not
you're	you are	wasn't	was not
he's	he is	weren't	were not
she's	she is	don't	do not
they're	they are	doesn't	does not
we're	we are	won't	will not
he'll	he will	wouldn't	would not
we'll	we will	hasn't	has not
they've	they have	haven't	have not
I've	I have	there's	there is
it's	it is	here's	here is
isn't	is not	who's	who is

Contraction Activity 18

Write contractions for the following pairs of words. Don't forget the apostrophes.

Example   he is *he's*

1. they are _____

2. it is _____

3. do not _____

4. does not _____

5. she is _____

6. I am _____

7. there is _____

8. they have _____

9. will not _____

10. are not _____

11. has not _____

12. you are _____

Apostrophe Activity 19

Put apostrophes in all of the contractions and possessive words that require them in the following sentences.

Example   Theyre not going to the firemens ball Friday.

Revised   They're not going to the firemen's ball Friday.

1. The chipmunks buried a years supply of nuts in the trees hollow.

2. Were supposed to be at the Smiths home for dinner, arent we?

3. The womens tennis team and the mens team were defeated in the leagues championships.

4. Havent you found your sisters new sweater or your four brothers fishing poles yet?

5. Megs response to Jacks question wasnt at all surprising to the groups leaders.

6. Cant you figure a way to curb Fredas appetite for anchovy pizza and lasagna?

7. No ones frame of mind is any better than Howies when he isnt drinking.

8. The dogs and the cats arent supposed to be in Mr. Grumbleys study.

9. The governments belief in the economys recovery isnt accepted by Willies grandfathers.

10. Youve had a difficult time with Newtons law of gravity, havent you?

COMMONLY MISSPELLED WORDS

Misspelled words account for the largest number of writing errors. Spelling errors are a nuisance to the reader, and final drafts should be free of them. Spelling is a minor problem for many writers, but it is a big problem for others. This section introduces some of the most commonly misspelled words and gives you a few basic spelling rules to follow; however, if you have serious spelling difficulties, you might seek further assistance from your instructor.

The following is the first of a number of word lists that appear throughout this section. Each list groups words that follow similar spelling rules.

Spelling List One: Words Ending in ing

beginning	kidding	putting	stopping
boring	letting	riding	studying
coming	living	running	swimming
dying	planning	sitting	taking
flying	playing	slipping	writing
hitting			

Words ending in *ing* are frequently misspelled. Here are the basic rules that will help you decide what to do when adding *ing* to a word:

1. *Verbs ending in* e: Drop the *e* and add *ing* (boring, coming, riding, raking).
2. *Verbs ending in* y: Keep the *y* and add *ing* (studying, playing, flying).
3. *Verbs ending in a* short vowel* *followed by a single consonant:* Double the last letter and add *ing* (beginning, hitting, kidding, letting, planning, running).
4. *Verbs ending in a* long vowel† *followed by a consonant:* Add *ing,* but do *not* double the final letter (dreaming, eating, sleeping, cheating). Note: Writers have few problems with this rule, so the words were not included in this spelling list.

Spelling Activity 20

Following the spelling rules for adding *ing* to words, add the *ing* ending to the following words from Spelling List One.

---

* Short vowel sounds are found in words like *shŭt, rĭp, rŏt,* and *cătch.*
† Long vowel sounds are found in words like *hāte, frēe, bīte,* and *mōpe.*

1. come _____	**5.** study _____	**9.** ride _____	**13.** live _____
2. hit _____	**6.** run _____	**10.** stop _____	**14.** begin _____
3. play _____	**7.** write _____	**11.** bore _____	**15.** swim _____
4. plan _____	**8.** kid _____	**12.** put _____	**16.** let _____

Here is the second list of words that writers frequently misspell. Each list contains words that are similarly misspelled.

Spelling List Two: Words with ie *and* ei

achieve	field	neither
believe	friend	receive
deceive	grieve	relief
eight	height	review
either	neighbor	their

As you can see, each of these words contains either an *ei* or an *ie* vowel combination. Many writers misspell these words by turning the two letters around. Here are the basic rules for when to use *ie* and when to use *ei*.

1. In most words, the *i* goes before the *e* unless it follows the letter *c*. Then the *e* goes before the *i*, as in *receive, deceive*, and *perceive*.

2. If the *ei* has a long *ā* vowel sound, the *e* comes before the *i*, as in *neighbor*, *eight*, and *freight*.

3. You need to memorize some exceptions to the *i* before *e* rule: *height, either, neither*.

Spelling Activity 21

Write eight sentences using any two of the Spelling List Two words in each sentence. Use all fifteen words in the eight sentences. Spell the words correctly.

Example   You can <u>achieve</u> more in life if you <u>believe</u> in yourself.

The words in Spelling List Three are grouped together because writers often misspell them in the same way: by leaving out a letter.

Spelling List Three: Left-Out Letters

again	familiar	interest
always	February	opinion
clothes	finish	restaurant

schedule	sophomore	whether
separate	stereo	which
several	straight	while
similar	surprise	

Thus, *again* is misspelled as *agin, February* as *Febuary, interest* as *intrest, clothes* as *cloths,* or *whether* as *wether.* The letters are often left out because of the way many people pronounce the words. Three-syllable words such as *interest, restaurant, sophomore,* and *several* are often pronounced and spelled as two-syllable words: *in-trest, rest-rant, soph-more,* and *sev-ral.* The *wh* words are frequently pronounced and spelled without the *h* sound: *wether, wich,* and *wile.*

Because there is no spelling rule to cover the range of List Three words, you will need to memorize them. The best tip for helping you learn them is to *pronounce* the words correctly so that you won't leave out letters by omitting syllables or sounds.

Spelling Activity 22

Write ten sentences, including two different words from Spelling List Three in each sentence. Use the words in any order you wish, and spell them correctly. Underline the spelling words.

Example   I <u>always finish</u> my English assignments five minutes before class.

Spelling List Four contains words that are grouped together because they all contain double consonants that can cause confusion. The writer is not always certain which letters to double. Unfortunately, there is no rule similar to the rules covering words in List One and List Two to tell you which letters to double. You need to memorize the words in List Four so that you can easily visualize their correct spelling. Because these words are commonly used, you should know them well by the time you complete this course.

Spelling List Four: Double-Letter Words

across	dinner	parallel
arrangement	embarrass	success
attitude	immediate	surround
business	impossible	terrible
different	occasion	tomorrow
difficult	occurred	

Spelling Activity 23

Write nine sentences using any two of the words in Spelling List Four in each sentence. Use all seventeen words in your sentences.

Example   Sarah made a <u>business arrangement</u> with her banker for a loan.

Spelling List Five contains words that end in *ly*.

Spelling List Five: Words Ending in ly

actually	finally	lovely
busily	fortunately	naturally
completely	hungrily	really
easily	lively	unusually
especially	lonely	usually
extremely		

Writers who misspell *ly* words get confused about whether to drop a letter before adding the *ly* or whether to add an extra *l* to form an *lly* ending. The following simple rules should clear up the problems.

1. Add *ly* to the root word. Do *not* drop the last letter of the word (*lovely,* not *lovly, fortunately,* not *fortunatly*). An *lly* ending is used only when the root word ends in *l* (real/really, unusual/unusually, natural/naturally, actual/actually).

2. If a root word ends in *y,* change the *y* to *i* and add *ly* (busy/busily, easy/easily, hungry/hungrily).

Spelling Activity 24

Add *ly* to the root words listed here, following the rules just covered for adding the *ly* ending.

Examples   clumsy *clumsily*

          sane *sanely*

1. natural _____   **6.** unusual _____

2. live _____   **7.** real _____

3. hungry _____   **8.** fortunate _____

4. special _____   **9.** lone _____

5. busy _____   **10.** complete _____

11. actual _____   **13.** easy _____

12. final _____   **14.** love _____

SPELLING REFERENCE LIST

The following list includes more than one hundred of the most frequently misspelled words. You may use it as a convenient spelling reference when proofreading your drafts for errors. You may also want to select five to ten words per week to work on until you can spell every word on the list correctly.

accommodate	despair	knowledge
achievement	disappoint	laid
acquaintance	disease	led
acquire	divine	leisure
actual	efficient	license
against	embarrass	loneliness
alleys	exaggerate	loose
amateur	exercise	lose
amount	existence	luxury
apparent	expense	maintenance
appearance	experience	marriage
approach	explanation	meant
argument	extremely	mere
attendance	fascinate	naturally
beginner	forty	necessary
believe	friend	ninety
benefit	government	noticeable
boundary	grammar	obstacle
business	guarantee	occasion
certain	height	occurrence
chief	heroes	operate
comparative	huge	opinion
conscience	ignorant	original
controversy	imaginary	paid
convenience	immediately	parallel
criticism	independent	particular
dealt	intelligent	performance
dependent	interest	personal
describe	interrupt	physical

piece	procedure	shining
planned	prominent	similar
possess	promise	studying
practical	psychology	success
preferred	pursue	surprise
prejudice	really	tries
preparation	receive	truly
principal	recommend	villain
principle	repetition	weather
privilege	sense	whether
probably	separate	writing

HOMONYMS

Homonyms are words that sound alike but are spelled differently and have different meanings. The three homonyms most commonly confused by writers are *there, their,* and *they're,* which we cover in the next section.

There/Their/They're

Writers frequently confuse the words *there, their,* and *they're.* Once you understand the use of each word, you will have little trouble distinguishing among them. However, you should always proofread your drafts for *there, their,* and *they're* errors because they appear occasionally in most writing.

Here is the meaning of each word:

There   An introductory word often preceding *is, are, was,* and *were*
There are five goldfish in the pond. I think there is room for you in the bus.

A location
Your books are over there. There are the books I've been looking for.

Their   Possessive pronoun (belonging to them)
Their car was vandalized. Joe took their picture.

They're   Contraction for *they are*
They're going to get married on Sunday. I think they're beautiful slides of Rome.

Spelling Activity 25

Fill in the blanks with the correct word: *there, their,* or *they're.* Select the word or words that fit each sentence.

Examples   *They're* going to break the snail-eating record.

Their patience is waning.

There are four hummingbirds in the bird bath.

1. _____ are thousands of wheat fields in Kansas.
2. _____ webbed feet help mallards cruise across the pond.
3. _____ an unusual breed of turkey.
4. _____ is a need for voters to mail _____ ballots by June.
5. _____ coming at 9:30, but _____ will be no one home.
6. _____ new sofa will be at _____ house by morning.
7. Plant the marigolds _____ , _____ , and _____ .
8. _____ learning algebra faster than _____ cousins did.
9. Is _____ a phone in _____ store?
10. _____ taking _____ time in _____ .

Spelling Activity 26

Write your own sentences using *there, their,* and *they're* as directed.

Example   a sentence beginning with *their*

Their schedules for the fall semester are full of errors.

1. a sentence beginning with *there*
2. a sentence beginning with *their*
3. a sentence beginning with *they're*
4. *there* and *their* in the same sentence
5. *there* and *they're* in the same sentence
6. *their* and *they're* in the same sentence
7. *their, there,* and *they're* in the same sentence
8. *there* three times in the same sentence.

Spelling Activity 27

Here is more practice using the words, *there, their,* and *they're* correctly. Remember, *there* is an introductory word or shows location, *their* is a possessive pronoun (belonging to them), and *they're* is a contraction for *they are*. Fill in the correct form in each blank in the following paragraph.

Example   *Their* shoes are new, but *they're* not bragging about it.

_____ is no doubt that Henrietta and Hank are nervous taking the test. _____ hands are shaking, and _____ frowning intently. _____ pencils are moving rapidly over the test booklet. _____ backs are hunched in effort. _____ working at a feverish clip, but _____ is a good chance they won't finish. It is a long and difficult test. _____ are one hundred multiple-choice questions and five essay questions. Finally, Henrietta and Hank stop at the bell, put _____ pencils down, and relax _____ minds. They've done _____ best, and _____ satisfied.

Confusing Duos: List One

A number of word pairs often confuse writers. They can slip erroneously into anyone's paper. The problem is not misspelling a word but using the wrong word in the wrong place. Here are some of the more commonly confused pairs with some information to help you tell them apart. (This is the first of two lists of confusing duos.)

Accept	to receive (I <u>accept</u> your gift. Joy <u>accepted</u> the award.)
Except	to exclude, leave out (Everyone is going bowling <u>except</u> Millicent.)
A	comes before words beginning with a *consonant* (<u>a</u> book, <u>a</u> slug, <u>a</u> dog, <u>a</u> cat)
An	comes before words beginning with a *vowel* or *vowel sound* (<u>an</u> apple, <u>an</u> orange, <u>an</u> answer, <u>an</u> herb)
Advice	what is *given* to someone (Joe gave me some very good <u>advice</u> about my major.)
Advise	the verb meaning to give advice (Joe <u>advised</u> me to major in computer technology.)
And	conjunction joining words or groups of words (George is going, <u>and</u> so am I.)
An	comes before words beginning with a *vowel* or *vowel sound* (<u>an</u> apple, <u>an</u> orange, <u>an</u> answer, <u>an</u> herb)
Are	present tense of *to be* for plural subjects (The gifts <u>are</u> on the table.)

Our	possessive pronoun, belonging to us (<u>Our</u> plans are uncertain. We'll go <u>our</u> separate ways.)
It's	contraction for *it is* (<u>It's</u> going to snow today. <u>It's</u> a rough exam.)
Its	possessive pronoun (The tire lost <u>its</u> tread. <u>Its</u> flowers are drooping.)
Know	to have knowledge, to understand (I <u>know</u> the answer. He <u>knows</u> his limits.)
No	none, negative (<u>No</u> one minds. There is <u>no</u> smoking in the library. I say "<u>no</u>.")
Mine	possessive pronoun, belonging to me (That book is <u>mine</u> <u>Mine</u> is the red jacket.)
Mind	to behave, to oppose (The dog <u>minds</u> well. I <u>mind</u> your eating my lunch.)
Past	time gone by (In the <u>past</u>, you have always done well. Your <u>past</u> is your business.)
Passed	(You <u>passed</u> my inspection. His fever <u>passed</u> hours ago.)

Spelling Activity 28

Fill in the blanks with appropriate words from the list of confusing duos.

Example   <u> No </u> one cares where we sleep tonight.

1. Mattie paid _____ way into the park last night.

2. For breakfast I'd like _____ apple, _____ omelet, and _____ banana.

3. Everyone seems to be having a good time at the party _____ you.

4. If Shandra takes my _____ , she'll forget about working.

5. Do you know why _____ so foggy this month?

6. We are planning to spend _____ honeymoon in Tulsa.

7. I don't _____ if you borrow my sweater tomorrow.

8. I enjoyed studying with you this morning, _____ I hope we can do it again.

9. Fenway was too tired to be good company to _____ guests.

10. Do you _____ if we take up where we left off yesterday?

11. Jack would _____ you to take _____ aspirin and _____ hot bath.

12. Your case is _____ exception to _____ rule.

Confusing Duos: List Two

Here is a second group of confusing word pairs to add to your list:

Choose	present tense verb (I <u>choose</u> the present with the green bow.)
Chose	past tense of *choose* (Yesterday I <u>chose</u> to stay home from work.)
Quit	not to finish, to give up (John <u>quit</u> his job with General Motors.)
Quite	completely, wholly (Are you <u>quite</u> certain of the time? That was <u>quite</u> a show.)
Quiet	opposite of noisy (Please be <u>quiet</u> in the hospital. I would like a <u>quiet</u> moment.)
This	singular word that identifies or locates (<u>This</u> is a great story. <u>This</u> table is new.)
These	plural of *this* (<u>These</u> are the best stories I've read. <u>These</u> tables are new.)
To	preposition of many uses (We went <u>to</u> the game. Look <u>to</u> your leader. Sheila belonged <u>to</u> the Modernes. <u>To</u> my knowledge, no one is missing.)
Too	also, in excess (We are going to the game <u>too</u>. You have done <u>too</u> much work for one person.)
were	past tense form of *to be* with plural subjects (They <u>were</u> here a minute ago!)
Where	indicates location (<u>Where</u> are you going? Do you know <u>where</u> the dishes are?)
Through	preposition of movement or passage (<u>Through</u> the years, you've grown more lovely. We glanced <u>through</u> the book.)
Threw	past tense of *throw* (He <u>threw</u> the ball through the window. Mildred <u>threw</u> out her boyfriend.)
Your	possessive pronoun, belonging to you (<u>Your</u> books are a mess.)
You're	contraction for *you are* (<u>You're</u> the first person to call since the trial.)
Then	indicates time (<u>Then</u> you can go home. I did my work, and <u>then</u> I slept.)

| Than | indicates comparison (You are smarter <u>than</u> I am. I saved more money this year <u>than</u> last.) |

Spelling Activity 29

Fill in the blanks in the following sentences with appropriate words from the list of confusing duos.

Example   Last night you *chose* to be by yourself.

1. _____ pickles from Julio's Deli are the spiciest I've eaten.

2. _____ do you think _____ going with my anteater?

3. _____ dog was found in the neighbor's flower garden.

4. I am not _____ ready to _____ on the project.

5. _____ _____ you when we needed relief?

6. I think _____ taking _____ test too seriously.

7. Jody went _____ the races three hours _____ early.

8. I enjoy a _____ evening at home listening to _____ records.

9. I hear _____ not sure _____ _____ tapes _____ left at school.

10. We went _____ the motions of reading our lines, but we didn't _____ have the feeling needed _____ move our audience.

11. Fred felt better _____ he had expected after the race, but _____ the exhaustion started setting in.

Spelling Activity 30

Here is a list of all the confusing duos covered in this section. Using the words correctly, write one sentence for each confusing duo. Underline the words.

Examples   your/you're

You're going to the library, but <u>your</u> brother isn't going.

are/our

<u>Are</u> you going to take <u>our</u> advice about taking vitamin C?

1. choose/chose

2. quit/quite/quiet

3. this/these
4. through/threw
5. to/too
6. were/where
7. your/you're
8. there/their/they're
9. accept/except
10. a/an
11. an/and
12. advice/advise
13. are/our
14. it's/its
15. know/no
16. mine/mind
17. past/passed
18. then/than

Index